The Battle of Britain

The Battle of Britain

John Frayn Turner

Pen & Sword
AVIATION

First published by Airlife in 1995
Reprinted in this format in 2010 by
Pen and Sword Aviation
An imprint of
Pen and Sword Books Ltd
47 Church Street
Barnsley
South Yorkshire
S70 2AS

Copyright © John Frayn Turner 1998, 2010

ISBN 978-1-84884-243-4

Typeset in 10.5/13pt Palatino
by Mac Style, Beverley, E. Yorkshire

Printed and bound in Great Britain
by CPI UK

Pen and Sword Books Ltd incorporates the imprints of Pen and Sword Aviation, Pen and Sword Maritime, Pen and Sword Military, Wharncliffe Local History, Pen and Sword Select, Pen and Sword Military Classics and Leo Cooper.

For a complete list of Pen & Sword titles please contact
PEN & SWORD BOOKS LIMITED
47 Church Street, Barnsley, South Yorkshire, S70 2AS, England
E-mail: enquiries@pen-and-sword.co.uk
Website: www.pen-and-sword.co.uk

CONTENTS

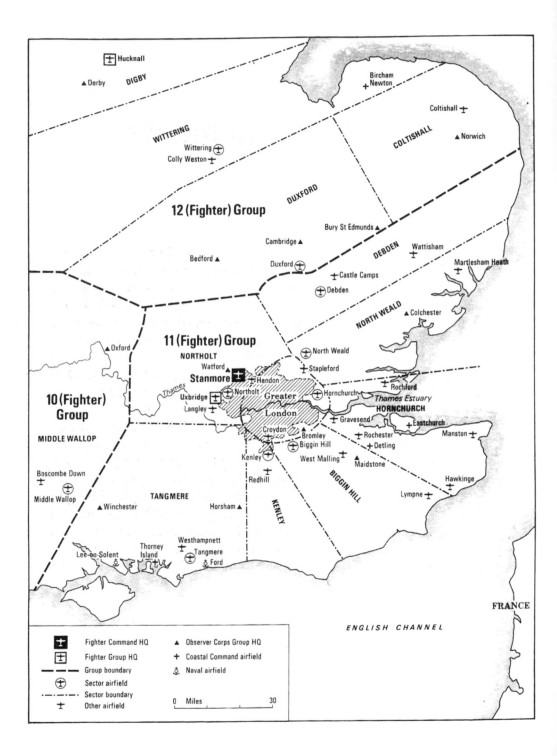

Fighter Command map

- ☩ Hucknall
- ▲ Derby   **DIGBY**
- Bircham + Newton
- Coltishall +
- **WITTERING**
- ⊕ Wittering
- Colly Weston +
- **COLTISHALL**
- ▲ Norwich
- **12 (Fighter) Group**
- **DUXFORD**
- Bury St Edmunds ▲
- Cambridge ▲
- Wattisham +
- **DEBDEN**
- Bedford ▲
- ⊕ Duxford
- Martlesham Heath +
- + Castle Camps
- ⊕ Debden
- ▲ Colchester
- **NORTH WEALD**
- **11 (Fighter) Group**
- ▲ Oxford
- **NORTHOLT**
- ⊕ North Weald
- Watford +
- + Stapleford
- ⌖ **Stanmore**
- + Hendon
- Rochford +
- **10 (Fighter) Group**
- *Thames*
- ⊞ Uxbridge
- ⊕ Northolt
- *Greater London*
- ⊕ Hornchurch
- *Thames Estuary*
- **HORNCHURCH**
- Langley +
- + Eastchurch
- + Gravesend
- **MIDDLE WALLOP**
- Croydon +
- ▲ Bromley
- + Rochester
- Manston +
- ⊕ Biggin Hill
- + Detling
- Kenley ⊕
- West Malling +
- ▲ Maidstone
- + Boscombe Down
- + Redhill
- **BIGGIN HILL**
- Hawkinge +
- ⊕ Middle Wallop
- **TANGMERE**
- **KENLEY**
- Lympne +
- Middle Wallop
- ▲ Winchester
- Horsham ▲
- Westhampnett +
- Thorney + Island
- ⚓ Lee-on-Solent
- ⚓ Tangmere
- ⚓ Ford
- **FRANCE**
- *ENGLISH CHANNEL*

Legend

- ⌖ Fighter Command HQ
- ⊞ Fighter Group HQ
- ▬ ▬ Group boundary
- ⊕ Sector airfield
- ·–·–· Sector boundary
- + Other airfield
- ▲ Observer Corps Group HQ
- + Coastal Command airfield
- ⚓ Naval airfield

0   Miles   30

Acknowledgements

In a conflict on such an epic scale as the Battle of Britain, it is clearly impossible to cover every single sortie of every aircraft. I have sought to convey the overall story and also to focus on a few of the pilots and squadrons. These represent the achievements of The Few as a whole. I have chosen to deal in detail with 12 Group because I feel that its activities have not hitherto been put into the perspective of the entire battle. Of course I appreciate that 11 Group bore the brunt of the air fighting and acknowledge it freely and fully in the text. But no matter whether the participating pilots were in 10, 11 or 12 Groups, they all contributed to the eventual victory – and so did their counterparts on the ground, both men and women.

In addition to the list of general references, I would like to acknowledge, with sincere thanks, first-hand or other help from the following: Peter Townsend, Johnnie Johnson, Hugh Dundas, Alan Deere, Douglas Bader, Geoffrey Page, Tom Gleave, Richard Hillary, John Hannah, John Cunningham, Peter Brothers, E.S. Marrs, then P/O Stevenson, R.F. Hamlyn, Joan Pearson, Felicity Hanbury, then A.C.W. Cooper, then S/O Petters, Joan Hearn, R.S. Gilmour, John Sample, Gilbert Dalton, Richard Hough, Denis Richards, David Masters, J.M. Spaight, Jim Coates and Winston Churchill. Part of the final chapter is based on material in the official history *Royal Air Force 1939–45* Volume 1 by Denis Richards.

CHAPTER ONE

Hurricane and Spitfire Prelude

The Battle of Britain was one of the crucial conflicts in the history of civilization. It started officially on 10 July 1940 and ended on 31 October 1940. But the story goes back to the birth of the two famous fighters – the Hurricane and Spitfire. For without them there could have been no battle at all. The date was 1933: only six years before the war and seven before the Battle of Britain. At that time, the Royal Air Force had just thirteen fighter squadrons. Eight were equipped with Bristol Bulldogs, three with Hawker Furies and two with Hawker Demons. All were biplanes, with fixed propellers and undercarriages.

The idea of the Hurricane was born in October 1933 when its designer, Sydney Camm, submitted a first design to the Air Ministry. By December 1934 a wooden mock-up of the single-seat, highspeed fighter monoplane existed and in the following August the first prototype was underway. On 6 November 1935, Flight Lieutenant P.W.S. Bulman, chief test pilot of Hawkers at the time, took off on the first flight. The small silver monoplane climbed off a grass strip that was surrounded by the banked curves of the famous Brooklands racing car track.

Germany was rearming rapidly and to many men like Winston Churchill it seemed that time was already getting desperately short. With the maiden flight of the Hurricane, a sense of urgency was beginning to be instilled into the British government, too. All went well throughout the early tests and on 7 February 1936 Bulman was able to recommend the fighter as being ready for evaluation by the Royal Air Force. This came a mere three months after that first flight, a tribute to Sydney Camm's design. Two other pilots who participated in some of the early experimental work were Philip Lucas and John Hindmarsh.

On 3 June 1936 – three years before – the war Hawkers accepted a contract to construct 600 aircraft. Within a week they had issued fuselage manufacturing drawings. Soon after this, the Hurricane received official approval from the Air Ministry. Never before had such a big order been awarded in peacetime Britain. It proved in retrospect to have been a historic turning-point in the outcome of the Battle of Britain.

In the course of production, Hawkers had to make a number of modifications. As a result of rigorous tests of the original prototype by the RAF, several snags had appeared. Not surprisingly, in a comparatively revolutionary design. During the 1937 flights simulating high-speed combat duties, canopies of the closed cockpit were actually lost on five occasions, but the trouble was eventually cured.

The first production model of the Hurricane, with a Merlin II engine, made its maiden flight on 12 October 1937: only two years before the war now. Seven weeks later, seven aircraft were in the air. The Merlin II engine change put the overall production programme back. Even so, the first four Hurricanes for the RAF reached 111 Squadron at Northolt during that December and a dozen more came along in January and February 1938.

The British public became dramatically aware of the new super-fighter when Squadron Leader J. Gillan, Commanding Officer of III Squadron, took off on 10 February 1938 from Turnhouse, Edinburgh, just after five o'clock on a gloomy and wild winter dusk. Gillan ascended to an altitude of 17,000 feet and flew over the clouds without the aid of oxygen. An 80-mph wind whistled him southwards at a great speed for those days. About 40 minutes

Prototype Hurricane.

later, he dipped his Hurricane into a dive, registering an air-speed of 380 mph. Once below the clouds, he made out Northolt aerodrome in the early evening darkness – 'startled at the realisation that the ground-speed was likely to be in the region of 450 mph'. The actual statistics for the flight were as follows: 327 miles from Turnhouse to Northolt in 48 minutes at an average ground-speed of 408.75 mph.

A fighter, which far outstripped anything that preceded it, had shown its paces. By the spring of 1938, RAF Kenley was the second fighter station to see the Hurricane, when 3 Squadron received its quota of eighteen aircraft. The strength of a squadron in the air was twelve, its total strength eighteen. The six extra were held as immediate replacements for unserviceable aircraft.

As the international situation became more menacing through 1938, the British people derived reassurance from these squat-looking but effective Hurricane fighters snarling above them in the skies. By September 1938, five RAF squadrons had received Hurricanes. This was the time of the Munich Crisis, when Neville Chamberlain appeased Hitler, but in so doing gave Britain crucial extra time to produce more aircraft. It was as well that the war did not break out then, instead of 1939. Perhaps Mr Chamberlain has been unduly maligned in some quarters for his stance.

Meanwhile, the intervening year enabled the Royal Air Force to double its Fighter Command strength. From the total of nearly 500 Hurricanes actually delivered to squadrons and to the reserve, about three-quarters were built in that vital year between the Septembers of 1938 and 1939. When war finally started on 3 September 1939, eighteen squadrons of RAF Fighter Command were equipped with Hurricanes.

At the time of the Munich Crisis, deliveries of the other famous fighter, the Spitfire, were only just starting. The Spitfire story goes back even further than that of the Hurricane. The Spitfire was descended from a dynasty of seaplanes competing in the celebrated Schneider Trophy contest. The award went to the aeroplane with the fastest average speed over a set course. R.J. Mitchell was the designer of the Spitfire and a decade earlier he had been responsible for the first British Schneider Trophy hope – the S.4 monoplane seaplane. Unfortunately this crashed before the 1926 contest took place. The next year the Schneider Trophy was held at Venice and the British entries were three S.5 seaplanes developed from the S.4. Royal Air Force personnel formed the flying team and they won the Trophy that year.

The next Schneider Trophy year was 1929. With the endorsement of the Air Ministry, the S.6 went into production. Mitchell made a change to Rolls Royce engines, giving the famous makers a mere six months for the job. The venue for the event was Spithead off the Hampshire coast, where the S.6 faced the redoubtable Macchi seaplanes from Italy. The British pilot,

Flight Lieutenant H.R.D. Waghorn won the Trophy at an average speed of 328.63 mph.

So Britain had won the Trophy twice. A third victory and it would be hers permanently. But in the bleak economic climate of 1931, the British government refused further financial support. However, Lady Houston stepped in privately, offering £100,000 for the purpose. Mitchell had only time to improve his S.6 into the S.6B.

This time the British had no competition. The Italian and French entries literally could not get off the water, so the British were the only starters. They just had to complete the course to win the Trophy outright. On 13 September 1931, thousands of people – including myself when very young! – lined the coast at Southsea, Gosport and elsewhere to see Flight Lieutenant J.W. Boothman average 340.08 mph over the stipulated course. On the same day, Flight Lieutenant Stainforth set up a new world speed record of 379.05 mph and on 29 September he increased this to 407.05 mph.

After that Mitchell and his staff felt that their work could best be channelled into developing a high-speed monoplane landplane fighter. As soon as the Air Ministry announced its specification for a day-and-night fighter monoplane with four guns, Mitchell urged his firm to tender. His Supermarine F7/30, however, was not approved by the government – but it did act as an indispensable link between the S.6B and the Spitfire. In any case, a new official specification was out for an eight-gun monoplane fighter. The projected machine-gun power had thus been doubled, and at the same time the government decided that the gun most likely to meet the needs of the new fighter would be the American Browning. Supermarine's restyled F7/30 to cope with the new requirement.

Just four months almost to the day after the first flight of the Hurricane, the Spitfire prototype was flown on 5 March 1936 from Eastleigh airport. The aircraft was under the charge of Captain 'Mutt' Summers, chief test pilot of the Vickers group. An onlooker described the new machine as 'a highly polished silvery monoplane that looked almost ridiculously small, with a seemingly enormous wooden propeller'. The machine took off, the undercarriage went up, and in a minute the Spitfire became a dot in the Hampshire sky. Then Mitchell had to convert the prototype into the production version, complete with eight-gun armament.

In 1936 the British public had not heard of either of the two magic names – Spitfire and Hurricane. The Spitfire appeared in public for the first time on 27 June 1936 at the famous prewar RAF Hendon Air Display. The prototype Hurricane flew on the same day, skimming the crowd just before the Spitfire. It marked the very first time the pair had flown in proximity – but not the last!

The First of The Few. R.J. Mitchell designed
the immortal Spitfire fighter but never lived
to see it in production.

The order was placed for Spitfire production and the agreement dated
3 July 1936. The contract was for 310 Spitfires to fulfil the plan of that year for
500 Hurricanes and 300 Spitfires to be in service by March 1939. In those
days, this sort of mass production represented a vast task to an aviation
manufacturer. The Spitfire's stressed skin construction called for tooling that
was both expensive and time-consuming. Tragically, that heroic figure
R.J. Mitchell died on 11 June 1937 when only 42 – before he could see the first
Spitfire off the production line. He has rightly been called 'The First of The
Few'. The first Spitfire was in fact flight-tested in May 1938.

That autumn of 1938, RAF Fighter Command had 29 fighter squadrons. Of
these, only five had Hurricanes. Pilots of the other 24 squadrons were flying
obsolete biplanes with fixed undercarriages, insignificant fire-power, and
maximum level speeds of around 220 mph. This was just one year before the
war.

The first Spitfire to go into the Royal Air Force reached 19 Squadron at
Duxford on 4 August 1938. The rate of arrival after this historic fighter landed
at the Cambridgeshire airfield was just one a week. Numbers 19 and 66
Squadrons, both also at Duxford, were the first two to be equipped with
Spitfires during the next weeks. On 8 March 1939, it was officially announced
that the Spitfire maximum level speed was 362 mph at 18,500 feet and that its
rate of climb was around 2,000 feet per minute. At long last Britain had a
fighter comparable to any in the world. These two squadrons were followed
by 41 Squadron at Catterick in Yorkshire, then 74 and 54 Squadrons, both
stationed at Hornchurch in Essex.

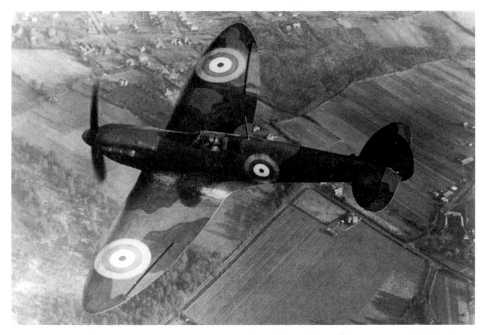

Prototype Spitfire.

Messerschmitt Me l09E with Daimler-Benz engine.

In July 1939 a two-pitch airscrew (coarse and fine) was fitted to the Spitfire, increasing its top speed to 367 mph. In August, less than four weeks before the outbreak of the war, these airscrews were being fitted to all production Spitfires. On 3 September 1939, there were already 400 Spitfires in service, and over 2,000 on order. That was a very different state of affairs from a year earlier. But Britain was still short of fighters and, worse still, short of pilots suitably qualified to fly them.

Douglas Bader described the Spitfire and Hurricane as 'two matchless fighters, born of British genius, produced by British craftsmen and, in the event, sustained by the whole British Nation'. It was these two fighters, flown by The Few, which would either win or lose the Battle of Britain.

CHAPTER TWO

From Dunkirk to Day One

The scene: Dunkirk. The date: late-May to early June 1940. In the skies over Dunkirk, the Royal Air Force met and mastered the Luftwaffe although those on the ground did not always know it. This was not yet part of the Battle of Britain. It was merely a preliminary skirmish. Yet two names taken at random symbolized the spirit which would later win the battle and enable Britain to prevail. These were Pilot Officer Alan Deere and WAAF Corporal Joan Pearson.

New Zealander Alan Deere crashed seven times altogether – and actually had nine lives in all. The first two escapes happened around the time of Dunkirk. Number one caused him 'little trouble' so he did not really count

France: 1940. Pilots of 1 Squadron race to their Hurricanes.

that. It was late-May when his real adventures began. In due course they were threaded right through the Battle of Britain proper.

Deere was with 54 Squadron on patrol over Calais when he shot down two Messerschmitts. Within two hours he was back over Calais when his squadron ran into fifteen Heinkel IIIs and nine Me 110s. They claimed eleven destroyed without loss, one of them being credited to Deere. On that initial day, Alan Deere flew for seven hours twenty minutes.

Two days later he was flying at 20,000 feet over Dunkirk again, when the squadron attacked Ju 88 bombers and 20 Me 110s making for two British destroyers on escort or evacuation duty. The Spitfires dived to the attack. Deere set an enemy aircraft alight and followed it down to see it crash on a beach near Dunkirk itself. During that dive he experienced for the first time what it was like to be attacked. For an instant he was spellbound by the sight of the tracer bullets streaming past his wings. There was a terrific bang. He was flung upside down, diving straight at the sea 1,000 feet below, and only managed to pull out of his descent just above the surface. As he headed for home, he saw a hole in his port wing nearly big enough to crawl through, but he managed to fly the Spitfire to England and land safely on a flat tyre. It was a cannon shell exploding in the tyre that had upset him and all but sent him crashing into the sea. That was the first escape. But as he said, he did not really count that one.

Next day the evacuation of the British forces from Dunkirk was in full swing, and 54 Squadron went over to protect the troops from German bombers. Deere dived after a Junkers 88 at 400 miles an hour and sent it down

Lockheed Hudson over the historic armada evacuating British Expeditionary Force from Dunkirk.

in flames before the end of the patrol. On the following morning, he was given command of a flight and sent to patrol the beaches again. They were crowded with troops. A dense cloud of smoke from burning oil tanks blotted out the sky over the actual port. It was a few minutes after four O'clock in the morning when he arrived with his Spitfire over the beaches. At once he began to chase and close on a Dornier 17.

The tail-gunner of the bomber opened fire at extreme range to try to drive off the Spitfire. Unluckily for Alan Deere, some shots hit his aeroplane, causing the glycol to start leaking and then pouring from the fighter. Despite this Deere continued to return the fire of the Dornier for as long as he could see ahead. But the Spitfire had been so completely disabled that Deere had no alternative but to make a crash-landing somewhere along the beach. He managed this, quite an achievement in the desperate circumstances, but the impact between aircraft and shoreline knocked him out. Coming round a minute or two later, Deere immediately became aware of the engine smoking furiously. Not wishing to risk being burned, he ripped off his straps, got clear of the cockpit, and sat down on the beach. At that moment he could only curse his bad luck rather than appreciate how fortunate he was just to be alive. Deere had commanded his flight for barely one hour before being shot down for the second time in a few days.

He had actually crashed several miles from Dunkirk. The rest of that day became one long struggle for him, as he became part of the mass British retreat. He had never seen anything so terrible as the ruins of Dunkirk. He got to the evacuation beach at last and was so worn out that he crept into an old ice-cream shed and fell sound asleep. Awakened by crowds of tired soldiers milling on the beach he took his place in the inevitable queue to get away. Eventually they were all able to board one of the destroyers continually arriving at that particular pier. Enemy bombers flew overhead. As Deere said later:

> After nearly five hours of dodging bombs we sighted the white cliffs of Dover. Here we berthed and I was soon clambering ashore, thankful to be on good old English soil again. I arrived back at my home station next day hardly twenty-four hours after my departure, twenty-four of the most adventurous hours I shall ever hope to spend.

After twelve days in continuous action around Dunkirk, Deere and the rest of 54 Squadron were rested. They returned to active service in the middle of June.

So Alan Deere had demonstrated the sort of opposition that the *Luftwaffe* could expect in the air. Corporal Joan Pearson showed the same spirit on the ground. While Deere was flying over Dunkirk, Joan Pearson was serving at the Fighter Command station of RAF Detling in Kent. The air was in Joan's blood and she had been learning to fly herself before the war. Now she felt she was doing the next best thing by helping the Royal Air Force. It was 30 May.

The WAAF quarters were located near the Detling airfield, and the girls heard aircraft taking off during that evening. Joan was off duty and went to bed as usual. She dozed into a fitful sleep soon after midnight. It was hard to sleep soundly as aircraft were regularly revving up and patrols going out or returning. Being in the medical branch, she was always on the alert, even when not on duty. It seemed somehow instinctive.

About 1 am Joan awoke at the approach of a particular aircraft sound. It was not the noise of a normal fighter. More like a fighter-bomber. An engine had cut out; she could tell that at once. Before she could do much else except sit up in bed, she heard a reverberating, rending crash followed by an uncanny second's silence. Then the sound of a roaring engine.

The aircraft had landed near the WAAF quarters. By then Joan's duty trousers and fisherman's jersey were on, and she was groping out of the hut in the black-out. She could not even remember if she had put on boots or shoes. All she knew suddenly, here she was – running over wet, dewy grass; footfalling across the cement road; stumbling towards the guard house. A few flames were moving in the air and there must have been some sort of noise from the crash. It scarcely registered as she ran. A twinkling light. That meant the ambulance or blood wagon. She must warn the guard to undo the gates quickly to let it through. The guard grunted as she ran by him. He knew her, and she shouted to him: 'The ambulance is behind.'

She kept running hard towards the crash and she came to an RAF policeman. 'You can't go over there,' he yelled, trying to stop her climbing the fence. But she did. Men were shouting for the doctor and the ambulance. Joan yelled: 'They're coming.'

Fire crackled from the crash. The nettles in the ditch on the far side of the fence stung her. She was near the crash scene now. A figure panted up and she saw another one silhouetted against the flames. An airman tried to drag at someone in the aircraft. Joan told him: 'Go and get the fence down for the ambulance.'

She knew there were weapons aboard the burning aircraft, which could go off. Yet she struggled to drag the pilot free from the flames. He was seriously hurt by the crash and groaned with the pain. Joan decided to render first-aid on the spot, in case of further damage. Another of the aircrew had been killed outright by the crash-landing.

Joan fought her way through the wreckage, stood on it, and roused the stunned pilot. Somehow amid scalding heat she stripped off his parachute harness and found that his neck particularly was hurting badly.

Burning oil tank destroyed by the RAF at Dunkirk. Other bombs damaged railway marshalling yards.

'Keep clear,' he gasped weakly at her, thinking of the bombs. But she stayed with him and helped him out of the cockpit. It was then that the petrol tanks blew. Joan lay down quickly and tried to shield the light from his face, as he was suffering from extreme shock, only really semi-conscious. Somehow again she got him completely clear of the aircraft, and about 30 yards off; holding his head carefully to prevent further dislocation or injury. She still had the bombs at the back of her mind.

It was then that a 120-pounder erupted. Instinctively she hurled herself on top of the pilot to protect him from blast and stray splinters. There was one more bomb still to go. Meanwhile, Joan continued to comfort him. He was conscious now and, in his state of shock, seemed most concerned about a small cut on his lip in case it showed! An airman crawled up and lent Joan his pocket handkerchief to tend the pilot while she waited for the ambulance to arrive. Joan thought subconsciously that the bomb seemed to have taken all the oxygen out of the surrounding air.

She felt it must be only a matter of seconds before the other bomb went up, so she ran to the fence to help the medical officer over with the stretcher. The pilot could soon be safe. In a few moments they got him aboard the ambulance.

Just in time. For the second bomb burst with an earthquaking explosion. More blast and splinters. But by then they were safely on the blood wagon and on their way to the sick quarters. Joan went straight on duty to see to the pilot's wounds herself, finishing for the night about 3 am. Sick parade was at 8.30 am as usual. She was there as usual. Seven weeks later, Assistant Section Officer Joan Pearson got the Empire Gallantry Medal later to be converted into the George Cross.

The Battle of France was lost. The British Expeditionary Force was forced to evacuate through Dunkirk. All its equipment was being left in enemy hands. No equivalent loss of material had ever happened in history. The Royal Navy, Royal Air Force, merchant seamen, and civilian boatmen were all contributing to the salvation.

Dunkirk meanwhile would rank among the battle honours of the RAF. Beside the tidewater, there stood thousands of weary troops awaiting embarkation – and offering ideal targets for attack from the air. Along the coast lay ships and craft of every conceivable kind, waiting their turn to rescue these men. And again presenting a perfect target from the air. The Luftwaffe bases were not far off. Conditions could scarcely have been more propitious for them to annihilate the British forces. But it never happened. The air attack was met and broken by the RAF. Our fighter squadrons were second only to the Navy in saving the BEF. Pilots hurled their aircraft on the enemy. broke up their formations, spoiled their aim, made accurate attack difficult, and generally harried them for the best part of a week until the evacuation was nearly complete.

Many squadrons took part in the furious air fighting and the protective patrols. Number 222 under Squadron Leader 'Tubby' Mermagen was just one of them – with Douglas Bader as a relatively raw flight commander! For several days they took off from Martlesham or Hornchurch or elsewhere at 4.30 am bound for Dunkirk. The black smoke over the beaches spread ever wider, ever denser. Number 222 Squadron was not in the thickest of the fight but even so they set an Me 109 on fire and it crashed. But two of the squadron pilots were missing ...

June now. From less than a mile overhead, they saw the ever-changing epic of Dunkirk. Most of the ground forces had got away by then – including Alan Deere! Only the valiant rear troops remained. By 3–4 June Dunkirk was over. Bader happened to fly on the very last patrol over the beaches on 4 June. The remnants of equipment, the craters, the wrecks, could never fully convey all that had occurred there. Then the pilots headed home for a brief rest. They had been on duty non-stop for over a week – and they slept around the clock almost twice over. But the immortal evacuation had been accomplished and over 335,000 troops were brought home safely to English shores. The Royal Air Force had acquitted itself with honour. No one yet knew what lay ahead of them.

That same day, 4 June, Winston Churchill told Parliament:

> There was a victory inside the deliverance. It was gained by the Royal Air Force. There was a great trial of strength between the British and German air forces. Can you conceive a greater objective for the Germans in the air than to make evacuation from those beaches impossible? And to sink all those ships which were displayed to the extent of almost a thousand? Can there have been an objective of greater military importance and significance for the whole purpose of the war than this? They tried hard and they were beaten back; they were frustrated in their task. We got the Army away.

The fate of Britain would now depend on victory in the air. Hitler knew that the prerequisite for all his invasion plans was winning air supremacy above the English Channel and the chosen landing places along our south coast. The preparation of enemy embarkation ports, assembling the transports needed, minesweeping passages to the British beaches – all these would be impossible unless free of air attack. For the actual crossing and landings, complete mastery of the airspace over the transports and beaches was the decisive condition. So the enemy answer would be the attempted destruction of the RAF and its system of airfields lying between London and the coasts.

The Luftwaffe had been engaged to its limit in the Battle of France and the German navy similarly occupied in the recent Norway campaign. Fortunately, they both needed a period to recover. The pause was certainly convenient for Britain and the RAF, as virtually all its fighter squadrons had at one time or another been operating in France and over Dunkirk. So the Luftwaffe recuperated and redeployed for its next job. There could be no doubt what this would be. Hitler must invade and conquer England, or face prolonging the war indefinitely, with all the implications and complications involved.

Though the Battle of Britain did not start in earnest until the following month, the Germans started air activity over Britain within 48 hours of Dunkirk. In fact, there had been earlier raids in May and the first week of June, but only stray sorties. On 9 May for instance, bombs fell in a wood near Canterbury. Later in the month, more were dropped in the south-east, Yorkshire and East Anglia. During the Dunkirk period, bombs exploded in Norfolk, Sussex, Lincolnshire and Suffolk. Then on the night of 5–6 June, just after Dunkirk, attacks were made on east coast aerodromes and ports. Bombs fell near Bircham Newton and Horsham St Faith. A dozen high explosives also disrupted the airfield at Hemswell, one hitting a hangar. A few also exploded at the Alexandra Docks in Grimsby.

On the next night, too, bombs were reported near four airfields – Upwood, Cranwell, Mildenhall and Feltwell – all famous names in RAF annals but not all necessarily fighter stations. A stray bomb fell on the roof of the United Steel Rolling Mill Scunthorpe, and another on John Brown's works. On 7 June, East Anglian and Lincolnshire aerodromes again seemed to be the main targets. Bombs were aimed at half a dozen airfields, but activity was still on small scale nuisance raids more than anything else. On the same night, an enemy bomber crashed at 1.49 am near Eyke, three miles from Woodbridge.

It was a fortnight after Dunkirk before hostile air activity reached any real strength. About 100 enemy aircraft crossed the various coasts on 18 June and dropped bombs on eastern and southeast England. They caused casualties of twelve civilians killed and thirty injured. Scunthorpe, King's Lynn, Waddington and Louth were targets, but the enemy suffered several losses, too, due to close co-operation between searchlights and fighters. Just after a Heinkel III shot down a Blenheim fighter, Flt Lt Duke-Woolley of 23 Squadron destroyed the He Ill, which ended up near Sheringham. Squadron Leader O'Brien, also of 23 Squadron, went for another He 111 over Newmarket racecourse, damaging it severely. But O'Brien's aircraft was hit, too, and he had to bale out. His navigator and air gunner were both killed. F/O Barnwell was reported missing after helping to shoot down yet another He III into the sea off Felixstowe. Others crashed near Cambridge and as far away as Margate. F/O Petrie of 19 Squadron had to bale out with bad burns and was hurried to hospital at Bury St Edmunds.

On 19 June, comparable raids killed eight civilians and injured some sixty. Other raiders laid mines in the vital Humber zone, while bombs fell near Louth, Grimsby, Withernsea, Hemswell and Scunthorpe. Then on the night of 21 June, heavier enemy thrusts were represented by about 100 hostile aircraft on the plotting tables. Aerodromes and towns were again on the receiving end: airfields in Norfolk, Suffolk and Lincolnshire, and the towns of Grimsby, Hull and Lowestoft. Bombs were actually reported from a dozen East Anglian areas: Harleston, Wattisham (where I later flew at 1,500 mph!), Colchester, Bircham Newton, Coltishall, Harwich, Newmarket, Orfordness, Digby, Duxford, Wittering and Winterton. As well as bombing Louth, the enemy also machine-gunned searchlights there. The beam of a searchlight always made the ground crew vulnerable to such an air attack.

24 June: some seventy enemy were plotted, though thick cloud precluded any interceptions. A slight switch of targets made East Anglian airfields and Midlands industrial areas the main objects of attention. For the first time one or two bigger towns and cities began to be visited: Derby and Coventry as well as the usual ten-or-so airfields. On the next night, Grimsby and Hull had some

bombs. Night fighters, or rather night fighting, was still at a relatively primitive stage, but air patrols fared a bit better. P/O Morgan of 222 Squadron shot down a He III, though he sustained severe injuries when his own aircraft crashed soon afterwards. Rugby and Wolverhampton figured among the night's ten locations where bombs exploded – still on rather a restricted scale.

Two fighters had to force-land during an unsuccessful attempt at finding the enemy on 25 June, but neither of the crews were hurt. Leicester, Coventry and Stafford all had a few haphazard bombs, while airfields were awakened more than once by the crump of explosions on earth. Then two nights later again it was the same story of aerodromes and Midlands, industrial targets plus the new ingredient of the Liverpool area. So scattered bombs fell right across the country from Grantham in the east to the Wirral Peninsula.

29 June saw the first experience, though not the last, of bombs around Birmingham and Stoke-on-Trent. On the last night of June, a Blenheim fighter of 29 Squadron crashed near Kneeton at about 1.30 am. Pilot Officer Sisman and Sergeant A. Reed were both killed. They were believed to have been pursuing an enemy bomber which was eventually brought down further south.

These rather desultory but casualty-causing raids went on as July opened amid rain, low cloud and hence poor visibility – all restricting fighter retaliation to raids. On 2 July, 32 incendiaries were sprayed north-east of Coventry at 1.23 am, while seven bombs burst in the suburbs of Ipswich. In early July enemy air attacks were largely concentrated on ports and coastal shipping, though inland goals were not neglected. On 4 July, quite a heavy raid on the Portland area resulted in an auxiliary vessel being set on fire; a tug and a lighter sunk; and some buildings turned to rubble. Eleven civilians were killed in this single raid. Then at nine minutes past midnight on 5/6 July, nineteen bombs burst near Spurn Head, followed by a further batch south of Saltfleet. On 7 July a stick of bombs straddled the airfield area of West Rainham.

Down south now in these early days of July, Alan Deere was back in action. He took his flight up to 8,000 feet to patrol over Deal in Kent. Seeking enemy raiders reported leaving Calais, they encountered a silver seaplane, twelve Me 109s flying at about 1,000 feet, and another five well behind at 6,000 feet. Deere led a section of Spitfires to attack the five Me 109s, and having disposed of one of them he saw another coming up in his rear mirror. Doing a steep turn to meet the enemy head-on over the Goodwin Sands, he fired at the same time as the German. Deere described the rest of the action himself:

We were dead head-on and he was right in my sights. I don't remember whether I thought about avoiding a collision by breaking away, but things seemed to happen so suddenly. The first awakening was a large nose looming up in front of me. There was a terrific and horrible thud and then my aircraft began to vibrate so violently that I thought my engine must surely shake itself off the bearers. Black smoke poured into the cockpit and flames appeared from the engine. I reached to open the hood in order to bale out, only to discover that his propeller had struck the front of my windscreen and the whole fixture was so twisted that I could not move the hood.

I could not see for smoke, but managed to ascertain that I was headed inland. Nearly blinded and choked, I succeeded in keeping the airspeed at about 100 miles an hour. The engine had now seized and I was just waiting to hit the ground. Suddenly there was a terrific jerk, and I was tossed left then right and finally pitched forward on my straps, which fortunately held fast. I seemed to plough through all sorts of things and then stop.

The remains of my ammunition were going off in a series of pops, and the flames were getting very near the cockpit. I frantically broke open the hood and, undoing my harness, ran to a safe distance. My eyebrows were singed, both my knees were bruised, but otherwise I was uninjured. The Spitfire was blazing furiously in the middle of a cornfield and had left a trail of broken posts and pieces of wing, plus the complete tail unit extending for 200 yards.

That was Alan Deere's third escape of his seven crashes and nine lives. The next day was more routine. He was back on patrol. His further adventures overlap into the Battle of Britain proper.

Douglas Bader was promoted and given command of 242 Squadron. This was the only Canadian squadron in the entire RAF at that time. Most of its pilots came from Canada naturally; only a month or more earlier they had been flying in France, and they had suffered badly – losing some eight of their strength. They needed someone tough to pull them together again. A man did not come any tougher than Bader. He had lost his legs in a flying accident in December 1931 and argued his way back into the RAF after the outbreak of war. Number 242 Squadron was regarded as fully operational on 9 July. They had mere hours to wait for their first encounters and victories. The next day, 10 July, marked the official launch of the Battle of Britain.

So during June and early July the Luftwaffe revived and regrouped its formation and established itself on all the French and Belgian airfields selected for the forthcoming fight. Meanwhile by its reconnaissance and tentative probing forays, it was seeking to measure the character and scale of the opposition it might meet. It was on 10 July that the first heavier onslaught started.

CHAPTER THREE

The Battle Begins

The Battle of Britain. Before beginning the actual battle, we must know the disposition of the principal RAF forces and who led them. Fighter Command comprised three main Groups within the area of the conflict. Number 11 Group took the strain of the battle and was based across south-east England in Kent, Surrey, Sussex, part of Hampshire, and north of the Thames in parts of Essex, Cambridgeshire, Suffolk, plus an equivalent region north-west of London. Number 12 Group were generally immediately north of this line. And 10 Group were more towards the west country.

Hugh Dowding in charge of Fighter Command. Some said he left too much to Keith Park, commander of 11 Group.

Trafford Leigh-Mallory led 12 Group with imagination – though it was not always appreciated by Fighter Command Headquarters.

The various commanders involved were as follows: Air Chief Marshal Sir Hugh C.T. Dowding was the Air Officer Commanding-in-Chief, Fighter Command, whose headquarters were at Bentley Priory, Stanmore, Middlesex; Air Vice-Marshal K.R. Park was AOC 11 Group; Air Vice-Marshal T.L. Leigh-Mallory AOC 12 Group; and Air Vice-Marshal Sir C.J.G. Brand AOC 10 Group. The first three of these four commanders figure vitally in the story a little later on. Most of the squadrons who were destined to fight in the battle had their bases in 11 Group, but it is still open to question whether it was necessarily wise for these bases to have been situated so vulnerably and so near the attacking airfields in France and the Low Countries: particularly bases like Manston, Hawkinge and Lympne. All were within sight of the French coast and hence the enemy.

10 July

Day One of the Battle of Britain dawned wet, became dry but cloudy and eventually cleared. As so often, it opened with enemy reconnaissance aircraft reporting back on damage done in previous raids and also checking on the weather.

Air Marshal Sir Keith Park in the cockpit of his Harvard some years after the Battle of Britain. He was C-in-C, 11 Group.

Dowding escorts the King and Queen on tour of Fighter Command HQ.

Despite the rain, 66 Squadron at Coltishall in 12 Group was scrambled before breakfast – so no scrambled eggs. Pilot Officer Charles Cooke led a section of Spitfires above the lower drizzle and into summer sun. Their target was a Dornier 17, which between them they managed to destroy. It churned into the North Sea off Great Yarmouth, and the section of three Spitfires were back on Norfolk soil for a belated breakfast. This was merely a brief overture to a day featuring a fight with 100 or more aircraft participating.

Another Dornier was on reconnaissance a bit later off Kent when it sighted a Channel convoy steaming for the Straits of Dover. The enemy attached importance to the role of these lone Dorniers, for a force of Me 109s was shepherding it. A flight from the soon-to-be-famous 74 Squadron, 11 Group, was scrambled to intercept from their over-forward base of Manston. On a clear day from here they could see Cap Gris Nez all too distinctly. The Spitfires managed hits on the Dornier, although they were surrounded by what looked like a squadron of the Me 109 escorts.

This little bout was in turn a precursor of the main dogfights of the day. By mid-morning the Luftwaffe were aware of the convoy, and sent a fresh squadron of Messerschmitts to the Dover area to coax or hoax some RAF fighters to take off. Biggin Hill Spitfires responded to this challenge, intercepted them, and exchanged brief bursts without major result on either side: almost like an inter-change of calling cards. Thus ended the morning of Day One.

Between one and two o'clock, radar picked up an enemy assembly in their already familiar rendezvous region of Cap Gris Nez. It was clearly 11 Group territory, though much later 12 Group disputed this claim. Five RAF squadrons took off, including 32 and 111, the former reaching the Dover airspace first. Their Hurricanes saw two dozen Dorniers and nearly twice as many Messerschmitts, 110s and 109s. When 74 Squadron arrived soon afterwards, J.H. Mungo Park hit a Dornier, while an Me 109 was struck right over Dover town.

As if to underline the power of the defence, Squadron Leader John Thompson led his Hurricanes of 111 Squadron straight for the bombers. This unnerved the German crews and their well-drilled v-formation quickly broke rigid ranks. One Hurricane got too close to a Dornier and they smashed. The enemy bomber went down with all its aircrew. One wing of the Hurricane flailed off and the fighter spiralled into home waters. The pilot, Tom Higgs, was lost but an English air-sea rescue craft picked up two of the German crew, so half of their number survived.

Meanwhile the convoy had reached the Straits of Dover, as more dogfights raged overhead and above the harbour. The silhouette of the historic crenellated castle etched itself on the hill overlooking the east side of the town. Amid all the confusion in the skies, at least 100 combined aircraft were slogging it out at several hundred miles an hour. The five squadrons of 11 Group plus the sixty-odd original enemy aircraft. At length the Luftwaffe broke off the attack on the convoy, with damage to only one vessel and the loss of Tom Higgs in his doomed Hurricane.

There was only time now for momentary mourning. Far away in the west country, almost exactly the same number of enemy aeroplanes were nosing for Falmouth and Swansea. The only difference was that whereas the Channel battle had been against twenty-four Dorniers and forty mixed Messerschmitts, all sixty-odd aircraft aimed at the two western targets were Junkers 88s. Through no fault of its own, 10 Group responded rather late and none of the bombers was hit. Falmouth and Swansea, on the other hand, were struck quite severely, causing inevitable casualties. The respective aircraft losses for the day were thirteen German and six British, though no further RAF pilots were lost after Higgs. He has gone into history as the first pilot fatality of the official Battle of Britain.

Up in 12 Group a section of 242 Squadron patrolled over a convoy ten miles off Lowestoft. Sub-Lt Gardner – seconded from the Fleet Air Arm – had the most decisive combat of the trio. He noticed an aircraft four miles north-east of the ships. Catching it up, he established it as an enemy – always important when under stress. Then he dived to the attack in direct line astern. Next he came in fast on the port side. His fire struck both the port engine and the undercarriage. After another attack, the Heinkel either crashed or pancaked into the sea. In the two or three minutes before it sank, one of the crew climbed on to a wing ... that was all Gardner saw. This was a cross-section of the aerial activity on Day One. There were 113 days yet to come before 31 October, not all as comparatively quiet as this.

11 July

Day Two. The second page of a book not yet written. At this stage, no one knew how long it would be, nor whether it would have a happy ending. Number 10 Group in the west country seemed vulnerable. Based at Box in Wiltshire, the Group had four sectors: Middle Wallop, St Eval, Filton and Pembrey. There were four squadrons each of Spitfires and Hurricanes plus a few Blenheims and even Gladiators. By this date their strength was less than this.

Mixed fortunes marked the day, perhaps foreshadowing lessons to be learnt by both sides on a larger scale in succeeding weeks. The first of two Junkers 87 *Stuka* raids resulted in their large force of escorting Me 109s getting the better of an argument with a small flight of Hurricanes and then half of 609 Squadron of Spitfires from Middle Wallop. Two precious Spitfire

Junkers 87 *Stuka* dive-bomber
releasing its weapons.

pilots perished in this melee. But Hurricanes from 601 Squadron, Tangmere, Sussex, within 11 Group, redressed things when they claimed two bombers and a pair of escorting Me 110s in a raid on the port of Portland. The Bill was of course a prominent landmark from the air and guided raiders to the naval base. Portsmouth also received a raid, as well as scattered shipping on this generally overcast day. The losses logged were German twenty, British four.

On this day, cannon and machine-gun fire actually raked parts of old Portsmouth. My wife – née Joyce Howson – and other Admiralty staff were hurrying across the courtyard of the Old Grammar School building when the firing followed them to their air-raid shelter. Civilians were already in the forefront of the battle. Meanwhile the anti-aircraft defences were beginning more and more to be involved with the aerial fighting, often adding to abstract impressions in sight and sound.

Elsewhere, 11 July meant a memorable date for Douglas Bader. It marked the occasion of shooting down his first aircraft in the battle. He had already been credited with at least one over Dunkirk. Reports reached 12 Group that a bomber was attacking Cromer in wretched weather. Bader decided he would try this on his own. He took off amid heavy rain and sighted the bomber, a Dornier 17, a couple of miles off the Norfolk coast. At an altitude

Legless legend Douglas Bader and his Hurricane of 242 Squadron.

of only 1,500 feet, he made two assaults. Through the rain-spattered windscreen, he saw his tracer hitting home. One brief burst from the enemy rear-gunner lit up the gloom. After he returned to base, Bader heard a report from the Observer Corps at Norwich that the Dornier had been seen to crash into the sea immediately after the attack.

12 July

The contest switched back and forth from the west and 10 and 11 Groups to the east and 12 Group. Amid fog patches near the North Sea, a convoy ploughed sluggishly when attacked by Heinkels and Dorniers. The enemy made obstinate thrusts against the ships when met by Hurricanes from 12 Group. In the following scraps, the RAF suffered two fighters lost and some damaged.

At 8.24 am an enemy squadron crossed the coast near Felixstowe. Sections of 17, 19 and 85 Squadrons went for them 'in no uncertain manner'. The Germans veered off in the direction of the Convoy BOOTY but they were quickly caught. Several Dornier 17s were shot down. Throughout the running engagement, the RAF lost one Hurricane and its pilot, Sergeant Jowett, listed as missing.

In un-July-like weather involving thunder and a general depression, activity ranged as far north as Aberdeen, in a small enemy prod; south to Channel ships; and west to Wales. So England, Scotland and Wales were included in one day. The losses later agreed were German seven, British six. It was clear that these forays by the Luftwaffe must presage far larger and more concentrated, focused mass-raids. If not invasion. But where? And when?

13–18 July
In the uneasy interim, nearly a week passed with rather reduced air activity in continuing poor climatic conditions. Fog, rain, cloud, showers typified this phase, with the statistical outcome for the six days between these dates: German twenty-one lost, British twelve. Enemy targets were mainly in the pulse areas of Dover and Portland, plus Swanage, Norfolk, Scotland, and the Sussex coastline. While dealing with figures, too, in the four weeks from that first serious raid on 18 June, 336 civilians had already been killed and 476 seriously injured. Not as heavy as later, but not negligible.

19 July
Four fighters had entered the Battle of Britain with Royal Air Force roundels: Hurricane, Spitfire, Defiant and Blenheim. Already the Blenheim was seen progressively less against the Luftwaffe. On this day, the Defiant was to face the inevitable truth, too. In theory, the two-man fighter seemed comparable to its brace of immortal partners, but in practice the idea of a separately-operated gun turret behind the pilot's position was proving considerably

Gunner of Defiant fighter straps on his parachute as the pilot gets into the cockpit: Kirton-in-Lindsey, 25 July.

too schizophrenic for anyone actually flying the machine. And it only had four machine-guns instead of the eight arming the Spitfire and Hurricane.

The Defiants of 141 Squadron had barely landed at the vulnerable forward airfield of Hawkinge when they had to refuel and received instructions to keep guard on convoys clinging to the Kent coast between Dover and Folkestone and beyond at either end. The historic clifftop Leas at Folkestone could hardly have provided a more panoramic viewpoint of what happened soon afterwards.

This was really a baptism of fire for the untried Defiants. Three-quarters of the squadron had taken off from their Hawkinge plateau airfield amid the hills behind Folkestone. These gallant nine fighters with eighteen aircrew, began convoy patrol in the dangerous skies over the Straits. A squadron of Me 109s spotted them, to be joined by a second squadron. Already the odds were nearly three-to-one against. The Defiants and their crews were trapped and shot into the Channel. Not all nine, but certainly six. Towards the latter throes of the tragedy, No III Squadron of Hurricanes under Squadron Leader John Thompson raced on to the scene to salvage three of the Defiants. Of this trio, all the pilots managed to survive, but one of them lost the air-gunner.

The severe lesson would be digested quickly and the Defiant seemed doomed to a status less exposed than twenty-odd miles from enemy-held coastline. So 19 July went down as a rare day when the British losses of eight exceeded the enemy's two aircraft. Not fatal to the course of the battle, because for one thing there was a known reason: the Defiant and its flawed conception for the flexible, fluid, and ultra-fast air warfare now being seen and developing daily. The victors would be those who assimilated their experiences – good or bad. In fact, the victors would be the survivors.

At the other end of the scale, a lone raider circled the Humber–Hornsea region, loosing bombs near an Army post on the coast north of Hornsea. The bomber descended to a mere 100 feet and machine-gunned the post together with a cluster of bungalows occupied by troops. The soldiers valiantly but vainly tried to shoot him down with their Bren guns. On occasion it was still this sort of small-scale almost personal war: not for much longer.

20 July

English Channel shipping again formed a focus for enemy attention on the next day. One convoy was steaming east when discovered. Attacks on shipping developed in two very distinct areas, one off Lyme Regis – shades of Thomas Hardy and John Fowles – and the other in the much-churned waters off Dover. Hurricanes and Spitfires of 11 Group met Me 109s towards the summer evening.

In this particular match, the score was 4–2 in favour of the RAF, while the total tally that day came to 9–3. Night raids flew as far north-west as the Mersey, again a foretaste of destructive attacks along that heavily-peopled and industrialized strip culminating in the crucial port of Liverpool itself. A footnote to the day: 66 Squadron found an aircraft mis-identified to them as a Blenheim fighter. When challenged by them, the rear-gunner replied with tracer fire. They realized their error quickly.

21–31 July

For the four days up to 25 July, it was the same pattern on the same limited scale of operations. Daytime raids on shipping and night-time mine laying to try to tie up or destroy our vessels in the regions of major harbours and ports. But that was really a sub-plot in the overall campaign. The Channel, south, and east coasts were the shipping lanes pinpointed by the Luftwaffe.

Never at a loss for some rather devilish device, the Germans dropped whistling bombs on Honington during early morning attacks on 22 July, while magnetic mines laid in the Humber were promptly swept up by the Royal Navy. On the following night of 23 July, bombing along the east coast embraced the breezy resort of Skegness as well as the more customary Humber and Grimsby areas. Skegness was in fact the locale for Royal Navy training – at the former Butlin's holiday camp. Then on 24 July, also in East Anglia, P/O Cutts of 222 Squadron participated in a successful attack on He 111s while patrolling over Convoy PILOT. But Cutts ran right out of fuel in his enthusiasm and had to attempt a forced landing on the sea: no minor feat. Luckily he was picked up uninjured and another precious pilot was saved. Dowding would be grateful for that over the next two months. The losses for the four days before 25 July were: German twenty-one, British nine.

The next little landmark date was in fact 25 July. The enemy took advantage of improved weather and consequent bombing visibility to go for an especially substantial convoy hoping to trail through the Straits of Dover unnoticed. But the enemy made a triple-pronged onslaught at this somewhat unwieldy force of ships. German naval E-boats combined with Junkers Ju 87 *Stuka* bombers and even the big guns ranged around Cap Gris Nez. The new factor in this encounter was that all three elements of the enemy forces acted in unison – army, navy and air. Between them they could claim that out of the struggling convoy of twenty-one ships, eleven were either sunk or seriously disabled. Bad as this loss obviously was, the sinking also of two Royal Navy destroyers must have been thought even more alarming.

In the air itself, the dogfights went on. As usual at this earlier stage, the onus fell wholly on 11 Group, which found that its fighters added up to only one-quarter as many as the combined Junkers and Me 109s. The quality of

'Sailor' Malan in uncharacteristic pose as Group Captain of a fighter station.

54 Squadron of Spitfires was already especially established, but these odds were proving too much. One of the squadron's casualties was Flight Lieutenant Way, acting as a flight commander. An Me 109 pilot had killed him before his Spitfire eventually crashed uncontrolled. Despite the heavy aerial odds against the RAF, losses persisted in their favour. On this day they were German eighteen, British seven.

As a direct outcome of losing approximately half the convoy on 25 July, it was decided, perhaps rather belatedly, that as soon as could be arranged all future convoys should only use the confines of the English Channel after darkness. It would take a little time to instigate this change of plan. And moreover, the enemy's accounting for those two destroyers decided the Admiralty to move other RN battle craft of this and similar type from the extreme vulnerability of Dover harbour to the slightly safer, or at least more distant, port of Portsmouth. This was a wise decision, if again made rather tardily. The date of the decision was 28 July, and on the same day the celebrated South African, 'Sailor' Malan, led his 74 Squadron to a victory that read, for the RAF as a whole, 18–5.

On the fine morning of 29 July, the Luftwaffe chose Dover harbour and a couple of nearby convoys for 50 *Stukas* bombers under the umbrella of half-as-many-again Me 109s. Hurricanes and Spitfires tore to the skies over the stricken township, and together with the enemy attackers brought the total of aircraft towards 200. The quantities were mounting inexorably. From this mass conflict, reports insisted that four *Stukas* and a single Spitfire went down to the sea or land. After the *Stukas* over Dover came Junkers 88s

Sergeant Pilot of 610 Squadron in his Spitfire on 30 July.

skimming low over a convoy. On 29 July the sea losses included yet another destroyer sunk by enemy action. The sooner the daylight convoys stopped the better. Despite the growing scale of the aerial action, losses for the day were restricted to eight German, three British.

So it went on until the end of the month. More shipping hit; the balloon barrage protecting Dover and its harbour was also made a target. Lesser activity further north, where there was still time to breathe and report minor incidents. F/O Woods-Scawen of 85 Squadron espied a Dornier 17 about 45 miles east of Felixstowe. He chased it all the way to the Dutch coast, when he saw pieces falling from it. But then he took a quick sideways look at his fuel gauge, made a mental calculation, and swung around rapidly for home. He got there. 12 Group sent up 1,101 patrols during July, involving 2,668 operational flights. Although this was fairly small beer besides 11 Group, three DFCs were awarded: to Wing Commander J.H. Edwardes-Jones, Squadron Leader J.S. O'Brien, and Flight Lieutenant B.J.E. Lane. Adding up the official figures of losses for the first three weeks of the Battle of Britain, they came to German 155, British sixty-nine.

During the last day of July, Raeder told Hitler that the earliest date for any projected invasion of Britain would be – 15 September. An ironic choice in view of later stages in the story.

CHAPTER FOUR

Enter Bomber Command

1–7 August

As August opened, the enemy consolidated their plans for 'the final conquest' as Hitler put it rather too grandiosely. The Germans were due to launch large-scale attacks after 5 August on the Royal Air Force as a whole and everything connected with it: fighter stations; their aircraft in the air; aircraft on the ground; aircraft in the stages of being manufactured; and all suppliers relevant to the air war. The date of 15 September was still on the Nazi cards. After neutralizing the Royal Air Force, the air assault on London would be almost a formality – with the implementation of the invasion – Operation Sealion – just as smooth. That was the theory.

By the start of August the Luftwaffe had gathered 2,669 operational aircraft comprising 1,015 bombers, 346 dive-bombers, 933 fighters, 375 heavy fighters. Göring, in charge of the Luftwaffe, never set much store by

Göring and his staff officers on the Channel coast.

Operation Sealion: his heart was in the absolute air war. And his consequent distortion of the arrangements disturbed the German naval staff. The destruction of the RAF and our aircraft industry to them was only a means to an end: when this was accomplished, the air war should be turned against British warships and shipping. They regretted the lower priority assigned by Göring to the naval targets, and they were irked by the delays. Shortly afterwards they reported to the German supreme command that the preparation for mine laying in the Channel area could not proceed because of the constant British threat from the air.

Meanwhile – air attacks did continue. In mixed weather for early-August, ships remained targets, while various scattered inland targets presented a wide net – the Midlands, South Wales, Liverpool, and an aircraft factory in East Anglia. They could not get much more scattered than that.

On its first day, August was heralded with hostile raids and accompanying bombs near 12 Group airfields Wattisham and Martlesham Heath. The enemy clearly knew their locations well. Number 242 Squadron were still on regular convoy patrol and F/O Christie, P/O Latta, and Sgt Richardson flew over a convoy that evening.

All three came in contact with the enemy. Richardson saw a Junkers 88 at 6.55 pm. Flying only 700 feet above the North Sea, the bomber had black crosses on the side of its white fuselage. The Junkers tried to regain cloud cover. Richardson pressed home two attacks and the enemy's starboard engine stopped. Thick grey smoke trailed from the Junkers. The bomber began a very shallow dive and when just a few feet above the water its nose rose steeply so that the tail touched the sea first. The aircraft broke in two and sank within about 30 seconds. Sgt Richardson circled the scene and saw a

Aftermath of the attack on oil storage tanks at Shellhaven on the Thames, 7 August.

rubber boat break surface on top of the wreckage – and drift away slowly from it. Only a single survivor was glimpsed in the water and he vanished from view soon afterwards. No one appeared to be in the rubber boat …

Losses for the first three days of the month were German 9, 4, 4, British 1, 0, 0. Then on 4 August, only twenty-six years after the outbreak of the First World War, the figures were nil on either side, with scarcely any air action anywhere. Three further days of poor weather curtailed the losses to German 6, 1, 2, British 1, 1, 0. These came from fights during some desultory attacks on the shipping lanes. In retrospect it seems fair to presume that the enemy were preparing furiously for their orders to launch the massed raids on RAF targets. The next day, 8 August, marked the start of resumed increased combat, though still not targeted on airfields.

8–10 August

The first important phase of the Battle of Britain was from 8-18 August. Over this period, hundreds of enemy bombers with appropriate quantities of fighters attacked shipping and ports on the south-east and south coasts, at points between North Foreland (11 Group territory) and Portland (10 Group territory). On 8 August, a convoy steaming westward past Dover was the first to risk it in daylight for a fortnight. As the merchant ships and their naval escorts scampered for the Portsmouth-Southampton waters, the enemy raids started from Dover onwards and went on intermittently for hours. Junkers 87 *Stukas* followed its progress down-Channel and so the air battles centred around airspace shifting further and further from the Straits of Dover. Number 11 Group found the *Stukas* vulnerable to their attack and downed

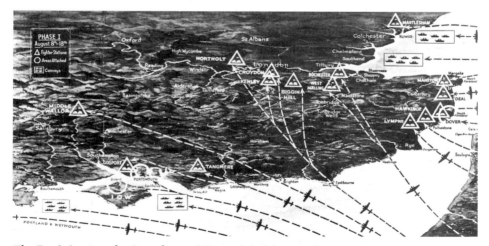

The Battle begins: the first phase of Göring's bid for aerial supremacy.

eight of them. But both sides lost fighters in considerable numbers with the RAF accounting for many Me 109s. Dogfights flared as far as the Isle of Wight, where the number of enemy aircraft present was put at 160. Two ships of the convoy were sunk. During the afternoon more than 130 enemy went for another convoy, off Bournemouth this time. Altogether the air encounters lasted almost continuously from 9 am until 5 pm and ran from Dover to Bournemouth. The day's losses were German thirty-one, British twenty.

As if to warn of the urban raids to come, the Luftwaffe ventured that night against Bristol, Birmingham, Liverpool and Leeds. The war was getting to be more nationwide all the time. But the big offensive still had to wait a few days. More inclement weather on 9 and 10 August reduced enemy thrusts to the minimum. Losses on the former date were five German, four British. On the latter: 0-0. The barrage balloons over Dover still irked the Germans and they had some rather abortive shots at reducing the number.

11 August

Before the battle changed gear and locations, there was one more day of south coast attacks. These went for the main areas: Dover was one. For centuries its castle had stood there as a sentinel against Continental incursion. Now the fisticuffs or arms were miles over it. The losses on this day were to surpass even those of three days previously. The second focus area was from the Isle of Wight down to the much-raided Portland/ Weymouth environment.

Göring launched about 200 aircraft in eleven waves against Dover. Number 11 Group were warned in reasonable time of the build-up and they met the masses of the Luftwaffe head-on. Pilot Officer Stevenson of 74 Squadron of Spitfires was one of those who clashed overhead. Speeding down from Hornchurch, over the Thames Estuary, he sighted his first Me 109 of the day. This was what happened next:

'I climbed up to him. He must have thought I was an Me 109 but when he suddenly dived away I followed him and gave him a two-second deflection burst. The enemy aircraft lurched slightly and went into a vertical dive. I kept my height at 15,000 feet and watched. I saw the enemy aircraft dive straight into the sea fifteen miles south-east of Dover and disappear in a big splash of water.

'I then climbed to 23,000 feet up-sun and saw a formation of twelve Me 109s 2,000 feet beneath me, proceeding north of Dover. It was my intention to attach myself to the back of this formation from out of the sun, and spray the whole formation. As I was diving for them, a really large volume of cannon and machine-gun fire came from behind. There were about twelve Me 109s diving at me from the sun and at least half of them must have been firing deflection shots at me. There was a popping noise and my control column became useless. I found myself doing a vertical dive, getting faster and faster.

'I pulled the hood back. I got my head out of the cockpit, and the slipstream tore the rest of me clean out of the machine. My trouser leg and both shoes were torn off. I saw my machine crash into the sea a mile off Deal. It took me twenty minutes to come down. I had been drifting eleven miles out to sea. One string of my parachute did not come undone, and I was dragged along by my left leg at ten miles an hour with my head underneath the water. After three minutes I was almost unconscious; then the string came undone. I got my breath back and started swimming. There was a heavy sea running.

'After one-and-a-half hours, an MTB came to look for me. I fired my revolver at it. It went out of sight, but came back. I changed magazines and fired all my shots over it. It heard my shots and I kicked up a foam in the water, and it saw me. It then picked me up and took me to Dover.'

Swinging the scene westward, the Luftwaffe made a mass attack on Portland and Weymouth plus a number of smaller raids at other points. According to German sources, the wharves and equipment of Portland harbour, the repair shops, storage tanks, and the dam connecting the latter with the mainland were wrecked. Shipping in the harbour was 'almost destroyed'. Actually the sum total of the damage was interruption of naval communications, an oil tank was set on fire, and some minor damage done by splinters to one of HM ships. No vessel was sunk or even disabled. The port carried on, and as an attack on the naval base the raid was a costly failure to the enemy.

Taken in isolation the day would have been a major event in aerial warfare, but compared to those encounters from the following day onwards it has receded to just another piece in the mosaic of the battle. The Germans lost thirty-eight aircraft and crews, Britain thirty-two – the highest for either side to date. Some eight Fighter Command squadrons met the dual threats in good time – thanks to radar warning. The enemy kept up its night raids on the north-west and west. The weather was set fair for the mid-August week, so all seemed also set for the battles to come. And radar was to be a key concern after one more night.

12 August
This was destined to be anti-radar day. The enemy intended to neutralize these tiresome warning stations which had been helping Fighter Command

Classic shot of a Spitfire flight banking steeply in a fast turn.

to get its Hurricanes and Spitfires airborne and heading for the areas of potential targets. The Germans appeared to have decided that such measures must be undertaken only as recently as nine days earlier. Targeted today were radar stations as far east as the Thames Estuary and as far west as the Portland region. The five destinations during the day were Dover, Dunkirk (in England!), Rye, Pevensey and Ventnor in the Isle of Wight. The installations all tended to be conspicuous by their very radar towers, so the attackers would have some assistance.

After leaving their Calais-area airfields, the anti-radar bomber force split into sections for their specific targets. The radar towers overlooking Dover could hardly be hidden to the force flying towards them. It was ironic that the early warning installation at Dover could not in fact foresee the enemy section heading for it. One moment the fighter-bombers were approaching low over the sea and the next the weapons had been released. Amazingly, though, the metallic towers did not collapse, nor was the damage at all serious. Dunkirk was slightly inland from Dover. The Luftwaffe force found it comfortably and dropped their bombs accurately. The same thing happened as at Dover. Despite damage, Dunkirk radar station was able to go on operating non-stop.

The next radar goal was reckoned to be the simplest one of all to attack. It was at Pevensey, near Eastbourne. This raid turned out to have more serious

German bomber crews being briefed for attack on English ports.

Delayed action at RAF Hemswell. This bomb did not burst so was blown up later by the station's armament officer. Other RAF stations suffered more severely from enemy action.

consequences. Eight bombs, each exceeding one thousand pounds, hit the technical installations. Several buildings fell; RAF personnel lay dead and wounded; and the explosions severed communications. Despite the damage to structures and the casualties, principal buildings somehow survived – so the worst losses were human rather than material. This was an early example of what the WAAF, as well as male RAF, would be facing in the forthcoming battle.

At the exposed site near Rye, that ancient Cinque Port beyond the Romney Marshes, the enemy once more could not really miss the radar masts. Their bombs blasted huts to smithereens, but the sturdier main blocks survived. Emergency power supplies were quickly switched in to reconnect each radar station with their headquarters. This was a prerequisite to later repairs.

The damage was purely temporary, but before the radar network in the south-east could really be re-established, the RAF failed to receive radar warning to scramble when enemy forces flew towards sea convoys in the North Foreland and Thames areas. The Foreness radar station had not been targeted by the early morning raids and so the first hint of the large enemy air presence heading for the convoys came from this source. Royal Air Force fighters already airborne could not reach them in time, nor could others be directed there. Another attack by Junkers 87s on the convoy off Ramsgate fared less happily, but four Hurricanes from several squadrons failed to survive the action – and two of the pilots were lost.

While all this was being waged, the enemy flung major forces at mixed targets in the Hampshire–Dorset–Isle of Wight triangle. In Hampshire, Portsmouth again and factory targets there, as well as at Southampton. The key aviation focal point here was naturally Woolston, where the Spitfire was being built. Dorset meant Portland once more. And the Isle of Wight could only mean the prominent and crucial radar set-up overlooking Ventnor. In peacetime how many thousands had holiday memories of summers at Ventnor and nearby Shanklin and Sandown. The attacks started at mid-morning from airfields in France virtually due south of the Isle of Wight. Over 200 aircraft comprised this phase of the day's raids: 100 of them Ju 88s and about 120 Me 110s. If radar failed to pick up this force promptly, the Royal Observer Corps managed it – albeit rather distantly from points along the Sussex coast. Number 10 Group got the warning and Hurricanes of 213 Squadron headed eastward from Exeter under Squadron Leader McGregor. Spitfires flew from elsewhere.

The Germans came in fast. Their target might be Portsmouth or Southampton or even more distant Portland. They parried anti-aircraft fire from every conceivable source at ground level and sea level. Then just as they reached the eastern extremity of the Isle of Wight, they veered for the Ventnor radar towers. Was it possible that I had spent a holiday at adjoining Bonchurch only a handful of years previously? The Junkers 88s found that

Messerschmitt Me 110CV two-seat fighter.

the ground fire did not really reach them as they came in for a non-steep bomb run over the radar cluster. The select Luftwaffe force all managed to hit home with their four bombs apiece. The calm of the little island resort nestling under the hills was instantly supplanted by the ensuing cataclysm. The Germans had carried out their task but they were far from home.

Spitfires of 152 Squadron from Middle Wallop and Hurricanes of 213 from Exeter pounced on the Junkers 88s. The enemy force commander was hit and died in the air before the bomber crash-landed in Isle of Wight parkland. The other three aircrew survived the landing. Between them the RAF fighters and anti-aircraft defences shot down ten more Ju 88s. While the Ventnor radar was being attacked, on the mainland across the water Portsmouth got an intense midday raid. The respective results of each attack were that the Ventnor installations had been worse hit than the others further east, but was operating again by the significant date of 15 August; and the citizens of Portsmouth suffered some 100 casualties. Bombs fell on the outskirts of the Dockyard area and set fire to a store; they caused some damage to a jetty; and sank two small harbour service craft. The main railway station – Portsmouth and Southsea – had several craters, while a number of buildings, including a brewery, were set ablaze.

Presaging the imminent launch of enemy onslaughts on airfields, the three most forward of all were hit on this same day: Manston, Lympne and Hawkinge. Various vics of bombers with their Me 109s descended on Lympne, set on the tree-clad hills overlooking the Romney Marshes, at quarter past eight. Spitfires of 610 Squadron from Biggin Hill met them. Without suffering worse than damaged aircraft, the Spitfires shot down two enemy.

Junkers 88s hit Hawkinge at teatime. This was the airfield overlooking Folkestone. Its surrounding terrain had historic connections, with Caesar's Camp within a mile or so. Now other invaders were in the vicinity. Several squadrons seemed more or less ready: 501, 32 and 64. Despite their numbers, the fast-flying Ju 88s released their loads on target, leaving hangars and other perimeter structures either destroyed or afire. Craters pitted runways but Hurricanes led by Michael Crosley managed to land there somehow – an obstacle course in piloting skill. Despite damage and the occasional unexploded bomb, Hawkinge stayed open for business – the business of servicing and refuelling fighters.

Not only was Hawkinge liable to be bombed, but the airfield was also subjected to long-range cross-Channel shelling from the German shore batteries. So it could be bombs or shells at any hour of the day – as at teatime today.

Just down the road from Hawkinge airfield lay the local pub – the quaintly-named Cat and Custard Pot. It was not a particularly pretty inn, but a friendly one. And it was the local for pilots from Hawkinge on their evenings off-duty. It represented a brief escape from the reality of their daily lives. Today no aircrew were drinking there. In fact it was fortunate to be still standing in view of its proximity to the airfield.

Occasionally there would be one of the regular pilots missing from the bar. But no one commented on it. The same sense of gaiety would prevail: forced gaiety if they were ever to admit it. Faint echoes of their laughter still resound round the walls seventy years later. And these walls bear witness to some of the names of those who flew from Hawkinge in 1940. And those who died.

The still-vulnerable location of Manston, almost on the cliff edge of the Kent coast looking towards France, meant that it was always bound to be a soft target. And yet Spitfires were supposed to fly to and from this airfield. Number 65 Squadron was just about to take off when several of the dozen pilots saw roofs of a hangar literally lifting off. Roughly the same number of bombs fell on Manston as on Lympne – 140-odd. And yet all except one of the Spitfires struggled up through the aftermath of this havoc. They were placed in an invidious situation aeronautically, with virtually neither altitude nor pace. But their very position luckily proved their salvation and the enemy could not really manoeuvre to make an attack. An Me 110 actually crashed into the midst of the maelstrom on the ground caused by its own air force.

The RAF and the Army carried out continuing emergency repairs on both Hawkinge and Manston, so that they were ready for the next phase on 13 August. But what had been achieved on 12 August? The enemy thought that not only had the three front-line fighter stations been pulverised out of commission, but that the radar warning stations and system would not be able to operate. They were wrong on all assumptions. Three test raids on the coast resulted in the hastily improvised radar repairs spotting the bandits long before they arrived over England. Only Ventnor remained as yet non-operational. All but five of 11 Group's eighteen squadrons had been in action and achieved these results: German losses thirty-one, British twenty-two. Half the British pilots were killed and half safe. Peter Townsend and his 85 Squadron were about to join 11 Group from further up-country.

If ever Britain needed a fillip to morale it was after the radar raids. The Royal Air Force supplied it that same night. Bombers had been quietly going about their business of retaliation against Germany for a while now. On this night the target was the vital Dortmund-Ems canal and the raid went down into the records through the particular gallantry of one man among many Flight Lieutenant R.A.B. Learoyd.

This is why:

Twenty-seven-year-old Roderick Learoyd led eleven twin-engined Hampden bombers on the raid against the old aqueduct on the Dortmund-Ems Canal. The purpose was to upset traffic on this vital waterway used to transport raw materials for the enemy's heavy industrial area. Learoyd and his crew of three climbed aboard the Hampden just before 8 pm. The others were navigator bomb-aimer P/O John Lewis (later killed on active service), wireless officer Sergeant J. Ellis and rear-gunner Leading Aircraftman Rich. Some of the aircraft were detailed for the actual attack, others for diversionary strokes.

It was a good flying night – cloudy and with a half-moon. The journey out was uneventful except for the usual flak from batteries along the route. The cloud continued right up to the edge of the target zone, where they emerged into a clear moonlit sky. Two of the Hampdens failed to locate the aqueduct. They did the next best thing and attacked Texel Island instead.

Eight of the remaining nine bombers made high-level and low-level attacks on targets in the vicinity of the aqueduct, and also on the aqueduct itself. There were five aircraft, including Learoyd's, engaged in the attack proper. They were to go in one by one over the waterway and Learoyd had

Peter Townsend, second from right, in Scotland with fellow pilots before they moved south for further action.

been detailed to go in last of all. As the bombs were fitted with a ten-minute delay, they were timed to attack at two-minute intervals from zero, which meant that the last bomb should be dropped at zero plus 8 and the first bomb was due to explode at zero plus 10. The timing of all the aircraft had to be very accurate to avoid mutual interference and to ensure that all aircraft were clear of the target before the first bomb went off.

Zero hour was 11.10 pm.

Due to the splendid work of Learoyd's navigator, they were over the target at 11.00 pm. Learoyd could see it quite clearly in the light of the moon as he circled at 4,000 feet, waiting for the other four machines to go in one after the other. Fully alive to the importance of the aqueduct, the enemy had concentrated scores of searchlights and anti-aircraft batteries along both banks of the canal.

The resultant firing was intense, as flak flailed the air at the exact altitude they were flying. But worse was to come, for Learoyd and the others. As he stooged around, waiting for their turn to go in, he saw one of the Hampdens hit and catch fire. It climbed to about 1,000 feet, then its nose dropped before finally spinning to the ground in flames. From reports received later, they learned that the crew had been taken prisoners-of-war.

It was now Learoyd's turn to come in over the aqueduct and let his bombs go. By this time another Hampden had been hit and was burning on the ground. In order to obtain the best possible view of the aqueduct, they had to get it as directly as possible between them and the moon. So coming down to 300 feet at a distance of four to five miles north of the target, Learoyd commenced his run in, the aqueduct being silhouetted against the moonlight. Within a mile of the target he came down to a mere 150 feet. By this time, however, the enemy had got their range to a nicety, and was blazing away with everything.

Flak fingered away large chunks of the bomber and they blew to earth like so many scraps of silver foil. Still Learoyd went in. Now his Hampden was being hit over and over again. It tottered across the sky, lurching increasingly as large pieces continued to flake off it. Virtually blinded by the glare of the tracery from searchlights, Learoyd had to ask his navigator to guide him in over the target. This he did with the utmost coolness and precision. Suddenly Learoyd heard him shout:

'Bomb gone.'

It fell the short distance through that shell-studded sky of flashes, light and intervening dark. The delayed-action bomb was fitted with a parachute which, provided the altitude was sufficiently low, gave them a chance of seeing just where it fell. Learoyd heard a triumphant shout from the wireless officer:

'Got it!'

The bomb had fallen on the aqueduct, which was destroyed as a result of the combined efforts of the five Hampdens. Their object was successfully accomplished. Then for home. After the attack eight of the eleven bombers got back to Scampton, looking the worse for the experience, between 1.30 am and 3.40 am. Two had crashed. That left one – Learoyd's.

The Hampden was in bad shape. Amongst other damage, the hits received had put the hydraulic system out of action, so that neither landing-gear nor flaps would function normally. If the system had not been completely destroyed, the emergency compressed-air bottle would operate the undercarriage. They would not know this until the lever was pulled just prior to landing ...

Meanwhile Learoyd flew the wreck of a bomber with superlative skill. He managed to coax it through the lane of flak and out over the North Sea. Soon after 2 am they were over home ground. Learoyd called up Scampton and told how he was fixed. The middle of the night could not be considered a suitable time to try to land a badly damaged Hampden with inoperative landing-flaps and useless undercarriage indicators. Not wishing to risk crashing the machine in the Lincolnshire darkness, Learoyd said that he would stooge around until dawn, when he would have a better chance of making a decent landing.

So for two-and-a-half hours they flew around in the crippled aeroplane. At 4.53 am in the pellucid light of the Fenland dawn, Learoyd brought the Hampden in for an emergency landing without mishap. That bottle must have worked after all. There was no injury to any of the four aircrew nor further damage to the riddled aircraft. Learoyd and the other three trod the dewy airfield in a fine August morning. The air was wonderful. The world was, too. Just to be alive was enough. But suddenly they were all damned tired. Roderick Learoyd was subsequently awarded the Victoria Cross.

CHAPTER FIVE

Eagle Day

13 August

This was Eagle Day for the Germans: when the air assault would really begin in full teutonic earnest and the sky cleared for the invasion by sea. Deep cloudbanks belied the meteorology predictions for fine weather. So although seventy-four Dorniers took off soon after 0500, only an hour later Göring put off their mass-plan until a time to be determined. For some inexplicable reason, this force never received the orders to defer their raid. The result was that they reached the English coast without their Me 110 escorts. And so the plan continued for one group to head for Sheerness and the other for Eastchurch. The former had Royal Navy targets; the latter, ones on the Isle of Sheppey.

Rather belatedly, because radar had not spotted them, the enemy were met by 74 Squadron of Spitfires under 'Sailor' Malan and then two Hurricane squadrons, 111 and 151. 'Sailor' Malan commanded 74 Squadron throughout the battle and its subsequent record of battle honours provided ample proof of his leadership qualities. In worsening weather, some of the Dorniers never got to their target of Eastchurch. They were badly shot up on the approach by 74 Squadron, Malan getting one of the Dorniers. After bombing Eastchurch, they ran into 111 Squadron under Tommy Thompson. Flight Lieutenant Roddick Lee Smith fired his Hurricane's weapons from some 300 yards. Then a Polish pilot of Malan's squadron had to bale out. The losses on the enemy side were five Dorniers destroyed and six damaged. One fatally-hit bomber ended up in woodland, with its aircrew of four all alive. The end of Eagle Day for them. This morning represented just one of the innumerable sorties by 'Sailor' Malan, whose eventual accredited victories amounted to a staggering thirty-two.

Meanwhile the enemy thought that Eastchurch was one of Fighter Command's numerous south-east airfields, but although there were some Spitfires on the base, it belonged to RAF Coastal Command. The bombs killed quite a few RAF ground crew. Some of the personnel had not yet risen when the first explosions occurred. For the rest of the morning, a lull fell over the air and ground alike – apart from the clear-up after three raids-by-mistake.

Alan Deere again – and two more escapes. But not for a few hours. It was the afternoon. The build-up began in the Cherbourg area, where nearly 300 of the enemy set their noses north towards the most westerly of the fighter groups, No. 10. They were supposed to bomb to blazes everything connected with this group. But another principal target in the same general direction was Southampton. Number 10 Group had only put up two squadrons of Hurricanes, 43 and 257, by the time the enemy overflew Southampton Water. The raid was on the town. This grew increasingly apparent each second. Fatal casualties were counted throughout the town, while the enemy also made the famous docks a primary target area. Militarily, the results were not so serious, and the nearby Supermarine Spitfire factory escaped any attention at all. The full force of 10 Group fighters were beamed in to the area by the Middle Wallop sector controllers. One RAF station in this sector was Warmwell, and this became the focus for a hopeless quest by some *Stukas*, which could not identify it through the still-poor conditions.

Similarly, other types of bombers, the Ju 88s, never actually traced the headquarters of the sector at Middle Wallop itself. Others also seeking Middle Wallop were Ju 87s which had Me 109s in company. Spitfires of 609 Squadron, actually based at Middle Wallop, found this force. Their commanding officer, George Darley, flew right through the Junkers, to be followed by his squadron. They concentrated more on the bombers than the Messerschmitts and disposed of six dive-bombers to four Me 109s. So the *blitz*-type thrust against 10 Group did not succeed.

It was still Eagle Day and the broadly dispersed raids shifted their focal area from 10 Group back to 11 Group. In other words, from the west to the east. Detling, Lympne, Rochester. Cloud persisted and the Germans relied again on dive-bombers to try to pierce the way to their targets-plus fighter support.

The ancient city of Rochester somehow seemed to elude the Ju 87s, which were met by Hurricanes of 56 Squadron. But Ju 87s and their accompanying hordes of Me 109s got through to the exposed fighter station of Detling. Neither air nor ground defences moved a finger or anything else before the bombing. And it proved tragically successful. A score or more aircraft eliminated on the ground; hangars, air-raid shelters and accommodation all remorselessly hit. The fatalities numbered sixty-eight, including the station commander plus a cluster of other officers. This attack on Detling left a trail of devastated buildings and some serious questions as to how 11 Group were so stretched.

Re-enter Alan Deere. Leading his Spitfire squadron against 100 Me 109s, he caught a German so intent on a flaming Hurricane that he failed to see the Spitfire pilot, who blew him to bits in the air. But a minute or two later, Deere himself, intent on another victim, was caught in much the same way and forced to land. That was his fourth escape. The fifth followed almost immediately.

This attack by Spitfires of 54 Squadron on a formation of 200 bombers and fighters resulted in Deere adding to his mounting score. After watching three German bombers floating down in flames, Deere chased two enemy fighters right across the Channel and was surprised to find himself over Calais Marck aerodrome. As he turned northward, five Me 109s dived on top of him. So he was being attacked over an enemy held airfield: the prospects did not seem promising. This is what followed:

'Bullets seemed to be coming from everywhere and pieces were flying off my aircraft. My instrument panel was shattered, my eye was bleeding from a splinter, my watch had been shot clean off my wrist by an incendiary bullet, which left a nice diagonal burn across my wrist, and it seemed only a matter of moments before the end.

Alan Deere, right, was shot down seven times and survived. He was credited with some eighteen enemy aircraft destroyed.

'Never did it take so long to get across thirty miles of sea and never had my aircraft gone so slowly. My good old Merlin engine carried me safely across, however, and I had just reached Folkestone when my pursuers broke off the engagement. None too soon. Two minutes later my engine – I was now at 800 feet – burst into flames. Desperately I tore my straps off, pulled back the hood and prepared to bale out. I was still doing about 300 miles an hour, so I pulled the stick back to get a bit more height.

'At about 1,500 feet I turned on my back and pushed the stick hard forward. I shot out a few feet and somehow became caught up by the bottom of my parachute. I twisted and turned, but wasn't able to get either in or out. The nose had now dropped below the horizontal and was pointing at the ground, which appeared to be rushing up at a terrific speed.

'Suddenly I was blown along the side of the fuselage, hitting my wrist a nasty smack on the tail. Then I was clear. I made a desperate grasp at the ripcord and with a jolt the parachute opened. None too soon. I hadn't time to breathe a sigh of relief before I landed with a mighty thud in a plantation of thick shrubs.'

Those shrubs probably saved his life. As he lay there, shaken but unharmed, on the outskirts of Folkestone, his Spitfire went up in flames in the next field.

The day's events could be translated into the respective losses: German forty-five, British thirteen but only three pilots of RAF fighters were in fact killed. That night of 13 August saw the enemy extending its industrial bombing policy as far as an aircraft factory at Belfast and the Castle Bromwich works turning out Spitfires. The total numbers involved were small and the damage done limited. Meanwhile British bombers in the form of three squadrons of Whitleys made the long journey to attack targets at the Italian cities of Turin and Milan.

On the following day, Alan Deere was on duty with a strapped-up wrist as evidence of his latest escapade. And two days later he had just shot down an enemy when his Spitfire was disabled and he had to make a forced-landing. He did not even count that as one of his escapes. His sixth one came a little later.

14 August

In retrospect it was easy to see why the Luftwaffe flew few sorties next day. Orders had gone to them already for the following one: 15 August.

Nevertheless, they had to make appearances in sufficient strength on 14 August. Hence a force of Me 110s made the five-minute flight across the water to Manston. The trouble with these far forward bases was that the raiders could be come and gone so quickly, even though they might have been detected on radar as blips assembling over the Pas de Calais. The damage to Manston by these low-level Me 110s was fairly shattering, though the surrounding ground defence got two of the enemy.

Just a few miles downcoast, approximately 100 aircraft belonging to each side were locked into combat overhead Dover. Two Hurricane pilots of 615 Squadron succumbed; two enemy were lost by their Me 109s; and 32 Squadron chalked up several forced-landings. The increase in scale and tempo can be gauged, however, simply by this 200-aircraft confusion of contrails now being considered limited in size. The day earlier, the enemy had made a total of one-and-a-half *thousand* sorties.

The rest of the raids on 14 August headed for the south, south-west, and north-west. Number 10 Group came in for another dose, in fact Heinkel bombers reached the HQ station of the Middle Wallop sector. Bombs exceeding one thousand pounds in weight exploded over an area of this Salisbury Plain airfield and destroyed Spitfires still lined-up in their hangars. Royal Air Force groundcrew were killed. Spitfires of 609 Squadron (West Riding) somehow got off the ground even as it was reverberating to the bombs all around. Despite craters on the airfields of both Middle Wallop and adjacent RAF Boscombe Down, the Spitfires landed at regular intervals for the inevitable injection of fresh fuel and ammunition. One of the Heinkels was shot down away to the east by two pursuing Hurricane pilots.

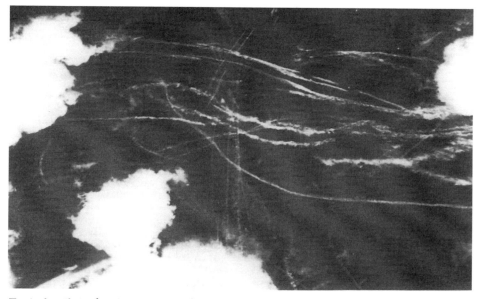

Typical trails in the skies over southern England.

One of these was John Dundas, brother of the celebrated 'Cocky' Dundas. Three Heinkels flew far north of Wiltshire – to Cheshire. They found and bombed Sealand airfield, though losing one of their small group while over Cheshire's county town, the old walled city of Chester. A strange contrast to the Roman occupation of old. The day's losses: German nineteen, British eight.

Night raids from 12–14 August covered the wide spectrum of York, Harrogate, Leeds, Pocklington, Flint, Ilkeston and Horncastle. On the last of these three nights, Birmingham, Leamington and Wolverhampton were all bombed quite heavily, too. One sidelight on this night was the sight of empty parachutes dropping in Derbyshire and Yorkshire. This turned out to be a rather feeble attempt by the Luftwaffe to cause some sort of panic among the local populace of those stolid counties. They were supposed to wonder if parachutists had landed. They had not.

CHAPTER 6

15 August

Phalanxes of bombers. That was the only way to describe the massed ranks of aircraft that Göring despatched on this day. It was destined to be one of the historic dates in the Battle of Britain. The other one came a calendar month later. Considering how crucial 15 August was to become, aerial activity began rather late. At half past eleven, to be precise. This morning strike was engineered by sixty Ju 87s with their umbrella companions of fifty Me 109s.

The force flew over the Kent coast in fine weather along the line Dungeness to Dover. Number 11 Group sent four squadrons up as soon as they got word. Numbers 54 and 501 Squadrons mingled with the 100-plus enemy. Royal Air Force airfields were still bombed, however, one being badly mauled. This was the unfortunate, though not major, airfield of Lympne. The advance fighter field, overlooking the vast coastal plain of the Romney Marshes, had also been hit again on the evening of 12 August after its earlier attack that day. So – three raids in as many days.

The difference in raiding policy on 15 August soon clarified, when Göring impulsively decided to throw in his squadrons from Norway and Denmark to attack targets in north-east England. These lunch-time raids involved both 12 Group and, remarkably, 13 Group – which spanned the latitudes from north Yorkshire across the Scottish border.

The northerly of the two assaults reached landfall first – not before meeting the RAF. At about 1 pm, sixty-five Heinkel 111s plus a score of Me 110s, all from Stavanger in Norway, came in further north than intended. They ran into 13 Group fighters already aware of their approach. The usual Spitfires and Hurricanes from four squadrons joined battle. They were 72 and 79 Squadrons, centrally situated; 41 Squadron Spitfires from Yorkshire; and 605 Squadron Hurricanes down from near Edinburgh. Numbers 72 and 605 met the enemy over the sea, while the other pair linked up in the Newcastle-Sunderland airspace. The enemy targets were RAF airfields in this Tyne-Tees zone. In the running dogfights, the Me 110s suffered as severely or even worse than the Heinkels. At least half a dozen of the Messerschmitts fell, while the bombers frantically got rid of their bombs almost anywhere. Some managed to drop them in the urban environs, but their main aim now was to veer round and survive the long flight back to base in Norway.

Then the more southerly of these two raids came in, flying due west. This force comprised fifty Ju 88s from Alborg, in Denmark – occupied by the Germans in the same way as Norway. They reached Yorkshire about 1.20 pm. The squadrons in 12 Group around the Humber area were scarcely expecting action. It was the first time that the Luftwaffe paid a mass day visit to the group. Suddenly they heard the scramble rasping out. At RAF Leconfield, 616 Squadron had been held in reserve up here for too long, according to most of its pilots – especially Hugh 'Cocky' Dundas. Raid 10 was initially plotted as 20+ enemy aircraft and then changed to 30+. Before crossing the east coast, it split into seven or eight separate small raids. The object of the attack clarified as being Driffield airfield.

Eagerly if somewhat surprised, 616 Squadron of Spitfires roared off, accompanied by a flight of 73 Squadron of Hurricanes. They were intent on dealing with the multi-pronged threat and climbed to 12,000 feet off Flamborough Head. 'Angels One Two.' When the enemy hove into rapidly

Beauty above the cloud ceiling – despite the Battle. Hurricanes on the prowl.

'Cocky' Dundas photographed as
Squadron Leader Hugh Spencer
Lisle Dundas.

enlarging sight, they turned out to be not 20+ or 30+ but 40+ Junkers 88s
escorted by Me 110s. The latter completely botched their protectice role, as
only a few were ever spotted by RAF pilots – and vice versa.

'Cocky' Dundas destroyed a Junkers 88 and damaged one. Of the total
bomber force, seven went down quickly, the rest keeping more or less on
course for their allotted goal of Driffield. Quite a few of them got through
and up to eighty bombs cratered the aerodrome and its environs. Three main
hangars were set on fire, complete with a number of aircraft parked inside;
the officers' mess was badly damaged and polished oak dining-tables
destroyed; and the anti-aircraft headquarters was hit. Seven aircraft on the
ground got variable damage and RAF and civilian ground personnel were
killed and injured. The war was closer – to aviators and those on the ground
alike. In this real taste of the Luftwaffe's might in 12 Group area, they paid a
substantial sum in aircraft and aircrew. Another bomber fell to local anti-
aircraft fire.

None of the RAF fighters were lost in these twin sorties, so the scoreline
registered a resounding defeat for the enemy in their initial north-east
England incursion from the two Scandinavian bases. It proved to be the first
and the last daylight gamble to this area. The Germans evidently thought

that their sorties in the south had attracted virtually all RAF fighter strength down there, depleting the north and leaving it undefended. Number 616 Squadron had been forced to forgo their pudding (or sweet?) at the sound of the scramble. It has never really been established whether or not they went back to finish the meal. On examination of 616's Spitfires and 73's Hurricanes, it was found that just one aircraft had been hit by a grand total of two bullets. Not a bad exchange for disposing of several bombers and their unlucky crews.

The plot had already moved south again as the enemy were retreating in disarray over the North Sea. Radar forewarned of exceedingly strong attackers heading for the coast. Eleven Group had some fifteen squadrons to meet the threat. Three were already patrolling and the other dozen could be called quickly to readiness. Even as Ju 87s had Hawkinge in their beady sights, mixed Spitfires and Hurricanes accounted for two of them. Twice this number of RAF fighters were lost in the melee, but none of the pilots – that was the important thing. Fighters could somehow be replaced more quickly than aircrew. And there was always the factor that British pilots baling out would land on friendly territory whereas the Germans would be taken prisoners of war.

After the earlier raid on Lympne, a mass of pock-marked grass from bomb craters, Me 110s roared in over the water to Manston in early afternoon. This time it was not bombs that caused casualties but gunfire from the Messerschmitts at something akin to zero altitude. Groundcrew casualties ran into double figures. Then followed another airfield raid around 3 pm on the East Anglia fighter base of Martlesham Heath. Twenty-five mixed Messerschmitts hit bulls-eyes without losing a single 110 or 109. They left behind them a smoking mass of stores, hangars and offices. In contrast to the Manston raid, though, no one was killed.

Both 10 and 11 Group were to be embroiled on a scale as never before. The discovery of enemy massing also further west on the French coast signified that 10 Group could expect to be airborne that afternoon or evening. Air Vice-Marshal Park in 11 Group and his counterpart AVM Brand in 10 Group combined to have fighters available from no fewer than fourteen squadrons. Initially the goals looked like being the coastal ones of Portsmouth, Southampton, Weymouth and Portland. Middle Wallop and Exeter could expect some attention, too, among 10 Group airfields. To match 300 enemy intruders, the defence mustered half that number of fighters – from fields scattered between Biggin Hill and Exeter in Devon.

But before this actually materialized, the south-east was coming into the aerial picture. As well as the Martlesham attack, the enemy reached Felixstowe and Harwich. Then about 3.10 pm, estimates of enemy up to 100 headed for Deal. Down the coast over Folkestone at 3.30 pm, the force approaching appeared to be half as strong again. Fighters were scrambled from some half-a-dozen airfields and although the enemy were numerically much superior, the defenders managed to prevent major penetration to their precious bases. Alan Deere was typical of many pilots in the Deal-Manston sphere.

Manston had been badly bombed. Weapons which had gone off on impact wrecked this airfield abutting the white cliffs. Unexploded bombs were still a danger. Alan Deere had shot down an enemy aircraft earlier, before he started his approach to land at Manston. But seeing the markers indicating bombs still to go off, he had to overfly at the final moments. He survived this, and the anti-aircraft fire from the perimeter of the airfield, and an Me 110 bent on catching him. The last act of Deere's eventful day was to be hit high above the old, weatherboarded, colourwashed dwellings of Deal. He baled out yet again. For the fifth or sixth time, he was beginning to lose count.

Mid-afternoon now. Radar at Dover identified more masses which soon transpired to be ninety Dorniers under the watchful eye of 130 Me 109s. There just were not enough RAF fighters to be spread over the whole south-east. It was like trying to cover a large slice of bread with a small spoonful of jam. Three squadrons squared up to these 220 enemy – 64, 111 and 151. The immediate result was six Hurricanes lost to two Dorniers. The enemy bombers were bisected into twin prongs heading respectively for Eastchurch and Rochester. The target at the former was, of course, the airfield. At Rochester they aimed at the factories making the aircraft. Not fighters, true, but vital four-engine bombers made by Short's. This factory and another called Pobjoy's were both pulverized and their lines of production put back – in fact until after the battle was won.

They came in their hundreds.

Those massed groups from Normandy and even further west reached Hants and Dorset (the name of an old bus company of the times!) about 5.20 pm. While the Luftwaffe were still over the Channel and heading for Portsmouth/Southampton and Weymouth/Portland areas, Spitfires and Hurricanes flew out to intercept them. The total of German aircraft was 200–300, the RAF numbers about half as many. But the fighters represented the maximum force assembled at a single time so far. Over one hundred.

The individual and collective scraps attained an intensity and ferocity scarcely seen before this day. The outnumbered RAF drove back much of the force around the airspace overhead Portsmouth, Isle of Wight and Southampton and also over Portland. They inflicted losses and prevented more than a minority of the bombers actually dropping loads. The enemy did get well beyond Southampton in one thrust and damaged aircraft and hangars at Middle Wallop.

But it was above the ports of Portsmouth and Portland that the desperate fights went on. Royal Air Force fighters literally limped back to their bases; the Germans were firing fanatically over intervening airspace, even though they knew often that their own aircraft could not survive and certainly not fly alone. Messerschmitt Me 110s and Ju 87s fell most frequently to the defenders. And away to the west, 87 Squadron commander Ian Gleed took a flight of his Hurricanes from Exeter towards the Portland battle zone. The reported enemy strength there was 120. Gleed's force totalled exactly five fighters – odds of twenty-four to one. Flying right at them, Gleed is reported to have said:

'Come on Chaps, let's surround them.'

They scored successes, though Australian Johnnie Cock crash-landed in the sea and was later picked up by an air-sea rescue craft. In another part of this Channel saga, pilot Richard Hardy was hit by fighter fire and had to forceland in France. Badly wounded, he was extricated from his Spitfire by the German air force, who made him a prisoner of war. It might have been worse.

Evening now, but still the hundreds of combats rattled on. At 6.15 pm, sixty or more enemy were plotted nearing the familiar stretch from the rather off-white Dover cliffs to the desolate wastes at Dungeness, with its wooden homes of fishermen. In a matter of minutes, four squadrons were up yet again. They made their first contact over Folkestone. The stately old resort had never seen or heard such activity in its history. Below, the twin hotels of the Grand and the Metropole had been taken over for the duration by the Services. Meanwhile, another enemy group used the flats of Dungeness to fly in fast via country routes to its goals of airfields. Biggin Hill and Kenley particularly, or any alternatives as circumstances dictated. They sped along over Tenterden – that eighteenth-century sheepmarket town – and so to Tunbridge Wells.

While other enemy forces were being beaten back over the Maidstone sector, some Me 110s and 109s did slip through the Kent net and across the Surrey border. Biggin Hill's 32 Squadron and Croydon's 111 caught them and shot down several. Hurricanes of 111 under Squadron Leader John Thompson attacked as the enemy were in the act of bombing 111's own station of RAF Croydon – the old civil airport. The enemy hit the usual cross-section of Royal Air Force buildings including a fighter repair plant. Thompson forced one of the 110s to crash-land, with both its aircrew safe. More prisoners of war. The enemy bombed not only Croydon but West Malling too, killing one or two groundcrew. Nearby aircraft factories also came in for more loads. The toll of casualties on the ground at Croydon was tragic seventy-odd killed and a higher number hurt. That was as near to London as the Germans had got in strength, but Croydon was too close to ignore. Many people of Greater London saw and heard the battles and the bombs.

Most of the Me 109s in this strike escaped, but as had happened more than once, the Me 110s were not so fast and lost six of the force of fifteen. The overall balance for the day was much in Britain's favour. The Germans had admittedly hit Driffield and Rochester – and in the evening, Croydon. But at what a cost to the 1,790 aircraft employed – 520 bombers and 1,270 fighters. The final figures for 15 August were German losses seventy five, British thirty four. No irreparable damage was done to RAF airfields, although eight had been hit:

Lympne, Hawkinge, Manston, West Malling, Croydon, Martlesham Heath, Driffield and Middle Wallop.

Could the first three survive? Should they continue to be used? Should they ever have been located there? Were they so vital for refuelling purposes? No one had time to ask these questions, let alone answer them. The abundantly clear fact then was that Göring still seemed to be attacking southern towns, but RAF airfields looked like becoming his main targets very soon.

Winston Churchill and Dowding kept a close eye on events, of course, but it was left to Park to conduct much of the hour-to-hour warfare and make the minute-to-minute decisions. Churchill seemed satisfied with this arrangement, even though Park's brief really only covered 11 Group, instead of maintaining an overall view of the whole country and its resources. But the organization could hardly be modified in the middle of the battle. Churchill had a few observations in the light of the historic events of 15 August:

Commenting on Göring's decision to raid manufacturing cities north of the Wash, he said that the distance was too great for their first-class fighters, the Me 109s. They would have to risk their bombers escorted only by Me 110s which, though they had the range, had nothing like the quality – which was what mattered.

'Accordingly, about a hundred bombers with an escort of forty Me 110s were launched against Tyneside. At the same time a raid of more than 800 aeroplanes was sent to pin down our forces in the south, where it was thought they were already all gathered. But now the dispositions which Dowding had made of the fighter Command were signally vindicated. The danger had been foreseen. Seven Hurricane or Spitfire squadrons had been withdrawn from the intense struggle in the south to rest in, and at the same time to guard, the north. They had suffered severely, but were none the less deeply grieved to leave the battle. The pilots respectfully represented that they were not at all tired.

'Now came an unexpected consolation. These squadrons were able to welcome the assailants as they crossed the coast. Thirty German planes were shot down, most of them heavy bombers (Heinkel 111s, with four trained men in each crew), for a British loss of only two pilots injured. The foresight of Air Marshal Dowding in his direction of Fighter Command deserves high praise, but even more remarkable had been the restraint and the exact measurement of formidable stresses which had reserved a fighter force in the north through all these long weeks of mortal conflict in the south. We must regard the generalship here shown as an example of genius in the art of war. Never again was a daylight raid attempted outside the range of the highest-class fighter protection. Henceforth everything north of the Wash was safe by day.

'August 15 was the largest air battle of this period of the war; five major actions were fought, on a front of five hundred miles. It was indeed a crucial day. In the south all our twenty-two squadrons were engaged, many twice, some three times, and the German losses, added to those in the north, were seventy-six to our thirty-four. This was a recognisable disaster to the German air force.

'It must have been with anxious minds that the German air chiefs measured the consequences of this defeat, which boded ill for the future. The German air force however had still as their target the Port of London, all that immense line of docks with their masses of shipping, and the largest city in the world, which did not require much accuracy to hit.'

Thus ended 15 August. Or nearly. The enemy were also maintaining a regular schedule of aerial mine laying around Britain. This always took place after dark and the night of 15 August was no exception to the pattern. Forty-two aircraft from the Royal Air Force's developing night fighters sought these mine laying intruders but with no success. These RAF pilots were unsung in the comprehensive battle, although later on they achieved celebrity when such men as John Cunningham led the night fighter forces in the Blitz. That remained in the imponderable future.

Heinkel He 111s en route to England. Not all would return …

CHAPTER SEVEN

16 August

In spite of the mauling sustained by the Luftwaffe, they came back as determined as ever the next day. This was typical of the Germanic plan of attack; inflexible in the face of changing outcomes. They were to throw from 500 to 600 aircraft into the fray – to the proportion of one bomber for every three fighters. Clearly one lesson had been learned. But they had only half-appreciated the hard facts of yesterday and previous days: that the most formidable aeroplane in the sky was a single-seater, one-engined, frontgun-firing fighter. It would outfly and outfight anything else except another of its own kind. The Germans did indeed send more fighters with their bombers, but a number of these were still the twin-engined Me 110s, which although quite fast, were lightly built and comparatively easy meat for either a Spitfire or a Hurricane.

The main targets today were more fighter airfields: Rochester, Kenley, Croydon, Biggin Hill, Manston, West Malling, Gosport, Northolt and Tangmere. In these climactic days of phase one in the battle, enemy losses were proving to be high, almost catastrophic. Between 11 am and noon, first enemy forces broke through an unusually ill-prepared defence system, to reach RAF West Malling in mid-Kent. They bombed the airfield itself, causing fresh craters after the station's previous poundings from recent raids.

Dorniers hit West Malling and it was this same type of bomber formation which was picked up on the way to the Thames Estuary via Dover. With its strong fighter support, the enemy amounted to three hundred in total, against one quarter as many British fighters that could be spared to greet them. James Leathart, commanding officer of 54 Squadron, flew at the head of a small force of ten. He aimed right for the core of the Dorniers, managing to disperse them in something akin to panic. Then the fearless, incisive lunges also revealed nerves among the Me 109 pilots and bombers and fighters lost several of their colleagues very quickly. This all happened

Hurricanes of 501 Squadron taking off, 16 August.

around noon. Down further into southern Kent, the sky darkened as more massed Dorniers advanced. Now it was nearly 12.15 pm and five defending squadrons went up, and climbed hard as they sped south: 266 Squadron Spitfires, 111 and 32 Squadron Hurricanes, and two other Spitfire units.

What ensued when they flew for the enemy hundreds was ruthless air combat. John Thompson led his 111 Squadron at the Luftwaffe in one lateral rank. Rodney Wilkinson and his 266 Squadron did likewise. Henry Ferris's Hurricane hit a bomber and both of them disintegrated. John Thompson saw the result of his worrying tactics at a Dornier when it went down near Ashford, then a sleepy little township. Number 266 Squadron turned things into life-or-death with the Me 109s. The enemy lost several, but they shot down five Spitfires. One of the three 266 pilots lost during these minutes was their commander, Rodney Wilkinson himself.

The strain was beginning to tell on both sides, which is not hard to imagine. The battle had already been on for a month and more. Eager young pilots were veterans, if they were still alive. Multiply by several hundred the experiences of a single pilot. One such was Flying Officer E.S. Marrs on this day of 16 August:

Hurricanes about to disperse.

'I got in a burst of about three seconds when – crash! The whole world seemed to be tumbling in on me. I pushed the stick forward hard, went into a vertical dive, and held it until I was below cloud. I had a look round.

'The chief trouble was that petrol was gushing into the cockpit at the rate of gallons all over my feet, and there was a sort of lake of petrol in the bottom of the cockpit. My knee and leg were tingling all over, as if I had pushed them into a bed of nettles. There was a bullet-hole in my windscreen where a bullet had come in and entered the dashboard, knocking away the starter button. Another bullet, I think an explosive one, had knocked away one of my petrol caps in front of the joystick, spattering my leg with little splinters and sending a chunk of something through the backside of my petrol tank near the bottom. I had obviously run into some pretty good crossfire from the Heinkels.

'I made for home at top speed to get there before all my petrol ran out. I was about fifteen miles from the aerodrome and it was a heartrending business with all the petrol gushing over my legs and the constant danger of fire. About five miles from the 'drome, smoke began to come from under the dashboard. I thought the whole thing might blow up at any minute, so I switched off my engine. The smoke stopped.

'I glided towards the 'drome and tried putting my wheels down. One came down and the other remained stuck up. I tried to get the one that was down up again. It was stuck down. There was nothing for it but to make a one-wheel landing.

'I switched on my engine again to make the aerodrome. It took me some way and then began to smoke again, so I hastily switched off. I was near enough and made a normal approach, and held off. I made a good landing, touching down lightly. The unsupported wing slowly began to drop. I was able to hold it up for some time and then down came the wingtip on the ground.

'I began to slew round and counteracted as much as possible with the brake on the wheel which was down. I ended up going sideways on one wheel, a tail-wheel and a wingtip. Luckily the good tyre held out and the only damage to the aeroplane, apart from that done by the bullets, was a wingtip which is easily replaceable. I hopped out and went off to the M.O. to get a lot of metal splinters picked out of my leg and wrist. I felt jolly glad to be down on the ground without having caught fire ...

Soon after 1 pm the Luftwaffe switched their next batch of bombers to Sussex and Hampshire: in particular, RAF Tangmere, 11 Group's westerly field, famous in 1941 as the base of the Bader Wing. Now though its fighters were scrambled even before the destination of the enemy came to light.

Almost anyone in western Sussex could have made visual contact with this mass of aircraft. With crystal clarity, the target of Tangmere was soon seen to be their destination. *Stuka*-type attackers made steep dives right on to the airfield. Electric trains plied along the adjacent Portsmouth-Brighton railway. Hangars erupted and took with them their contents of Blenheims and some of the station's precious Hurricanes. A dozen or more aircraft lost, in about equal numbers of Blenheims and Hurricanes. While bedlam broke out on the ground, 43 Squadron Hurricanes had taken off in good time and picked off seven *Stukas* with others hit. Screeching noise, then explosions, then fire and smoke, then the aftermath of craters, then the danger of delayed-action bombs. The feeling could never be conveyed adequately. Only by being there and knowing the fear.

Over into Hampshire now – and 10 Group. Like 12 Group in East Anglia, 10 Group had a limited fighter force. Naval targets at Gosport and Lee-on-Solent had been earmarked by the enemy. At Gosport the airfield was just near the golf course where I played as a boy. At Lee-on-Solent, the airfield was where I used to watch the seaplanes slide down the slipway in the 1930s. Damage did occur at both these naval air stations, but neither was an RAF fighter unit, so anything sustained by the bombing was less serious in hard terms. But the Portsmouth/Gosport/Lee-on-Solent complex would clearly continue to be in the very front line.

It was while the enemy were over the Gosport area that Flight Lieutenant J.B. Nicolson of 249 Squadron won the Victoria Cross.

It was symbolic of the whole battle raging in the cloud-flecked skies. James Nicolson was educated at Tonbridge School and became a pupil pilot in the Royal Air Force in 1936, when he was nineteen. He trained in his home county of Yorkshire. By 1940 he had married.

As France fell, he was moved to the south of England, and August found him a fully trained fighter pilot eager for action. It was not long in coming, for every day now Hurricanes from 249 Squadron hurled themselves into the air against the hordes of Hun bombers.

Answering the scramble signal, Nicolson thrust his Hurricane forward along the runway and into warm air. He had always shown terrific enthusiasm for air fighting and now in his first engagement his skill would at last be tested. He was impatient to get at the enemy.

Wild white trails streaked the sky over Southampton and the Isle of Wight. Nicolson was told to intercept enemy fighters. With other Hurricanes of his squadron, he made contact. Scrapping at 300 mph, the aeroplanes wove their weird exhaust fleece four miles over Southampton Water.

Nicolson took on one Messerschmitt but as he was still trying to get into position to attack, the German fired at the Hurricane. Four cannon shells

The only fighter pilot to win the Victoria Cross in the Battle of Britain: Flight Lieutenant J.B. Nicolson, centre.

screeched into it. One pierced the cockpit, injuring one of Nicolson's eyes; another hurt his foot badly; the remaining two damaged the Hurricane's engine and set fire to the gravity tank.

Petrol poured out of the tank, over the cylinders, and seeped into the cockpit below the control-panel. Flames started to spread and scorch the whole cockpit. The airscrew fanned them, until Nicolson could scarcely see the Messerschmitt's movements – hurt as he was in one eye. Now burns began to affect him, too, and he could only control the fighter with the greatest strain.

By now the lower part of the control-panel and the floor of the cockpit were burning, and the entire machine would soon be an inferno. Nicolson reached for the hood-release and struggled out of the searing cockpit, his limbs already badly scorched. But just as he forced himself up to jump, he saw a Messerschmitt in front of him.

Without stopping a second, he slid back into the flaming cockpit, took hold of the stick again, and his feet groped for the rudder bar. He hardly knew what he was doing or how he was doing it. The whole of the lower part of the Hurricane flared into flames. Somehow Nicolson kept the stuttering engine going, and sighted himself on the enemy fighter. His wounded eye was worse each moment. Up to his waist in flames, his hands blistering on the controls, he battled on until his range was close enough to be entirely accurate. Nicolson pressed the firing button.

A stream of bullets bore straight down at the enemy. The Messerschmitt reeled away mortally hit and careered to the ground; but Nicolson was still in a blazing furnace of a fighter. Summoning strength and will from somewhere deep within him, he struggled to raise himself a second time out of that candle of a cockpit. He operated the hood-release – and baled out. He pulled his ripcord, and then passed out, landing unconscious just outside Southampton – with bad burns on his hands, face, neck and legs. But as he was still drifting down – just before hitting the ground – one of the Local Defence Volunteers fired on Nicolson and hit him in his buttocks. He had been mistaken for an enemy pilot. This in addition to everything else endured.

Then they rushed him to the nearest hospital, where he hung between life and death for two days and two nights: a charred, charcoal colour. Then followed recovery, recuperation, and a fierce fight with authority to fly again. Finally he did fly, despite two illnesses and a car crash, becoming Officer in Charge of Training, South East Asia. Wing Commander Nicolson died in a Liberator crash in the Bay of Bengal before the war was over. He was the only fighter pilot to be awarded the Victoria Cross in the Battle of Britain.

Back to 16 August. The enemy went on with the attack, this time a renewed raid on the Ventnor radar installation – or what was left of it. And in early evening their bombers were sighted at four very distant coastal crossings, from Harwich beyond the Thames Estuary down to the Isle of Wight. The day ended on a small-scale note, but successful as far as the Germans were concerned. Somehow a pair of Junkers 88s got through all the inland defences up to RAF Brize Norton, Oxfordshire.

Here they were mistaken for British bombers and allowed to fly unimpeded right over the station. Their sixteen bombs between them wiped out forty-six RAF trainer aircraft, as well as causing considerable damage to the equivalent of a squadron of Hurricanes.

Once more the huge enemy force utilized throughout the day's three assaults were far from justified by the results and their losses. The enemy aircraft involved in the day totalled 1,720: 400 bombers and over 1,300 fighters. These figures could well be translated as meaning that the Luftwaffe was showing greater respect for the qualities of RAF fighters and their pilots. The losses were German forty-five, British twenty-one. Only three out of the eight airfields hit had been RAF fighter fields; the Germans blamed the rather misty conditions of the afternoon and evening for these errors. And a final postscript from the south. A Heinkel 111 fell to a sergeant pilot flying an unarmed Anson aircraft of RAF Training Command. Whether he rammed the enemy intentionally will never be known: but both aircraft fell to the ground intertwined and there were no survivors from the incident.

Another historic day concluded with 12 Group entering the fight. Birmingham and Coventry had been city targets, as well as the airfields. And even four or five other subsidiary civilian goals. Towards evening a flight from 19 Squadron returning from Coltishall to Duxford were suddenly diverted in mid-air to catch a raid near Clacton-on-Sea. The modest force of one flight stumbled on some eighty He 111s with fifty Me 110s far above them. The clock read 5.50 pm. The flight plunged into some of the 110s and a dogfight conflagrated in a tracery of abstracts: pink-flecked, torn trails. At least one or more of the Me 110s crashed on to the low-lying Essex marshlands.

P/O W. Cunningham was one of the handful of pilots in the scrap. He opened with a burst astern, followed by a longer one as the enemy stallturned – presenting its under-surface as a sitting target. Cunningham continued to fire as the enemy took a vertical dive from 12,000 feet to 2,500 feet, when it entered a cloud. Considering the speed of its descent and as the base of the cloud represented a height of only 1,000 feet, it would have been almost impossible for the Me 110 to pull out of the dive in the limited depth of air. If the RAF pilots had not sustained trouble with gun stoppages, more of the enemy would probably have been hit.

CHAPTER EIGHT

Biggin Hill and Kenley

17 August

The night raids persisted: in East Anglia, the Bristol Channel and the Home Counties quite near London. But though the next day, 17 August, was fine, the enemy took a 24-hour breathing space. This was welcome for both air forces, in view of the varied damage done – to German aircraft and crews and to British buildings, equipment, and most important of all, lives. By contrast with the 1,720 enemy sorties on the previous date, now only seveny-seven crossed the coastline. The damage could begin to be repaired to fighter airfields. Radar equipment could be put back into permanent order. Or in the case of Ventnor, the repairs could be carried on without the sudden appearance of dive-bombers from the Channel skies south of the Isle of Wight.

But the most serious RAF loss during the ten days between 8–17 August was that of precious pilots. Their lives and also the inability to replace them.

Czech fighter squadron flew Hurricanes and were welcomed back by their canine mascot.

Killed, missing, or seriously wounded came to a total of 154. Replacements were only materializing from training at the rate of sixty-three for such a period. Meanwhile, the Royal Air Force was still in the midst of its historic battle. And on this quiet day of 17 August, the only station to be under attack was again the unfortunate Lympne. The losses line read German three, British zero.

On this date, 310 Squadron (Czech) became operational at Duxford. The fanatical Czechs would be in action in just over a week and anything they might lack in mastery of the English language they more than made up in their spirit to get at the enemy.

The lull was short-lived. Like a rest for boxers at the end of an especially gruelling round. Between rounds, too, the RAF were being joined by squadrons of the Auxiliary Air Force. Six AAF squadrons flew Spitfires: 602 (City of Glasgow), 603 (City of Edinburgh), 609 (West Riding), 610 (County of Chester), 611 (West Lancashire) and 616 (South Yorkshire). They were all needed.

18 August

If only seventy-seven enemy aircraft attacked on 17 August, ten times as many were destined to surge back on this Sunday. Whereas targets had been more widespread up till then, the Germans decided to hit just two crucial fighter fields of Biggin Hill and Kenley. The day did not end like that, though. Their plan for Kenley was a three-pronged one: a triangular thrust by dive-bombers, then conventional ones flying at the customary higher altitude, and a zero-height strike.

The clocks read a little after midday as the nine low-level raiders raced in over the great beacon of Beachy Head. Visual reports from the ground put defenders on alert at once. The bombers flew at minimum height towards Kenley, using the main Sussex railway lines to guide them northward. Number 11 Group was already in action even as the observer warnings got through.

The nine low-level Dorniers swept through at 50-100 feet above the remote Sussex landscape, despite efforts by 64 and 111 Squadrons to get at them. Into Surrey where the Kenley defences were waiting. But the Dorniers suddenly poked up from behind trees and bombed their appointed targets with alarming accuracy. Only one hangar remained. And practically all the station's main structures were affected. Six Hurricanes were hit while stranded on the ground or actually on runways. And these runways themselves bore craters as instant evidence of the raid.

It all happened in the time occupied by the Dorniers overflying Kenley just once. Perhaps a mere ten seconds or so. They had taken the defences by utter surprise. No one can react in that period. But now the anti-aircraft

Observer Corps detect and plot height and course of hostile aircraft, passing back the information to the control centre.

swung round and fired. And a newly-developed invention called PAC rockets was used. These initials stood for parachute and cable. Each rocket launched 500 feet of cable attached to a parachute. This kept the cable up before gravity gradually took over. Then if an aircraft did happen to foul it, another parachute opened. The PAC rockets were fired in groups of nine and actually accounted for one of the Dorniers as it fled off. Anti-aircraft guns were credited with two more Dorniers and the rest were chased by 111 and 615 Squadrons.

This low-level hit had been intended as the last of the three on Kenley. But the other two were late arriving. The Junkers dive-bombers and Heinkels for high-level bombing were guided to the target by the visual effects of the devastating explosions. On the ground, the signals communications was one area worst struck, while the sector operations room had to be closed down at once. Meanwhile the raid went on amid the fighter defence.

Fifty bombers under their umbrella of many more Me 109s were still coming in towards Surrey. Though at odds of five-to-one against, Hurricanes of 615 Squadron tore into the fighters. They scored hits for certain, but lost four Hurricanes in the process. Three pilots survived, including the South

African colleague of 'Sailor' Malan, Dutch Hugo, who crashed at Orpington. Only through these heroic Hurricane pilots were six others able to brush away the fifty bombers left without their cover of Me 109s. Elsewhere, Squadron Leader Michael Crosley took 32 Squadron line abreast at Junkers 88s and Dorniers. They got at least one of each type. So not all the bombers prenetrated to Kenley, which was just as well.

Enough damage was done. The ground personnel – RAF and WAAF – behaved impeccably. They took their lead from the aircrew they were supporting and suffered casualties in exactly the same way. The bombers destroyed Kenley's hospital and killed one of the station's medical officers while he was sheltering. Fires took time to get under control; Kenley was without water; the runways were unusable; and personnel proceeded to deal with unexploded bombs. The postscript to the Kenley bombing came when its vital sector operations room was subsequently moved to a room in an empty butcher's shop in the nearby town of Caterham!

That was the Kenley raid. The Biggin Hill raiders encountered earlier opposition. Sixty Heinkel IIIs had forty Me 109s as their guardian angels. And there were Ju 88s and Dorniers en route as well. Number 610 Squadron of Spitfires under Squadron Leader John Ellis throttled for the Heinkels and got one. Number 32 Squadron from Biggin Hill itself also flew straight at the mixed bombers. Dogfights howled over Surrey, Kent and Sussex: the air was no respecter of county borders. And elsewhere offshoots of the Kenley attackers had detached themselves according to plan and went for nearby Croydon airfield again. West Malling, too, and the important Rollason aircraft factory.

But Biggin Hill was the next target, even though many of the raiders never got there either destroyed, deflected, or dejected. It turned out to be almost a replay of Kenley, anyway as far as the arrival times of the bombers were concerned. The Dorniers throbbed in low and earlier than scheduled, the others later. The nine Dorniers tore low over the little plateau-type area of Biggin Hill and ran up against PAC rockets again. Two of them got entangled and came down the short distance to earth. Together with the results achieved by 32 and 610 Squadrons, seven Dorniers of the nine failed to get back home.

This was the scene at Biggin Hill as the high-level raiders reached it. The RAF fighters were struggling to stop the bombers getting through. Practically all personnel not on vital ground work were sheltering. Fortunately the fighters interfered with the accuracy of the enemy attack, and their bombs were dropped away from the main buildings – though some inevitably registered on the airfield.

While high-explosive and delayed-action bombs ripped up ground around Biggin Hill runways, twenty-eight-year-old Sergeant Joan Mortimer was on duty in the station armoury during the raid. Though stacks of ammunition lay stored near her office, almost asking to be ignited, she manned the telephone, passing instructions to the various defence posts around the airfield.

As the raid got worse, she went on with her job and also managed to shout welcome encouragement above the din to airmen in the same building. At last the raid ended, but the tall, slim girl from Yorkshire, with blue eyes and brown hair, had not finished what she considered as her duties. She went outside the Biggin Hill buildings, and walking amid the smouldering aftermath, she calmly pegged out with red flags all the places on the aerodrome where unexploded bombs lay buried. When asked afterwards about her actions and her future, she said, 'Naturally I want to stay here and continue my work.'

Back aloft the battle flared down to Kent. Number 266 Squadron of Spitfires were sent down from Essex to patrol over Manston airfield. As most of them had landed there for refuelling, a force of Me 109s spotted some Spitfires already on the grass and others about to land. Machine gun and cannon fire from the enemy hit the Spitfires badly, leaving few free of some damage. Just across country at Ashford, five Me 110s were seen by Hurricanes of 56 Squadron. The Messerschmitts seemed uncertain as to what to do. Before they had come to any decision, it was too late and the Hurricanes out-manoeuvred them – despatching all five.

Aircraft of both sides were littering south-east fields, farms, and golf courses. And parachutes fluttering earthwards signified pilots saved. Few begrudged German pilots' survival, even if they were the enemy.

The action swung westward to Sussex and Hampshire. Here the Luftwaffe went for Gosport and Ford naval air stations and also RAF Thorney Island – a Costal Command station. The Germans believed that all three belonged to RAF Fighter Command. The force detailed for the tasks comprised 111 Ju 87 *Stuka* dive-bombers shepherded by an appropriate quota of Me 109s. As this air armada neared the Isle of Wight, it split into port and starboard groups. The Gosport raiders peeled off to port, the Thorney Island ones kept straight ahead, while those for Ford flew starboard. Ford was situated very near to the recently-raided RAF Tangmere in Sussex. Two squadrons of Ju 87s bombed the Gosport air station without interruption or loss. Gorse used to catch alight nearby in the summer. Now there were just bombs to cause the fires.

Things were less lucky for the Germans eastward at Thorney Island. Thorney lies two islands from Portsmouth itself, with Hayling Island in between. Here the Hurricanes of 43 and 601 Squadrons caught many of the dive-bombers before they commenced their descent, and so prevented many serious results on the ground. Bombs found their mark more worryingly at Ford airfield, and perhaps the worst effects from the RAF point of view were those at an additional target – the radar base of Poling. The bomb tally here came to ninety, leaving the place in as bad a state as Ventnor. It took a fortnight before it was back in full service, and this at a critical phase of the air battle. But the Luftwaffe losses were much more concerning to the enemy. Half of many groups failed to return.

Teatime. But with the long fine August evening, the raids were not yet done. The time: 5.30 pm. A hundred more bombers showed up on the plots, heading across the Kent and Essex coasts. Their goals were once more the fighter airfields bordering the Thames area. North Weald and Hornchurch in particular.

Eleven Group was still sustaining the brunt, apart from occasional 10 Group action to the west. Now it was sometimes the third sortie of the day for 11 Group men. 501 Squadron was just one of those taking off yet again. Risking their lives yet again. Flight Lieutenant George Stoney flew at fifty Dorniers entirely on his own, and disrupted the whole force before Me 109s pounced on him. He died somewhere in the area of the Thames Estuary … The end of the day came when many bombers failed to find their RAF airfields through worsening weather – and released their loads over the outskirts of the densely-peopled Greater London. Many civilians were being killed. The bare figures of aircraft losses read German seventy-one, British twenty-seven. This was in the face of odds reaching as astronomical a ratio as twenty-to-one.

The tactics of 11 Group in tackling the fighter and bomber formations by squadrons splitting into two was successful, and the quality of the pilots certainly veered much in favour of the RAF. But apart from all this, there remained that nagging twenty minutes which it took for our fighters to climb to a good operational height of 25,000 feet. Perhaps at least some of the southern airfields were pitched too far forward. After all, an airfield was only a facility for aircraft to be housed, to leave, and to return to safely. And of course for refuelling. But if it were too vulnerable, then why locate it there? Certainly when fighters had to climb away from an approaching enemy to gain enough height, something might be considered doubtful or even wrong. It has been suggested that when planning the position of fighter airfields in the 1930s, the threat was envisaged as coming from Germany – but no-one thought sufficiently of the chance that they would again invade the Low Countries and so progress as far as France.

Finally on 18 August in an evening attack in the Thames Estuary area, a single squadron of Hurricanes shot down nearly their own number without loss in just 50 minutes. That was the end of the day when the enemy aimed mainly for Biggin Hill and Kenley and lost seventy-one aircraft in the process. What was coming next?

CHAPTER NINE

The Five-Day Lull

19–23 August

The weather deteriorated for the next four days or more, but this did not stop aerial activity. It gave both sides a slight breathing space for repairs, regrouping, and counting the cost. But the Luftwaffe did as much as they could in spite of a generally heavy cloud-base. As if to keep the battle going, they chose smaller-scale raids on widely dispersed targets. Manston was always an easy one and they prodded at it again – and again.

Some celebrated squadrons were now fully operational in 12 Group, the latest being 74 Squadron ready at Wittering by 19 August. They would be moving south at any time. On this day, as well as bombing industrial zones, a quartet of bombs landed on Broughton airfield. Then at 2 pm a lone bomber emerged from fleecy clouds to hit Coltishall and cause instant casualties among civilian workmen there. A little later, other raiders made a

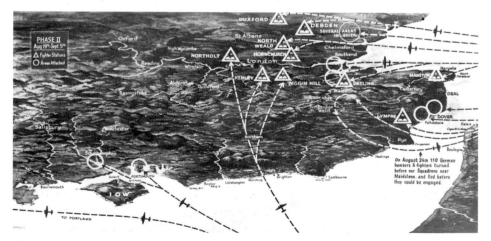

The second phase: the attacks move inland against RAF airfields.

Burnt-out forward part of Dornier shot down on 19 August.

hit-and-run strike at Hanington, fleeing into cloud the moment their bombs were released. But 66 Squadron probably disposed of a Heinkel 111 out to sea east of Cromer.

During the afternoon, Junkers 88s went for two western ports – Southampton and Pembroke Docks. The Southampton raid was not too serious, but one Junkers of the small force headed for Wales managed a direct hit on the Llanreath oil storage depot. The fire spread to ten of the adjacent tanks and burnt-out all but five of the total storage tank capacity there. More than this, the light from the fires beckoned other night-time bombers. German losses six and British three.

Night bombing of ports was on the increase presaging the blitz on London and other cities generally. Over the night of 19–20 August, the crucial north-west port of Liverpool received some of its first bombs from a squadron of Heinkel 111s, and there were also jabs at the Midlands. The rains came on 20 August, but Manston and Martlesham still had air-raid warnings and attacks to a minor degree. Far away in Yorkshire the newly formed 302 (Polish) Squadron of Hurricanes disposed of a Ju 88 into the North Sea. This particular date of 20 August, however, was made memorable by the phrase coined by Winston Churchill, who declared in his inimitable phraseology:

'Never in the field of human conflict has so much been owed by so many to so few.'

It was certainly true and would continue to be so for a further month and more. And at the same time Churchill reported to Parliament:

'The enemy is of course far more numerous than we are. But our new production already largely exceeds his, and the American production is only just beginning to flow in. Our bomber and fighter strengths now, after all this fighting, are larger than they have ever been. We believe that we should be able to continue the air struggle indefinitely and as long as the enemy pleases, and the longer it continues the more rapid will be our approach, first towards that parity, and then into that superiority in the air upon which in large measure the decision of the war depends.'

Even as Churchill was paying his tribute to RAF pilots, Douglas Bader lost his first young pilot Midshipman Patterson. He was shot down into the sea on a convoy patrol. With Fighter Command so short of pilots in the frantic build-up after Dunkirk, the Royal Navy seconded fighter pilots from the Fleet Air Arm. They were all without exception well trained and disciplined. There were three in 242 Squadron: Midshipman Patterson, Sub-Lieutenant Cork and Sub-Lieutenant Gardner. The first two were Royal Navy, while Jimmy Gardner was Royal Naval Volunteer Reserve. Gardner was the only one to survive the war.

21 August

It was still rainy weather, restricting the enemy to limited thrusts, again of the hit-and-run variety. Their goals were airfields, but only on a nuisance scale: southern England, south-west England, East Anglia. The respective losses reflected the scale. On 20 August they were German seven, British two. On 21 August, German fourteen, British one.

The first time that the three squadrons of what would become the Duxford Wing flew on the same day was 21 August. Not yet as a wing but separated by an hour or so. One of these was the Polish 302 Squadron; another was 611 Squadron of Spitfires; and the third was Bader's 242 Squadron.

At 8 am a raider slipped across the coastline and dropped five bombs on Bircham Newton, demolishing the married quarters there. Another did the same sort of thing at Stradishall airfield. Number 242 was the first of the Coltishall squadrons airborne. One flight patrolled over Norwich at noon. Flt Lt G.S. Powell-Sheddon, P/O Latta and Sub-Lt R.E. Gardner were the trio.

Over the cathedral city they saw a Dornier 17 twenty miles to their south. They fired but then found enemy tracer bullets etched through the cloud mask. They were all after it and in other circumstances might even have felt sorry for the occupants. The enemy port engine lit up like a gas jet in a strong draught. The fuselage also showed flame signs. Gardner closed to about 20 yards just the length of a cricket pitch away from the Dornier. Oil from the bomber actually clung to his Hurricane. No further firing came from the spiralling Dornier. Two of the crew baled out but the pilot stuck to his aircraft. It staggered on as he tried to pancake in a field on the far side of the village of Harleston. But he could not control the crippled Dornier and overshot the field. The bomber bounced into a small wood beyond the field and dissolved into a familiar mixture of smoke and flame. The fire consumed its black crosses and little else was left of it. Powell Sheddon landed with the other two at 12.37 pm to find he had a torn tailplane and a dent in the tailplane spar. These had been caused not by firing from the bomber but by fragments flying off it at close range – always an additional hazard to fighter pilots.

Bader also got his eye in within the hour. Although only detailed for 'local flying' and not ordered off, he took of in his Hurricane at 1 pm and climbed to 9,000 feet. He got in a couple of bursts at another Dornier near Great Yarmouth but could not report anything more definite than tracer striking the enemy bomber. The aircraft was duck-egg blue underneath with black on top. And as the enemy rear-gunner fired his machine gun from above the fuselage, weights attached to long wire were thrown out from under the fuselage. These weights passed beneath Bader's Hurricane causing no damage to it. It was a strange idea.

Number 611 Squadron had a section four miles east of 'bracing' Skegness. They spotted three Dorniers. P/O Brown attacked one and soon saw both engines fuming. His firing entered the Dornier – he could vouch for that visually. After breaking off the burst, he saw the Dornier vortex towards the North Sea with two or three of the crew baling out frantically. Would they survive the water even if they reached it alive? But before the bomber finally sent up a spume of seawater, other enemy bullets had penetrated both of Brown's wings, burst one of his tyres, and ripped through his rudder. Somehow he hobbled back to base to discover the extent of this damage.

22 August

Manston saw enemy aircraft heading for them again, while convoys in the Channel presented other targets. Fortunately, damage in all sorties seemed slight. But the Germans at this stage were sending quite a few Me 109s on freelance missions over the Kent coastal strip. Number 616 Squadron of Spitfires from Kenley took off to discourage them and a series of individual dogfights was the familiar outcome. The Spitfires did well, but when another batch of Me 109s arrived, 'Cocky' Dundas found that he and his aeroplane had both been hit. This is how he remembered it:

> 'White smoke filled the cockpit and I couldn't see the sky or the Channel coast 12,000 feet below. Centrifugal force pressed me against the side of the cockpit and I knew I was spinning. I felt panic and terror and I thought "Christ, this is the end. Get out, you bloody fool; open the hood and get out." I tugged the handle with both hands where the hood locked into the top of the windscreen. It moved back an inch, then jammed again.' – The Spitfire spun for several thousand feet, while he failed to open the hood wide enough. It opened eventually near to the ground. – 'Thank God my parachute opened immediately. I saw the Spitfire hit and explode in a field below. A flock of sheep scattered outwards from the cloud of dust and smoke and flame.'

'Cocky' Dundas had dislocated his shoulder and got splinters in his left leg.

The night raids did not cease. The list of areas attacked could hardly have been more geographically diverse: Aberdeen, Yorkshire, Hampshire, South Wales, Bristol, Filton. On the night of 22-23 August, a considerable tonnage of bombs fell on the aircraft factory at Filton and output was affected, while the enemy also hit the adjacent airfield.

23 August

In the early hours of 23 August, magnetic mines were laid in the Humber; bombs fell near Warrington; and another half-dozen towns were hit by widespread raids. One or more enemy bombed and machine-gunned the front-line town of Bridlington, at times flying a mere 50 feet over the boarding houses of the resort. None of 12 Group fighters could manage to make daytime contact in misty weather.

On the final night of this five-day phase of quieter daylight living and noisier nights, in excess of 200 bombers went for several areas visited previously – Bristol, South Wales, Cardiff specifically, and now industrial sites at Castle Bromwich, near Birmingham. The Dunlop rubber works were hit in this raid. Bombs were also recorded on the city itself, Kidderminster and King's Lynn. One of these could have been the bomb rendered safe in King's Lynn years later by Major Bill Hartley, as head of Bomb Disposal (and watched by me!). The 48-hour losses were, on 22 August, German three, British five; on 23 August, German two, British zero. It seemed that the raids in darkness were definitely proving safer for the enemy. With improved weather overnight, the next day looked like marking the resumption of the bigger battle. It did.

CHAPTER TEN

Battle in the Balance

24 August

On this day came the first of some thirty-five major attacks on the inland fighter airfields and aircraft factories in the space of under a fortnight including bombing residential districts in Kent, the Thames Estuary area and Essex.

Manston, Biggin Hill and Kenley were all used to being heavily hit. Now with a resumption of fine August weather came the mass airfields attacks. A breakfast-time lunge at Great Yarmouth proved merely a feint, for which the Germans were becoming adept, even obvious. Then follmved the almost routine assemblage of bombers far outnumbered by fighters over the Pas de Calais. They targeted Manston five times during this single day. They also flew for North Weald and the Essex station of Hornchurch. North Weald did suffer severely, but anti-aircraft gunfire ringing Hornchurch kept most of them at bay there. Perhaps it was as well for the morale of fighter Command, in the air and on the ground, that they did not know that these fanatically regular raids on airfields would go on and on for the following fourteen days. It is usually a lesson of life that it is better not to know the future, whether good or bad.

Several pilots claimed as many as five enemy aircraft destroyed in a single day. Sergeant R.F. Hamlyn managed this on 24 August. He was airborne with the rest of his Spitfire squadron just after five o'clock – am! This proved to be a quiet early morning sortie devoid of incident or interest. His next sortie came three hours later. Shortly before 8.30 am, three or four waves of Junkers 88s were sighted and attacked by the Spitfires before the enemy escorts could intervene.

Hamlyn settled for the end bomber of one formation and shot it down into the sea with a two-second burst. He had to throttle back quickly to avoid crossfire from the other bombers. He was immediately seen and gone for by an Me 109, which overshot him and in so doing presented him with a sitting aerial target. Hamlyn repeated the two-second burst routine and the Messerschmitt was sent smoking into the sea. Hamlyn and the squadron then returned to base for breakfast. However, it was not destined to be.

'As a matter of fact, I didn't get any breakfast at all. I only had time for a hot drink before we were ordered to stand by again, and by half-past eleven that morning we were patrolling the south-east coast.'

The squadron were soon in a typical series of dogfights with six Me 109s, which they chased away right across the Channel. Hamlyn followed one beyond the French coastline. He glimpsed Cap Gris Nez away below, before giving the enemy just three seconds of firing. He watched it crash into a French field near the coast.

Hamlyn and the others had time for lunch before the next scramble. This came about four o'clock and they found themselves flying towards the Thames Estuary at the low altitude of 5,000 feet. They saw the blobs of anti-aircraft fire bursting away to the north-east of them – Essex presumably. They made a maximum speed for the area and stumbled into twenty Me 109s escorting a similar number of Junkers 88s. The bombers were packed in tight formation.

The Spitfires went in head on. Hamlyn shot down two of the Me 109s, after two and three seconds of short bursts respectively. Hamlyn described how his fifth victim fell:

'The whole machine became enveloped in flames and pieces began to fly off. Finally, as it went down, more pieces came off, all burning. As it tumbled down towards the widening Thames Estuary, it was really a bunch of burning fragments instead of a whole aircraft. It was an amazing sight.'

As an illustration of the intensity and brevity of these encounters, none of Hamlyn's fights on that Saturday lasted more than five minutes.

Meanwhile, a large mixed force appeared in the Isle of Wight area at teatime. About the same time that Hamlyn was finishing his day's work. Number 609 Squadron of Spitfires saw them when the RAf fighters were still a mile lower than the massed clump of Luftwaffe. In this rather desperate tactical situation, the Spitfire pilots did their best, but could not prevent a powerful bombing raid on the port and city of Portsmouth. Some two hundred bombs whined down on naval targets around the harbour, while civilians were also among the fatalities. There were over 100 naval and civil deaths, a grim average of one for every two bombs dropped. The raid was one of many made on Portsmouth altogether by day and night. Being my birthplace, I felt especially strongly for everyone there. In this day of total war, Dover and Ramsgate heard and felt bombs, too. It was always a shivering experience.

The night raids virtually merged into the daytime ones. South Wales, Birmingham, the north-east coast and London itself received raids on the night of 24 August. The attack on the capital was reckoned to have been a mistake, however, and it did not recur for a fortnight at any rate. The scale of ceaseless aerial thrusts were back to full strength now, and during the devastating two weeks' raids on RAF airfields the enemy exceeded 600 daily sorties practically without fail. In fact, the average number of aircraft used all but reached 1,000 a day. The stepped up activity of 24 August resulted in losses of German thirty-eight, British twenty-two.

Central London's first casualties occurred on this night and the Air Ministry bulletin admitted that a good deal of damage had been caused again to Manston airfield. One final feature of the day was that 12 Group had its aggressive appetite whetted when 19, 310 and 66 Squadrons were eventually despatched to help 11 Group. They caught up with the Luftwaffe over the mouth of the Thames, but only 19 Squadron actually got near enough to fire. Sgt B.J. Jennings hit an Me 110 in the starboard engine and propeller – the latter falling off and dragging parts of the engine along too. After firing at another Me 110, Jennings witnessed the spectacle of its starboard rudder, tail fin and a major chunk of tailplane all floating and falling – almost as if weightless for an instant. Jennings never saw its anguished death throes as two more Me 110s arrived on his immediate air scene. He survived the day. Pilots were beginning to learn that this was as much as they could expect. Eleven Group had already long learned it. Leeds was one of nineteen places on the long list of night raid recipients.

25 August
The enemy were still intent on swinging their offensive action about from east to west, from 11 to 10 Group. North Weald again. The weather was hot there throughout the day. Aircraftwoman (ACW) Cooper was waiting to go on watch at 4 pm, when she heard the warning on the Tannoy. The North Weald fighters, including Geoffrey Page, had been up and down all day. But first came ACW Cooper:

'As we were hurrying to the shelters, we looked up and saw the enemy planes glinting in the sun and getting into formation – ready to do a run across the station. We were just down when the first bomb, a screaming one, fell near.

'There were not more than six WAAF and three RAF in our shelter. When the first bomb fell, we all involuntarily sat forward with our hands over our heads. I think we heard the second bomb. After that it was just a roar. All the corrugated iron of the shelter cracked. There was an incredible smell of explosives and the heat of the blast which swept through the shelter. The escape hatch had been blown off the hinges, and I shall never forget the smell of the heat.

'We didn't know when the raid was over. Eventually one of the men put his head out of the trench and heard firing. But soon it stopped. We found afterwards that the Tannoy had been blown out of action.

'My first thought was then of the Ops Block. We were due to go on duty at 4 pm, and it was almost that then. When we looked out there was a horrible sight. It's best forgotten. They'd hit a crowded trench quite near. In the next trench to ours, some RAF were taking a boy out with his shoulder off, and another who'd lost a leg. Two plotters who had been in that trench were helping.

'The first bomb had fallen within ten feet of the mouth of our trench, and blown up the concrete road between the trench and the WAAF quarters. As we were below ground level, we were all right.

'A WAAF sick quarter attendant had a bad time. She'd just left the sick quarters when she saw it blow up behind her. She staggered into a trench crying: 'It's all right, I'm safe,' and found she was alone. She stayed put till the end of the raid. Then she went out and as she was crossing the grass a delayed-action bomb went off. But she reached what remained of the sick quarters safely.

'We left the trenches and went first into our quarters where we found the beds riddled with bullets. We'd only got up a short time before. All the glass was out of the windows, and they'd machine-gunned the rooms.

'On the way to Ops Block we met the CO., Wing Commander Beamish, busy worrying about the water mains. He'd been up in the thick of it during the battle. We then took over in the Ops Room and the business of getting information through to Group was done by the WAAF. The lights and telephones were gone, and it looked like the black hole of Calcutta by candlelight. Operators from this station had never stopped for a minute, and we were all anticipating another attack.

'We worked in Emergency Ops all through the night. It was the first time we had been allowed on at night. Apparently they thought it would be too much of a strain.

'We couldn't go back to our quarters for a week. There were D-A bombs in the garden, and one had actually landed on my long-cherished cabbage patch. We slept on floors, anywhere we could find room. We had to carry water in buckets for 200 yards for washing up and everything else. A serious concern was our make-up, which we couldn't get. So we all bought powder and stuff at the NAAFI and carried our face around with us in the pocket of our gas masks. Then everyone wondered how we managed to look so smart and clean. The next air attack came soon afterwards ...'

P/O Geoffrey Page (eventually DSO, DFC and Bar) of 56 Squadron was returning to the officers' mess at North Weald that evening when he was told by the duty orderly that his mother had phoned him and asked to call her back as soon as possible. Getting through was not easy because of the aftermath of the air raid, but eventually he made contact with her.

'I'm very worried about you, darling,' she informed him.

As he had probably had several thousand rounds of enemy bullets fired at him during the day, he too had been a trifle worried about himself!

'I don't think your batman is drying your socks out properly, and you might catch a nasty cold ...' she continued.

The civilian population still had little notion of what was going on far overhead. Perhaps for relatives at least that was just as well. Anyway, Geoffrey assured his mother that he was safe and did not have a cold.

Meanwhile during the afternoon the patched-up radar station at Ventnor was able to announce the imminent arrival of another large unwanted flotilla. They materialized over the frequented Weymouth/Portland strip of Dorset. Three squadrons climbed to challenge them: 17 Squadron of Hurricanes, 609 Squadron of Spitfires from Middle Wallop, and 87 Squadron of Hurricanes from Exeter. Although the fighting took place from Portland inland, the target really turned out to be the airfield at Warmwell.

Both sides lost precious aircrew. The three squadrons were much in a minority, but took the edge off enemy intentions. The leader of 17 Squadron, Cedric Williams, fell to an Me 110 and was killed. Nearby one or two RAF parachutes billowed down over both Dorset and Wiltshire. Some thirty-six RAF fighters could not be expected to stop all the bombers reaching Warmwell, where rapid bomb-and-run tactics hit hangars. The Germans were again using more fighters than bombers, so it was not to be wondered that the relative loss figures tilted less in favour of the RAF. On 25 August they were German twenty, British sixteen. This foreshadowed the pattern for the current stage to 6 September.

Other areas attacked during the day were Portsmouth, Southampton, Dover, Folkestone, the Thames and Kent areas generally. It should never be forgotten that the residents remaining in both Dover and Folkestone could often actually see Occupied Europe, from Cap Gris Nez and beyond in the east to Boulogne and beyond in the west. Not a comforting sight.

A comforting item of news was released, however, after the night's activities of 25 August. True, the enemy raided twenty-one locations. But the Royal Air Force carried out its very first raid on Berlin. Officially this was not regarded as a reprisal for the raid on London. The British line was that the Berlin raid aimed against military objectives on the outskirts of the capital and these would have been attacked irrespective of the London bombs.

The statement stressed that the RAF bombing had been careful and selective, as opposed to the completely indiscriminate recent bomb-drop by the Luftwaffe.

26 August

Repeated raids to paralyse RAF airfields continued to be more or less foiled, with the infliction of the same steady losses. During this last week of August, however, the British loss of three airgunners was from Defiant fighters, now being employed far less than the Hurricane and Spitfire. While pilots were reading in their morning papers about the raid on Berlin, they did not have time to dwell on the news, for the enemy again started concentrated forays on airfields, as well as raids over the ports of Dover and Folkestone.

Debden in Essex became the aim of a Dornier force. Only six got through to the strategically placed airfield, but they were enough. The damage proved comparable to some of the attacks on the Surrey fields. Losses were inflicted on the enemy, but both 11 and 12 Group fighters felt the impact, too. Kenley's 616 Squadron lost seven aircraft, with two of the pilots killed and the other five safe. That was some small compensation.

Four squadrons of 12 Group went to help combat a raid over the Thames Estuary. Only 310 (Czech) Squadron under George Blackwood made contact. Twelve Group were becoming daily more frustrated at not being called on much, so it was a relief for them to be in action of any sort. Sqn Ldr Blackwood was leading 310 at 3.35 pm near North Weald when his dozen Hurricanes saw as many or more Dorniers. After one attack, Blackwood eyed one Dornier slightly apart from the rest, so he chose this one to attack. The range had halved to 300 yards and after he had fired, the bomber wobbled perceptibly.

But Blackwood suddenly smelt something burning. He looked around urgently in the confined cockpit, to see his starboard wing-tank blistering on the top side of the wing. He decided wisely to break off the attack and concentrate instead on survival. He then realized that his petrol tank was burning inside. About ten seconds later, the tank flared up, so Blackwood undid his straps and disconnected his oxygen tube. Following the prescribed drill calmly and quickly, he turned over the aircraft on its back and he simply fell out. Blackwood wafted down safely, landing in a stubble field with no personal damage. The harvest had been gathered. He felt the stubble as he landed. The result: one aircraft lost, one pilot saved.

Sergeant Prohal went for a Dornier first and then a group of Me 109s. Firing fruitlessly, he set course for the coast at the Clacton-Southend stretch. Over to the left, he saw what he thought was a Spitfire, but on flying closer he realised it was actually an enemy machine – unidentified. Prohal regained a level position at 5,000 feet, but as he did so another enemy loosed a short snap of cannon and gunfire at him. Bullets from the machine gun literally tore into his glycol tank, port wing and rudder. Prohal instinctively made a steep starboard turn. His cockpit became choked with vapour from the glycol. He could not see the compass, so he flew by the sun with the object of landing as soon as he saw the coast. By gliding from the altitude of the clouds, he came down to land level, with his undercarriage up and 3½ miles south-east of Hornchurch. The Hurricane made a forced-landing. Prohal was slightly wounded with splinters penetrating his shoulders, left arm and neck. But he was alive.

After the squadron had launched their offensive against the Dorniers, P/O Emil Fechtner followed an Me 110, aiming a burst of 1,200 rounds at him as the range shortened to 100 yards. The usual heavy black smoke from one of the enemy's engines left a trail from 15,000 feet downwards. Suddenly six Me 109s zoomed at him. He wisely found refuge in the clouds and set course for base. His action had been over Harwich. Now no ferries left that port for the Continent. Nor would they until the war was over. Fechtner flew fast for four minutes, crossing over the railway line and the road leading to Chelmsford and Colchester. Prudence had ensured his survival. So three pilots all lived. The score seemed to finish up 3-3. Quite a reasonable debut for the Duxford squadron. Twelve Group had to wait for a few more days before they could really claim action on the heroic scale.

Still 26 August. Around 4 pm, 150 enemy were assembled against Portsmouth, with the ratio of two-to-one fighters-to-bombers. Numbers 10 and 11 Group got nearly 100 fighters into the air, and at height, and at speed, for the oncoming Heinkel 111s and Me 109s. Three squadrons espied them in failing visibility, and deflected the main thrust of their raid, Portsmouth was duly grateful to have been spared much further damage after the bad experience of only two days previously. That was the last raid of the day, but the Luftwaffe went on into the night against Midland industrial factories in the Birmingham-Coventry conglomeration. The bombers came from both the south corridor and the east. Birmingham suffered a long and wrecking raid. People were slaughtered, though fires started did not spread too much.

Some eighteen other places, too, including a rare raid far west on Britain's second naval port of Plymouth. Sailors were finding they were safe neither at sea nor in port. Finally, between one and two hundred incendiaries rained on North Coates airfield, but with little fire damage.

27 August

Rain stopped play. Not quite true, but it did restrict daytime flying. Then after dark, the enemy resumed raids on airfields and urban factories. This was the one day of the fortnight when fewer than 600 individual sorties were logged by the enemy. The losses were lighter on both sides: German nine, British one.

But the night raids were the heaviest to date in the 12 Group zone. Both Birmingham and Yorkshire industry had hits, while the Humber docks received a share as well. Fires broke out near the Nuffield factory at Birmingham. The strategy was successfully tried of blacking out Birmingham and Norwich as far as searchlights were concerned. This made it harder for the bombers to navigate and to locate their targets with any accuracy. Twenty-seven places were bombed in all. An enemy seaplane alighted on the water off Mablethorpe and remained there for some considerable time!

28 August

Next morning the weather improved and airfield targets were in the Essex sector – Rochford and Eastchurch. The enemy seemed to have mistaken the latter for a front-line fighter station, as it was unlucky enough to be pinpointed for several sorties in August. The principal feature of this day was the mass meeting of fighters as the Luftwaffe sent great sweeps of them over the south-east. Hard-pressed 11 Group Spitfires and Hurricanes took off again – and again. Defiants, too, of 264 Squadron. But their days were numbered for daytime fighting, in fact this was their swansong. Twelve of the two-crew fighters were destroyed over only two or three days, with equivalent loss of aircrew. The main fighter types acquitted themselves as well as ever, including 85 Squadron of Hurricanes. Its renowned leader, Peter Townsend, and the rest of his squadron claimed half-a-dozen aircraft destroyed. And all of 85 Squadron landed safe and sound after the last sorties.

The enemy stepped-up the night raids still further. Out of the 600-or-so sorties, the main raid fell on the Liverpool-Merseyside strip of terrain. The estimates were that 160 bombers took part for little if any loss. The raids everywhere spanned six hours of darkness, from 9.20 pm to 3.30 am. Worst hit were Derby, Sheffield, Manchester, Barnsley, Leeds and of course Liverpool. Derby suffered a special volume of bombs.

But spare a second, too, for the rest of the targets that night, spread as far apart as Bircham Newton, West Raynham, Aylsham, Finningley, Horncastle, Melton Mowbray, Grantham, Digby, Daventry, Mablethorpe, Brackley, Spalding, Manchester, Goole, Grimsby, Louth, Warrington, Skipton, Crewe, Rochdale, Stenigot, Sealand, Northwick, Leeds, Huddersfield and Chester. Quite a list. Number 12 Group pilots read about it next day with mounting impatience. Only one more day to wait … The loss of figures for 28 August were German thirty, British twenty.

29 August

This followed the same pattern. The enemy made 600–700 sorties in daylight fighter sweeps, apparently pursuing the dual aim of attacking airfields and drawing RAF fighters into costly combat. Park was cautious in his reaction to reports of these sweeps, tending to conserve or rest his forces wherever possible. He did have to defend airfields when necessary, though, and so did Brand in 10 Group.

On 29 August, one of the great names in the Battle of Britain entered the scene. F/O Richard Hillary of 603 Squadron pressed the button to fire a burst

Peter Townsend, right, with his rigger and fitter, in Scotland before being moved south for further action.

at an Me 109 as it crossed his sights for a fraction of a second, He did not get the Me 109, so he scanned the sky for his own Spitfires. Instead, he happened on a Hurricane squadron flying in a trio of v-formations. They did not seem to have any protection, so he attached himself to them as a self-appointed tail-end Charlie.

Then bullets began to hit his port wing. Smoke belched out of his engine, so he thought quickly and aimed towards Lympne. As the engine might give out at any moment, he then thought better of it and settled for a Kent cornfield, where he made a passable landing. At any rate, good enough to allow him to climb from the Spitfire cockpit. It was lucky the corn had been harvested.

Continuing his story, Hillary was shot down five days later on 3 September, the first anniversary of the outbreak of the war. Badly wounded, he parachuted into the sea, to be picked up by the ever-vigilant Margate lifeboat. He recovered from his wounds and returned to combat, but died later flying at night …

The night raids throbbed through the late summer darkness. They went for Merseyside in roughly the same strength as on 28 August. It must be remembered that the Germans did not have inexhaustible supplies either of aircraft or aircrew, but the quantity, if not quality, balance still lay on their side. The day-and-night raids took the toll of losses as German seventeen, British nine. These three days were, in retrospect, a lull compared to what followed. August was to end on a near-desperate note. But it did mark the start of 12 Group's serious participation. Meanwhile, Berlin received Bomber Command raids on the nights of both 29 and 30 August. Good for British morale. Bad for enemy morale.

CHAPTER ELEVEN

Enter Douglas Bader

30 August

The enemy effort now concentrated on the RAF's inland fighter aerodromes. No fewer than 800 aircraft darkened the skies of southern England in a determined, desperate throw to neutralize the vital airfields of Kenley, North Weald, Hornchurch, Debden, Detling, Duxford, Northolt and Biggin Hill. Especially Biggin Hill. The name of the famous fighter station was synonymous with – and symbolic of – the Royal Air Force in the Battle of Britain. Eager young men thrusting into the sky. Perhaps a

RAF Hornchurch, 1 September. Spitfires of 222 and 603 Squadrons. The nearest aircraft was shot down over Maidstone three days later and its pilot, Fg Off J.W. Cutts, was killed. The second aircraft was that flown by Plt Off Richard Hillary on 3 September

fraction less eager now and a little more haggard, depending on their experiences and individual characters. Sometimes they were being called on to make three, four or even more sorties a day. When a single sortie could so easily be their last one.

It was Biggin Hill that took the biggest punch of the forty-eight-hour massed air armada over the final days of August. The station was at the heart of the 11 Group network and also situated in a key defence ring south of London. Biggin Hill had two raids, several warnings, and the worst damage and casualties.

Waves of Me 109s rippled over south-east England with some 200 Ju 88s. The bombers fanned out into their respective formations to navigate for their assigned airfields. It seemed at one stage that the 11 Group map was bedecked and bedevilled with enemy pilots everywhere. The RAF pilots could have been forgiven if they had complained of fatigue. But there was no time for fatigue, or trauma, or any other more modern battle syndrome. It was life or death. Numbers 266 and 79 Squadrons both made head-on counterthrusts at the invaders, with due success. And 85 Squadron of Hurricanes also followed this head-on technique to force a large enemy bunch to all points of the compass, in an effort to evade or escape. It was almost impossible to count the claims of victories – they were happening at such speed.

One 79 Squadron pilot, Donald Stones, was making a head-on air-butt when his Hurricane did actually hit a Heinkel 111. Little was left of the Hurricane as Stones went through his escape drill. He was not certain of the sequence of events afterwards, but he did somehow operate his ripcord instinctively at the right time and landed somewhere in the Home Counties. He broke one leg. Other RAF pilots had to 'take to the silk', as it was known, to survive the fanatical fighting of the day. Others force-landed, crash-landed, or simply crashed. Yet they did their brilliant best to thwart the threats to the stricken airfields and equally stricken groundcrew.

Balls of smoke lingered over several airfields, including Biggin Hill. Some enemy bombers blasted through twice to the base. In the words of the official history of the Royal Air Force 1939–1945 by Denis Richards:

> '… wrecking the workshops, M.T. yard, the equipment and barracks stores, the armoury, the Met. Office and – a grave blow at the morale of the airmen – the N.A.A.F.!. The attacks also severed the gas and water mains and all telephone communications on the northern side of the station. A direct hit on a shelter trench killed several officers and men …
> '

These bare facts only partially convey the human side of the raids. Personnel, male and female, could only shelter; they could not escape to another place. Their duty lay here, just as their pilots had no choice but to take off and fight, however they might feel. And they would all have seemed superhuman if they had not felt frightened.

The enemy also got through to an important industrial target well north of the capital – the Vauxhall works at Luton in Bedfordshire. Then, with every available squadron of 11 Group airborne or else refuelling, Park at last called on 12 Group for assistance again. It was what Bader and the others had been begging for all this time. They could not really comprehend the apparent demarcation between 11 and 12 Groups in the middle of such a critical conflict.

So here at long last was the first of many memorable days for Douglas and 242 Squadron. Throughout August they were always being held in reserve, however impatient they became. They heard the growing number of reports on the gathering momentum of mass attacks in the south and ached to join in the affray. True, they had been in action several times, Bader more than most of them. He could now get in and out of his fighter more quickly with his artificial legs than most of the pilots with their real ones.

Now it was the sort of war where a German flyer fired at a Hurricane pilot parachuting down from a wrecked fighter – and killed him. Early on 30 August they got the orders: Take off immediately for Duxford. Bader was at last to lead his Hurricanes into action in some force. Then came the word:

'242 Squadron scramble – Angels fifteen. North Weald.'

They were off. At 1626, 4.26 pm to us, 242 were ordered from Duxford to patrol North Weald at 15,000 feet on vector 190 degrees. Just north of North Weald they received vector 340 degrees. About then, too, Bader's piercing eyes noticed three unidentified aeroplanes below and to the right of the squadron.

'Bandits to west. Blue Section investigate.'

So the squadron was depleted of three Hurricanes and had ten remaining. Green leader drew Bader's attention to a large Luftwaffe formation on their left. He turned with the other nine aircraft to witness what was undeniably an awe-inspiring sight – particularly to any of them who had not previously been in action. There were a vast number of twin-engined aeroplanes in front now, flying in an easterly direction. Bader counted fourteen blocks of six aircraft – all bombers – with thirty Me 110s behind and above.

Eight-gun Hurricanes of two squadrons on way up to interception.

Altogether, 242 Squadron's ten Hurricanes had more than 100 enemy to tackle. Odds of ten to one. The bombers, Heinkels with perhaps some Dornier 17s as well, flew in tight formation stepped up from about 12,000 feet. Then came a gap of 1,000 feet, with a swarm of fighters ranged from some 15,000–20,000 feet.

Bader could not see any friendly fighters near, so he ordered Green Section to attack the top of the lower formation of fighters, while his flight of Red and Yellow Sections went into line astern to go for the bombers. Immediately Bader had detailed F/O A Christie to take his section of three to keep the Messerschmitts busy; this pilot from Calgary said 'OK, OK' with obvious relish, and away he streaked to deal with that vastly superior number of enemy.

There was no point in trying to deliver any formation attack and Bader's only object was to break up the formation and start a dogfight. The enemy bombers were flying at around 15,000 feet now with the middle of the formation roughly west of the reservoirs at Enfield and heading east. When first sighted they looked just like a vast swarm of bees. With the sun at Bader's back and the advantage of greater height, conditions were ideal for a surprise attack and as soon as 242 were all in position they went straight down to the Germans. Bader did not adopt any set rules in attacking – he just worked on the axiom that the shortest distance between two points is a straight line.

So he dived straight into the middle of the tightly-packed formation, closely followed by the rest of his flight – Red 2 was P/O Willie McKnight and Red 3 P/O Denis Crowley-Milling. The enemy immediately broke up

Douglas Bader with some of his Canadian 'chums' of 242 Squadron.

fanwise. He saw three Me 110s do climbing turns left and three to the right. Bader spotted McKnight veer left while he attacked the right-hand trio. Their tactics appeared to be climbing turns to a nearly stalled position to try to get on Bader's tail. He tried a short burst of nearly three seconds into the first Me 110 at nearly point-blank range as he was at the top of his zoom. The aeroplane seemed to burst into flames.

Willie McKnight went for a section of Me 110s and two aircraft broke off specifically to attack him. He succeeded in getting behind one of them and opened fire at 100 yards. He hit it and it spun towards the Essex earth. He at once went for a Heinkel group, executing a neat beam attack on the one nearest to him. Its port engine paused and then stopped. A second or so later, the bomber rolled over on its back as if wounded and finally started to smoke. Then it conflagrated and crashed, according to reports.

Meanwhile Bader continued his zoom and found a second Me 110 below and to his right, just starting to dive after a stalled turn. So he turned in behind the German and got a very early shot at about 100-150 yards' range. The enemy's evasive action consisted in pushing his stick violently backwards and forwards. The second time he did this manoeuvre, Bader got in a burst as he was at the top of his short zoom. He saw pieces fly off the enemy's starboard wing near the engine and then the whole of the starboard wing went on fire. The aeroplane fell away to the right in a steep sort of spiral dive, well on fire. Bader did not see anyone bale out of either of the Me 110s, although it is possible that they did so. He was too busy looking around to worry once they had caught fire. There was just not time to stop and think of consequences.

Bader noticed in his mirror an Me 110 coming up behind him and he did a quick turn – to see five or six white streams coming out of the German's firing guns. It seemed as if the pilot were using tracer in all his guns. As soon as Bader turned, the Me 110 put its nose down. Bader tried to catch it but could not, so fired no more. Not once did an Me 110 get sights on Bader's Hurricane. He saw nothing except Me 110s, though there were Heinkels and Dorniers in force as well.

One of these Me 110s was attacking Willie McKnight just about then, but the young Canadian pilot succeeded in getting behind. He followed the Me 110 from 10,000 feet right down to a mere 1,000 feet. The enemy used ultra steep turns to try and get clear, but eventually it had to straighten out or crash. McKnight opened fire at a range of thirty yards. The enemy's starboard engine stopped, the port one flamed. It crashed after having used a lot of rear fire at McKnight. He reported as seeing it go down alongside a large reservoir.

Denis Crowley-Milling flying Red 3 was left with a Heinkel open to himself. He attacked astern, giving the bomber a five-second burst. Tentative return rear fire soon stopped as the aircraft began an inexorable descent to earth. Crowley-Milling started to follow it, when tracer bullets from an Me 110 passed his starboard wing. He decided to nose away to port. P/O Hart saw the Heinkel go down.

Flt Lt Eric Ball led Yellow Section as Bader's own section broke up the enemy masses. He saw a single Heinkel circling, diving and turning – all at once, Ball took it from behind. He closed to 100 yards, using one-third of his ammunition. Both enemy engines caught alight and the bomber force-landed on an aerodrome full of cars near North Weald. Ball then chased a straggler Me 110. The enemy engine stopped dead and the aircraft lost height rapidly. Ball had the sun behind him during both these attacks – as per Bader's dictum.

At 5.05 pm, Sub-Lt R.J. Cork, RN, was flying as Yellow 2 between North Weald and Hatfield when he attacked an Me 110 in company with several other enemy fighters. Cork's beam attack hit its mark and the enemy executed a frantic stall turn with the port engine afire. There was no hope left for it as it had reached the point of no return, and seconds later exploded on the ground. Cork swung back to the scene of combat and an Me 110 burning in a field. Its swastikas still stood out against the dark green body.

Sergeant R.V. Lonsdale flying as Yellow 3 sought a Heinkel which had become parted from its formation. He pressed the button to start a prolonged ten-second burst beginning 300 yards away and ending only 50 yards off. The enemy circled like a wounded bird and eventually was claimed to have crashed in the same area as the Me 110 attributed to Cork. A

Legendary trio of 12 Group – two Canadians and one British. Willie McKnight, Douglas Bader, George Ball.

Hurricane could and did of course easily outfly and outrace an opponent like Heinkels or even Me 110s.

When Bader told Green Section to go for the top of the lower formation, F/O Christie as Green Leader launched a bull-like head-on charge for an Me 110 on top of the four layers. It arched off to starboard, diving as it went. Christie kept glued to its tail, spraying a burst from 50 yards astern. Something had to hit shortly, and oil started spouting, gushing, from the starboard motor. The petrol tanks burst, the Me 110 took a vertical dive and it travelled from 6,000 feet straight down into greenhouses about 500 yards from the reservoir at Ponder's End.

Green Section were flying behind Yellow Section when 242 saw the enemy originally. They received the orders to attack the fighters above them, but these quickly dispersed. So Green Section chose the bombers instead. Green 3, P/O N. Hart, stumbled on three in line about 1,000 feet below his Hurricane. As he started to dive, he saw Yellow 1 attacking the last one of the trio. Hart took the second bomber and sent it into a dive. He was just about to follow it down when he saw the first Heinkel making a steep right-hand turn. He turned inside it and used up all his ammunition on the bomber. It was reported to have plunged into a field with all the crew still aboard. Hart did not dwell there as three Me 110s began to chase him.

P/O Stansfield also attacked an enemy with Eric Ball. Stansfield first saw the straggler aiming eastwards. In the first of three attacks he silenced the rear gunner, who had opened fire with cannon. Both enemy engines were in trouble; smoke from the port, while the starboard stopped altogether.

Someone saw the Heinkel come down heavily on an aerodrome covered with wrecked cars. Three Germans staggered out of its remnants. Stansfield was Black 1 and Sergeant G.W. Brimble Black 2.

Brimble had followed Stansfield on to the Heinkel, firing from 250 yards. He saw Stansfield follow the bomber almost into the ground. Then Brimble broke away to find an Me 110 executing a gentle turn to port. He achieved a quarter attack and had the definite sight of the enemy actually striking the ground.

As Brimble flew across to rejoin his section leader, the next thing he knew was an Me 110 aiming straight for him. He opened fire instinctively at 350 yards and saw glass splinter in front of the enemy. The machine took a violent convulsive dive, as if in some fatal fever. Brimble did not see any more, as another Me 110 got on his tail. The rule was survival first.

Back to Bader and his advice about enemy aircraft on the tail of Hurricanes. As Bader climbed back to 12,000 feet from 6,000 feet, he could see no further enemy. He thought:

'Now, there's one curious thing about this air fighting. One minute you see hundreds of aeroplanes in the sky, and the next minute there's nothing. All you can do is to look through your sights at your particular target – and look in your mirror, too, if you are sensible, for any Messerschmitts which might be trying to get on your tail.'

That particular battle lasted about five or ten minutes, and then, quite suddenly, the sky was clear of aircraft. One pilot had sent a bomber crashing into a greenhouse. Another bomber had gone headlong into a field filled with derelict cars, hit one of them, turned over and caught fire. Another of

Back from action comes a Spitfire with flaps down ready to land.

242 Squadron had seen a twin-engined aircraft go into the reservoir near Enfield. Yet another pilot saw his victim go down with his engine flat out, the aeroplane diving into a field and disintegrating into little pieces.

Number 242 Squadron had not shot them all down, of course. The enemy had not waited for that, but made off home in all directions at high speed.

As Bader could spot no enemy despite his peeled eyes, he called Duxford by radio and was told to land. On the way he picked up Green Leader, F/O Christie, and also Blue Section. The infuriated Blue Section pilots had been sent off to investigate unidentified aircraft and missed the entire battle. They had not fired a single round between them and their language when they heard what they had missed was unprintable!

One thing Bader noticed with surprise was that he received no rear fire from the Me 110s and they appeared to be trying to fight with front guns only. This made the odds heavily in the Hurricane's favour. So – ten Hurricanes had fought and routed over a hundred of the enemy. Such was Bader's leadership and strategic skill.

As a result of this successful engagement, the notion of a larger formation than a squadron was conceived in the mind of Air Vice-Marshal Leigh Mallory. On this occasion, the squadron had been called off the ground in time to meet a large enemy formation under favourable conditions south-west of Epping. They had position, height and sun in attacking an enemy bomber formation without Me 109 escort. In the course of a congratulatory call from Leigh-Mallory that same evening, Bader said to him:

'If I'd had more fighters, we would have shot down more of the enemy.'

This rather memorable day ended with the all-too-regular raids on Merseyside. On the night before this, Liverpool, Warrington and Manchester had been targets, with the Observer Corps actually unable to plot raids for some time due to the holocaust around Warrington. Then on 30 August, it was Warrington again, with other industrial areas and East Anglian aerodrome. Watnall was bombed for the first time, four delayed-action devices being dropped near the camp. These killed two civilians. Watnall was the location of 12 Group Headquarters and it was a coincidence that this was a target selected on the same day that 242 Squadron first went into full-scale action.

The losses of aircraft for 30 August were German thirty-six, British twenty-six. They were still worrying days for both sides in different ways. Park and Dowding had a lot to ponder. Lack of pilots and aircraft; damage to their fighter airfields; what the future held in store; who would crack first. But Bomber Command provided a crumb of comfort – they raided Berlin again on the night of 30 August. And Munich just a day or two later. Two of Hitler's sacred cities.

CHAPTER TWELVE

Airfields Under Siege

31 August

The Hurricanes of 111 Squadron under John Thompson had fought on and on throughout August. Croydon airfield had been in the thickest of things, along with Biggin Hill. Now the squadron was to be withdrawn for a vital respite. Before this happened, two untried replacement pilots from the Officers Training Unit drove up to Croydon, complete with their equipment. Both were conscripted into action at once, before they had even unpacked. One got back injured from that first scramble. The other never returned at all … At this time, too, the legendary air ace, Bob Stanford Tuck, joined 257 Squadron of Hurricanes. He managed to inject indefinable spirit that revived a punch-drunk outfit.

This was the catalogue of some of the airfields again under siege today: Biggin Hill (twice), Hornchurch (twice), Kenley, Detling, Debden, Eastchurch, Croydon. Squadrons moved around flexibly as runways or facilities became unusable, or the threat of being caught on the ground became unjustifiable. Once more the imperturbable figure of Peter Townsend was written into the chronicles of the day. Emerging from the sound of furious combat over North Weald, Townsend was to sail back to British soil with a metal fragment or two in one foot. But that was later in the day.

Parachute-packing was one of the RAF ground trades on which lives literally depended daily. Pilots frequently fell safely to earth by parachute, quite often landing on golf courses – to the consternation of people actually playing there. It was an irony of the Battle of Britain that golfers should be enjoying a round while the struggle for civilization was being decided some four or five miles above their heads. It was war with the extra dimension of the sky.

The timetable of the bombing was: Debden during the morning; Croydon and Hornchurch at midday; Hornchurch and Biggin Hill each for the second time in the evening. The enemy caught three fighters of 54 Squadron actually on take off. The bombs began dropping just as the squadron had been scrambled. Eight aircraft got clear of the runway seconds before the blast of the first bombs. The other three were literally feet off the ground as the explosions blasted them. The Spitfires were destroyed in the air, yet their pilots were not. Sergeant Davies was taking off towards the hangars at Hornchurch. He was thrown back across the River Ingrebourne two fields away, scrambling out of his machine unharmed.

We left Alan Deere having survived five escapes. Now he was six miles up in the air – in a fight that started at 34,000 feet. He dived after an aeroplane he had shot down, when he found himself in the midst of a formation of Messerschmitts flying at 28,000 feet. One of the enemy promptly shot away his rudder controls.

As Deere dived away, his engine began to smoke ominously, indicating that the aircraft would probably go up in flames if he made a crash-landing. So he decided to bale out. Controlling the Spitfire by using the ailerons until he was down to 10,000 feet, he prepared to abandon aircraft. The vivid memory of how he had been caught a few days previously led him to adopt another method this time. He stalled the burning Spitfire and took a header over the side, as if he were diving off a springboard into a swimming pool.

Directly he saw the tail of his aircraft overhead, he pulled his ripcord and floated gently down, taking the opportunity of practising side-slipping by working the lines of his parachute. It was as well that he did practise, for he had to side-slip to avoid a farmhouse. Instead he landed right in the middle of a heavily-laden plum tree. You could say, plum in the middle. So much for his sixth and penultimate escape. That was actually on 30 August. Now it was 31 August.

As a change from being shot down, Alan Deere was next nearly killed on the ground. He had just made two sorties and was about to take off for a third when a formation of Heinkels bombed the aerodrome. As he opened his throttle, a bomb fell right in front of him. He seemed to be flung miles in the air, then he felt himself careering along the ground upside down – with his head scraping over the earth and squeezing him into a ball in the cockpit. He thought it was the end for him this time, but the aircraft stopped at last and he was still alive.

Every moment, Deere thought the flames would creep in on him, but a squadron colleague, Pilot Officer E. Edsall, managed to get the door off and haul him out. 'I was balancing on my head, so there was no danger of breaking my neck when I released my Sutton harness,' he explained later. His scalp was caked with earth and bleeding badly – and he was very dazed.

But otherwise he was unharmed. Deere finished that episode of a charmed life:

'When I saw the wreckage of my aircraft afterwards, I just didn't believe I had come out alive. The engine had been blown completely off, the starboard wing was some hundreds of yards away, the tail unit was nowhere to be viewed, and there was a furrow about 100 yards in length where I had ploughed along upside down. I think the engine being blown up saved me from fire, as there was a considerable amount of petrol in the tank.'

The wing and the tail were blown off his rescuer's Spitfire which drove ahead on the fuselage and came to a stop with the pilot unharmed. There was no trace of the third pilot who was taking off when the bombs dropped, and he was not found until a couple of hours later, when he was discovered knocked out, but completely unscarred and uninjured, along with his wrecked aircraft two fields away from the aerodrome. All three of the fighter pilots had extraordinary escapes.

Next day, Deere had concussion and a generally sore head. He was grounded by the medical officer, but ignored the injunction not to fly. Instead he shot down a Dornier into the River Thames. Altogether Squadron Leader Alan C. Deere destroyed seventeen enemy aircraft.

It was still 31 August. From a few fragments over the radio between ground controllers and aircrew, or air-to-air talking, an accurate scenario could well be imagined of what was happening three or four miles above the operations rooms:

'Tally Ho!'

'Bandits ahead of you.'

'Angels one five.'

'Prepare to break.'

'Attacking line astern.'

Then some sound effects of the battle followed by: 'Thought I'd bought it that time.'

'Getting short of juice.'

'No need for the blood wagon.'

This last line referred to the station ambulance. Perhaps humour was one of the qualities that helped them win.

RAF Kenley may not have been the primary target on 31 August, but its pilots were still in the thick of things. Tom Gleave took off from the familiar runway of Kenley in his Hurricane. This is what transpired next:

'A large raid was coming in from the south … I glanced up to see what we were chasing. Right above us were rows of Hun bombers – Ju 88s in line astern – and my aircraft was directly below one line of them and closing distance rapidly. I rocked my wings and then eased the nose up, taking a bead on No. 15 of the line of Huns and giving him a raking burst. I repeated the process on No. 3.

'I was about to pull up to attack No. 1 … when I heard a metallic click above the roar of my engine. A sudden burst of heat struck my face, and I looked down into the cockpit. A long spout of flame was issuing from the hollow starboard wing-root. The flames increased until the cockpit was like the centre of a blow-lamp nozzle. There was nothing left to do but bale out. The skin was already rising off my right wrist and hand, and my left hand was starting to blister, the glove being already partially burnt off. My shoes and slacks must have been burning all this time.

'I undid my harness and tried to raise myself, but found I had not the strength. I was comforted by the thought that I had my gun ready loaded if things came to the worst … I decided to pull off my helmet, open the cockpit cover and roll on my back so that I could drop out. My helmet came off after a determined tug: I opened the cockpit cover and that was the last effort I had to make. There was a blind flash, I seemed to be travelling through yards of flame; then I found myself turning over and over in the air … My hand instinctively passed over the harness release and on to the ripcord handle … then came a gentle jerk as I was pulled into the vertical position. I felt my left hip and head strike the ground simultaneously and then all was still.

'With an effort I stood up and surveyed the damage. My shoes still looked like shoes and I found that I could walk; why, I don't know, as my ankle and each side of my right foot were burnt and my left foot was scorched and had several small burns. My slacks had disappeared except for portions that had been covered by the parachute harness. The skin on my right leg, from the top of the thigh to just above the ankle, had lifted and draped my leg like outsize plus-fours. My left leg was in a similar condition, except that the left thigh was only scorched …

'Above each ankle I had a bracelet of unburnt skin; my socks, which were always wrinkled, had refused to burn properly. My Service gloves were almost burnt off, and the skin from my wrists and hands hung down like paper bags. The under-side of my right arm and elbow were burnt and so was my face and neck. I could see all right, although it felt like looking through slits in a mass of swollen skin, and I came to the conclusion that the services of a doctor were necessary.'

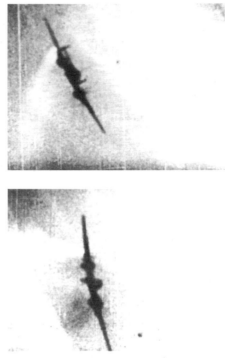

RAF pilot's-eye-view of an Me 110 at the moment of attack and immediately afterwards. Smoke from hits clearly visible.

The celebrated plastic surgery unit at East Grinstead had to create almost a fresh face for Tom Gleave. This creative surgery was achieved under the guidance of the famous head of East Grinstead, Archibald McIndoe. Gleave was typical of many pilots – fighter and bomber – who were treated for similar or comparable injuries as a result of burns.

Peter Townsend was a little luckier. He had been commanding 85 Squadron since May. On 31 August he climbed from Croydon in his Hurricane and saw results of a raid on Biggin Hill. He was closing on Me 110s with the squadron following him. As he put it afterwards, his only thought was 'to get those ill-mannered bastards who had disturbed our lunch, smashed our airfield, invaded our sky'. There were Me 109s above him. Townsend ran into tracer from all sides. He shot at an Me 109 and it 'belched black and white smoke'. He fired at another. Then a third one appeared – 'so close I could see the pilot'. He was about to fire at the Me 109 when an Me 110 pointed towards him. Peter Townsend took up the story from that second:

'My thumb was on the firing button, but I never fired. A blast of shot suddenly splattered my Hurricane, my left foot was kicked off the rudderbar, petrol gushed into the cockpit. The shock was so terrific that for a few instants I lost control and went into a steep dive. "Christ … " I heard myself say quite softly, as if I'd spilt some tea on the drawing room carpet. Over to the right a Hurricane was going down vertically, etching a black line of smoke across the sky.

'Then I straightened out. By some miracle, my Hurricane had not burst into flames. Sitting there in my blue jersey, sleeves rolled up, I had escaped the agony of Tom Gleave … burnt beyond recognition. My windscreen was scarred with bullets – how lucky that Dowding had insisted that we be at least as well protected as the gangsters of Chicago.

'But I still had to land, and did not fancy the densely wooded country below. So I baled out and watched my poor Hurricane dive into the trees and blow up. A house appeared below and at the back door two girls were looking up at me. Swinging in my parachute a few hundred feet above their heads, I called to them rather stupidly, "I say, would you mind giving me a hand when I get down?" For I was rather shaken, there was something in my foot, and I still had to fall into the trees.

'Missing a wood of old oaks by a few yards, I fell with a thump among supple young fir trees. After that mortal combat I felt idiotic sitting on my backside in a wood with a large hole in my shoe. My foot was in a mess, so I lit a cigarette and waited. A man burst from a thicket and levelled his rifle at my head. A policeman ran up. "Name and address, please," he asked as if he had caught me speeding. Speeding had yet to come. During the breakneck drive with Mr Sauter through the Kentish lanes to Hawkhurst I spent my most frightening moments since leaving Croydon.

'Mr Sauter delivered his prize to Hawkhurst Cottage Hospital, where the doctor looked at my foot: "I could sew it up, but there might be something in it." Of that I was convinced; it was beginning to hurt like hell. I was dying of hunger, too, since those Me 110s had done me out of lunch. A beautiful plate of scrambled eggs was brought …

'At 10 pm I lay in the operating theatre at Croydon General Hospital. The house surgeon, Mr Brayn-Nicholls, bent over me. "We'll try to save the toe," he said gravely. A mask was clapped over my face and the wailing air raid siren faded into oblivion. For me the battle was over.

'The squadron held out for a few more days. With its two night commanders and me out of action, Patrick Woods-Scawen took over. That evening he led nine Hurricanes out of the setting sun on to a group of Me 109s, sending down four.'

More than once during the battle, RAF pilots forced their German counterparts to land by bluffing them. On 31 August still, south of Maidstone, one Hurricane pilot ran out of ammunition after shooting down two enemy aircraft. He followed a third Me 109 right down virtually to ground level, flew alongside it, and pointed down to the Kent fields. Then the Hurricane pilot made a dummy attack, without firing, whereupon the German landed and threw up his hands. The RAF pilot threw him a packet of cigarettes and circled overhead to watch the Luftwaffe man being taken into custody by a patrol of local Home Guards.

There were various other similar incidents. K.W. McKenzie, from Belfast, also used up all ammunition. So he flew fast alongside an Me 109 trying to force it down into the sea. As this manoeuvre failed, he cut the enemy fighter's tail with his wingtip. This achieved the object and McKenzie himself escaped injury.

A Hurricane pilot even exceeded this exploit. He was out of ammunition but likewise determined that the enemy should not get away. He took the ultimate step of ramming the opposing aircraft, a Dornier, amidships. This tore off one of the bomber's wings, but the British pilot found his cockpit

German airman after parachuting from his burning aircraft. The ubiquitous British Bobby is taking down the full particulars!

swamped with glycol fumes. He had no option but to bale out – safely. Another RAF pilot, T.P.M. Cooper-Slipper, rammed and destroyed a German aircraft after his own controls had been all but shot away in a fight.

Twelve Group was asked again to help on 31 August. Although six squadrons were detailed, only 310 Squadron made contact. They hit a Messerschmitt 110 but in so doing they lost three fighters. P/O Aberhart was killed; F/O Coward was injured; and F/O Brinsden baled out safely. So one pilot was lost. Then just after lunch, 310 Squadron of twelve aircraft took off from Duxford with orders to patrol Hornchurch at 10,000 feet. North Weald also came within their remit. Flt Lt Sinclair was leading the squadron when they sighted fifteen Dorniers plus the protective screen of Me 109s in about the same numbers – milling above and below busily. In the ensuing dogfight, Sqn Ldr Hess was on the receiving end of several Me 109s. One overshot him and he took the German from below. He hit it and the Messerschmitt spun madly down. Hess broke off as a further pair appeared from nowhere. Then Hess and other Hurricanes countered by spotting a Dornier on the left outskirts of its group. He gave it the usual 4–5 seconds' burst. At 1,000 feet it straightened out from a dip and Hess pumped in the balance of his ammunition. The bomber went down near the River Roach. Three of the crew jumped out and put up their hands. They had had enough of the Battle of Britain. Everyone had.

Ten miles north-east of London, P/O Z.M. Maly's Hurricane was set on fire by fighters from the rear and out of the sun. Turning left, he met three Me 109s. After watching one plummet from his fire, he glimpsed a parachute unfurling four or five miles off. He did not know whose. Flt Lt J. Jeffries led a flight at some Dorniers around the 11,000 feet mark. He hit one and claimed it, since it was last seen 'ominously near ground level'. But later the rear-gunners of enemy bombers began to hit back. P/O Sterbacek and his Hurricane went down, while P/O Kredba baled out safely. P/O Emil Fechtner hit a Dornier's engine and cockpit. Part of the cockpit snapped away and the bomber dived on its port wing towards earth. P/O Zimprich shook off an Me 109 with an aerobatic shrug and counterstruck from the rear. The enemy dived but Zimprich did not see the end of the joust. Too often that was what happened. The squadron claimed five enemy shot down and most of that number probably were – certainly three.

Concluding the account of August in the official history of the Royal Air Force 1939-1945, Denis Richards said:

'But once again it was at Biggin Hill that the damage was worst. More telephone lines were severed; many buildings and hangars were destroyed; the operations room block was set on fire; and an emergency

Hurricanes on the climb.

room outside the station – in an estate office in the neighbouring village – had to be brought into use. The station still continued in action; but as the emergency equipment could not deal with the normal number of aircraft, two of the three squadrons had now to operate under the control of adjoining sectors.'

So Biggin Hill really suffered. As did Manston. In fact, the enemy had at some cost achieved their aim and put it out of use. Like Biggin Hill, RAF Kenley was operating but at only reduced efficiency. The last locations to be visited by the Luftwaffe in August were south-east radar stations and though normal service was interrupted, they came back after a few hours. Merseyside received its raid that night, along with Midlands targets. Night and day, the bombs oscillated down in the south, Midlands, and north. The losses: German forty-one, British thirty-nine. It was the worst day for RAF losses of the entire battle. How much longer could it go on?

CHAPTER THIRTEEN

The WAAF at War

1 September

The ordeal of the airfields went into September. The month opened with the sixth raid in three days on beleaguered Biggin Hill. Its buildings were by then unsafe – those still standing. Ground staff had to move vital gear into the open air. Somehow Biggin Hill went on working. Bombs fell and exploded or failed to do so. Men and women were frightened. Men of the RAF, women of the WAAF. Women like Corporal Elspeth Henderson, Sergeant Helen Turner, and Assistant Section Officer Felicity Hanbury.

At the start of the day's raids, ASO Felicity Hanbury, two other WAAF officers, and some RAF men, went to the nearest trench. The steady sound of our aircraft patrolling overhead turned to the zoom and roar of dogfights. Bombs straddled the airfield, getting louder as they came closer. So loud that Felicity clutched her ears. She thought that otherwise they would burst. The bombs were all around them now.

One fell a few feet from the entrance to their air-raid shelter. Stones and earth flew inside, and a blast of hot air pushed them sideways across the trench. Another bomb dropped near; and again the noise of aircraft engines, anti-aircraft guns, bombs and then machine-guns all made Felicity feel as though she were falling to bits. It was all over in ten minutes. Then came a lull, and they heard the throb of our aircraft returning to refuel and rearm. A messenger came to get the padre and another officer, as a trench had been hit at the far end of the aerodrome. They could only guess why the padre was needed.

Felicity went quickly to the airwomen's trenches by the guardroom. On her way past craters and debris, she saw her first dead person – a NAAFI girl lying in the hedge. Then she found that one of the airwomen's trenches had got a direct hit and the girls were buried underneath. The station officer came along at that moment and said they must get some volunteers to dig the girls out.

There was another trench at the other end of a horseshoe of houses. Felicity went to see the airwomen there and told them they could come out. A corporal ran off to fetch blankets. A bomb had blown in the end of the first trench, cutting off the entrance and killing a sick quarters attendant. The wounded were got out and laid on stretchers in the hedges; they coped with the worst.

Some went to sick quarters, others direct to hospital. Several girls had broken legs and arms. A stream of ambulances ferried them to the hospital for long after the raid.

In the trench shelter where the sick quarters attendant had been killed, Flight Sergeant Gartside's mind went blank after the bomb burst. The girls said she was conscious and issued orders as usual. She made them all laugh for a minute by trying to sit up after the shock and saying: 'Heavens, I've broken my back,' and then almost in the same breath, 'Heavens, I've broken my teeth, too'. The girls laughed with nervous reaction and did not worry any more till they were rescued.

When medical help came, the flight sergeant said: 'Look after the others. Don't worry about me. I'm all right.' She had, in fact, broken her back and spent some weeks lying on it in plaster before recovering enough to be invalided out of the WAAF.

Some WAAF quarters had been hit during the raid, but everything possible was salvaged to make them habitable for the airwomen. Felicity Hanbury went on working. She thought the cooks particularly were magnificent. The airmen's cookhouse was one of the few buildings which had not been affected. It was at the end of the aerodrome. The Army ground defence and the airmen were all fed from the WAAF cookhouse for some days. The WAAF cooks were frying sausages and mash for the men till long after midnight that first night. Felicity took hurricane lamps along, as the electric light had gone, and then she collected some food to take to the WAAF plotters on duty.

A bomb had fallen right in the middle of the station road, and burst the gas, electric and water mains. The heat and dust were terrific. The girls stacked up the dirty plates and later water-tanks came along and kept the cookhouse supplied.

Continuing the story, the WAAF officers slept in the commanding officer's quarters that night, as there was a delayed-action bomb in front of their own mess. Felicity went to bed about 2 am as there did not seem to be anything else to do, but she could not sleep much for delayed-action bombs kept going off. Also a cow kept mooing in the field opposite, and she thought it might have been hit. But it hadn't!

Then there was an air-raid alarm at 8.30 the next morning. The station broadcast was out of action, so two buglers stood outside the Operations

Three gallant WAAF girls all awarded the Military Medal for remaining at their posts under heavy aerial bombardment: Sergeant Joan Mortimer, Corporal Elspeth Henderson and Sergeant Helen Turner.

Rooms and bugled like mad! They all went down to the trenches, but the enemy aircraft were driven off. Raiders came again at 10 am, when Felicity was in the cookhouse and once more she heard the zoom of the dogfights, mingled with the whistling of bombs. But it did not sound very serious this time, and they joked in the trenches before soon going back to work. Another raid followed in the afternoon, when the Operations Room roof fell on the WAAF plotters, who were dug out without much harm. The attacks on Biggin Hill went on. Felicity Hanbury was awarded the MBE.

Meanwhile, the WAAFs were taking it all over Biggin Hill. Elspeth Henderson, from Edinburgh, was small and auburn-haired. Before the war, she had travelled a great deal and lived abroad, some of the time in Ceylon. She spoke fluent French and German. Helen Turner, from London, was among the early women recruits who worked with the Air Force in World War One, joining in the days of the Royal Flying Corps. She completed four years' service. Then for ten years she was a telephone operator at the Savoy Hotel in London and after that seven years in a similar job with an advertising agency. Now it was September 1940 and both women were corporals in the WAAF.

Enemy bombers throbbed once more over Biggin Hill. The two women were both on duty, Elspeth in charge of a special telephone line and Helen as the switchboard operator. The bombs began falling perilously near to their building, but both of them went on with their jobs although they knew they had only a light roof over their heads.

Then came a direct hit. Neither of them was hurt and they still carried on with their work. Elspeth said later: 'There was nothing much else we could do anyway, was there?'

Then the building caught fire, and the flames spurted and spat across the room. At last they were ordered to leave. Helen said:

'When we did leave, we had to crawl out through the wreckage, crawling through the broken-down walls to safety. I felt a bit sorry for some of the youngsters in the building at the time, because it was their first experience of bombs. I did my best to cheer them up.'

Elspeth Henderson and Helen Turner were awarded the Military Medal at the same time as Joan Mortimer. The commanding officer of Biggin Hill said:

'These three girls have shown amazing pluck in carrying on their work under the strain of falling bombs. I am proud to have them working on this station. There is no doubt that their example during two days of bombing inspired all around them.'

As well as the havoc at Biggin Hill, the first of September included raids on Debden, Detling and Eastchurch, with naval targets of Tilbury and Chatham. So the battle blazed on – and unknown or unnamed pilots, as well as the famed, contributed equally to its course. Pilots like the anonymous one of Max Aitken's 601 Squadron, whose Hurricane was hit during a dogfight.

'I felt a pain in my right thigh, felt the engine stop, heard hissing noises, and smelt fumes. My first reaction was to pull back the stick, but there was no response. That was at 19,000 feet where the combat ended. The next thing I remember is falling through the air at high speed and feeling my helmet, flying boots and socks torn off. Lack of oxygen must have dulled my senses. My Hurricane had disappeared. My parachute opened at 7,000 feet. About 2,000 feet lower, a Messerschmitt 110 fired at me while being closely pursued by Hurricanes.

'I landed in the water, just after seeing a motorboat pass about a mile away. My CO told me later that they did not see me coming down, although they saw a German parachutist about 200 yards away from me. After about 20 minutes, I saw a Hurricane search the bay, and I soon recognized it as belonging to my flight commander. He waved to me and spent some considerable time trying to inform a motor-torpedo-boat of my whereabouts, flying backward and forward between the boat and me. I was eventually picked up and taken to hospital, where my shrapnel wounds were X-rayed and dressed.

Just one snapshot in the overall battle, a cameo from one day.

The most remarkable achievement of Flying Officer H.M. Stephen, 74 Squadron, was that he claimed five enemy aircraft in one morning. This morning. Before breakfast he had accounted for two Me 109s. A little later he attacked some of forty Me 110s which were trying to bomb and attack a Channel convoy. Stephen got one. Later again the same day, he came across another Me 110 chasing a Spitfire. In his own Spitfire, Stephen managed to silence the rear-gunner of the Me 110, before later bursts sent the entire aircraft screeching into the sea. It was still before midday when Stephen found a fifth enemy aircraft. This last Messerschmitt was part of an escort for a formation of dive-bombers, but it had become detached from the rest. Stephen sent it spinning on to a beach below them. As well as claiming these five victories, Stephen also damaged three other aircraft. H.M. Stephen was the first member of the Royal Air Force to receive a 'field award' of the Distinguished Service Order. An honour for the Aberdonian pilot.

Night-time raids on 1 September went to Bristol, South Wales, the Midlands and Merseyside. Liverpool and Sheffield also both felt the fear of bombs bursting unseen at night, while Grimsby and Hull had similar experiences. Although the losses for the day were less than on 31 August, another first-time figure was that on 1 September the RAF lost one more aircraft than the Luftwaffe: German fourteen, British fifteen. This was not a precedent that anyone would want to be repeated.

The following few days up to 6 September were really a catalogue of previous raids. Only the destinations varied. But for the sake of chronology, here is how the battle fared for the last five days of this particular phase – before a surprise twist varied the plot of the story and also the plot as unveiled before the controllers of all the RAF fighter sectors.

2 September

Raids on: Biggin Hill; Lympne; Detling; Eastchurch; Hornchurch. Fighter squadrons beat off all the assaults but one. And here they harried the enemy so insistently that only one out of a hundred bombs fell actually on the target airfield. Quite a triumph. Perhaps the most serious damage occurred when bombs hit the Short Brothers aircraft factory at the Medway town of Rochester in Kent. Elsewhere now. Before the war, racing cars tore around the banked Brooklands track near Weybridge in Surrey; now the Vickers aicraft factory was turning out Wellington bombers there and became the victim of the other industrial raid of the day. The same northern towns were hit that night, plus Manchester and Sheffield. At Birmingham, the Nuffield factory sustained two hits in the vital machine shop and one on a pillbox near the entrance. Aircraft losses for 2 September: German thirty-five, British thirty-one. Still high on both sides.

3 September

The war was a year old. Above North Weald, Hurricanes shot down four Me 110s aiming for the airfield – for the loss of one fighter and no pilots. Two hangars blazed at North Weald, however, and communications were all but utterly cut. One bomb hit the roof of the station's new Operations Rooms, but did not explode. Slighter damage was done at Manston and West Malling. There could not have been that much left at Manston after all its travails.

Aircraftwoman Cooper and the others had just about recovered from the first air attack on North Weald. It had been a comparatively quiet week at the station. Not on 3 September. ACW Cooper:

'We had just got back to our quarters to get our things, and were allowed in one at a time so as not to disturb the D-A bombs (we were sleeping then in the barrack blocks) when the station had its second attack. That was at 10.45 am. We sat in trenches for about ten minutes while we heard a running commentary on the Tannoy. We had time then to be frightened. Hardly any of us hoped to get out alive.

'There was one WAAF in the trench who hadn't been on the station for the first raid. She insisted on staying at the entrance to see what happened. But at the first bomb, she came down with a rush.

'I sat on the bench and there was one plotter beside me and two others standing in front; and we all gripped each other. It seemed a much longer raid. They used H.E.s, anti-personnel bombs, which just touch the ground and explode with a terrific blast, and incendiaries.

'After the bombing, we heard machine guns firing off and thought they had got the ammunition dump. The decontamination centre proved to be far from bomb-proof. The M.T. yard was ablaze. The Ops. Block had been hit, but not much damage was done. There was a D-A bomb outside the telephone exchange. In fact, except the officers' mess, which survived both raids, there was hardly any building which hadn't been damaged. They got some of the hangars, but all our aircraft, of course, were up, except a few which were being serviced.

'I and two other plotters climbed into a civilian lorry and went off to Emergency Ops. All the service transport in the yard had been blown up. On the way, we thought there was another attack coming, but it was only our aircraft returning.

'We ran Ops from Emergency Ops, and worked all that day and through the next night. We had to cook for ourselves and the airmen.'

One girl at one fighter station in one day of the battle. Three hours later than the raid on North Weald, another fighter station was hit. This was Debden, which lay almost due north of ACW Cooper's station.

Section Officer Yates (née Petters) was at Debden in Cambridgeshire on that day:

'About two o'clock the siren sounded. Before everyone had got inside the trenches – about 15 seconds after the warning – there were the most earsplitting rumbles and bangs. I was just entering my trench when suddenly I found myself lying on the floorboards, having been hurled down four steps into the pitch blackness. The noise was so deafening and terrifying that our whole lives passed before us in a few seconds, which we certainly thought to be our last.

'Pieces of the trench fell upon us and my tin hat was knocked off. The bombing ceased and all we heard in the deathly stillness of the trench was the whine of diving aircraft and splutter of machine guns and the roar of our squadrons taking off. Then we smelt burning.

'Before we had time to utter a word or contemplate further, I heard a man's shout: "Come out of the trench. There's an unexploded bomb on top," and the girls' cry, "It's on fire this end." Out we filed and ran to the nearest trench, to find it full, and then to the next with no luck; so we had to throw ourselves on the ground.

'As we emerged from the trench, I thought immediately – This is like the picture *The Shape of Things to Come*. The buildings around us were damaged and many knocked down. Dust and smoke were in the air, and there was a solid ring of craters around us. Afterwards we counted fifty within 50 yards of our two trenches, and an enormous one just outside the entrance to our shelter.

'Then the all-clear sounded, and for the next hour a voice came over the Tannoy giving instructions. These were mostly about the positions of unexploded bombs, and where not to go. As one had to skirt the bombs by a range of 25 yards, it was very difficult to pick a route to anywhere. The playing-field was the only safe place, so the airwomen were assembled there and the roll-call taken, to find – by a miraculous piece of luck – that all were present, and only a few slightly injured, bruised, or cut by flying glass.

'Some WAAF drivers were caught in the M.T. yards, so dived under their vehicles. When they emerged, they found three large craters in the centre of the yard.

'One WAAF was washing her hair, and before she could remove the soap from her eyes and run to a trench, she had ceiling plaster falling

WAAF plotters at work in Operations Room of fighter station. They frequently sustained casualties but kept on working at their posts.

about her, so dived under the kitchen table. Those in the Ops Room carried on with complete coolness, although the lights went out, and telephones to the squadrons failed.

'After the roll-call, a job was found for most people. We discovered that the complete street where the airwomen were quartered was out of bounds. At least half the houses were unsafe, and unexploded bombs were around them. Many who had been off duty in their quarters came out in all states of undress – slacks, overalls, and some even in underwear – with only a coat or mac thrown over their shoulders. They couldn't get their clothes for several days.'

Her Majesty The Queen visited a station of Fighter Command soon afterwards and said to the senior WAAF officer there: 'I hear that your women are magnificent.' Altogether there were about 2,000 girls attached to similar fighter stations throughout south-east England.

During all these daylight raids, in flimsy buildings on many fighter aerodromes, WAAF plotters continued with their earphones pressed to their ears to keep out the inferno of noise from the torrent of bombs bursting all around. Steady and calm. Not a murmur, nor a movement, from a single one, though the buildings were often rocking, sometimes falling ...

WAAF radar operators plot and communicate warnings of all approaching enemy aircraft.

While one raid was at its heaviest, a squadron leader in charge of administration at his station was about to enter a shelter near the airfield when a bomb fell – wounding him badly in the legs. A WAAF who had been a nurse before the war ran over to him as he lay there helpless.

The squadron leader was losing blood very fast from the wounds. The WAAF immediately improvised a tourniquet and stopped the flow. The raid went on, and bombs continued to fall very close to them. Despite this danger, she helped a station medical officer to take the injured officer over to sick quarters. When the raid eventually ended, and it was safe to move about again, the squadron leader was removed to hospital. After he had been examined and treated by the doctors there, they declared quite definitely that the WAAF's prompt action had saved his legs from having to be amputated.

Twenty-four-year-old Corporal Joan Hearn was at the telephone of her observation unit when an air raid developed and bombs began to fall on the unit itself. Damage was extensive, and then several heavier bombs burst volcano-like alongside the block where Joan was working alone controlling her telephone.

The sudden sound was overpowering. All the windows of the block were blown in. Glass splintered over the floors. Heavy walls cracked and threatened to collapse. One of the main walls of two rooms had a jagged rent right down it and looked like caving in. But amid all the din and danger, Joan never moved from her instruments. Steadily she reported the course of enemy bombers over the phones, knowing how much the RAF fighters and anti-aircraft gunners needed the information. She went on telephoning the results of plots coolly, and in one of the most dramatic messages ever sent by a woman at war, she said:

'The course of the enemy bombers is only too apparent to me, because the bombs are almost dropping on my head.'

Joan Hearn was later awarded the Military Medal, one of six won by the WAAF in the Battle of Britain.

Still 3 September. Strong activity in 12 Group. Flt Lt J. Jeffries was with 310 and 19 Squadrons sent to help North Weald against 150 Dorniers and Me 110s. Jeffries chased an Me 110 which dived away. Steepening its dive, the enemy went vertically into the ground some ten miles north of North Weald. Sergeant Koukal of 310 saw the port main plane of a Dornier cut off a yard from the engine. At 10,000 feet one of the crew got out. The Czechs had been up for nearly an hour since take off from Duxford. They saw the enemy aircraft flying first in close herringbone pattern.

Flt Lt Sinclair caused a Dornier to catch alight. Sinclair was preserving 2,000 feet altitude advantage over the enemy – as well as the use of the sun. After the Germans bombed North Weald, they veered east for home. Sergeant B. Furst's single burst caught an Me 110, which took its flaming fuselage down to ground south of Chelmsford. By then, Furst had run out of ammunition. The sky was still black with Luftwaffe, though less formally distributed, more dispersed, than at the start. Flt Lt Jeffries was running out of petrol, not ammunition, so sped for home and glided down on a virtually empty tank. Expert piloting.

Number 19 Squadron went into action simultaneously with 310 and found part of the main enemy force returning east from a raid in the London area. At 20,000 feet, Sqn Ldr Pinkham could still see the result of the raid on North Weald. He also saw fifty bombers and 100 fighters. The latter were turning and twisting, searching and weaving. Attacking, Pinkham found that his guns had jammed … Then P/O E. Burgoyne took on a pair of fighters, and his starboard gun jammed. He was set on by two Me 110s, but shrugged them off with a flick from the stick of his Spitfire. He fired at another Me 110 until his port gun also jammed. These were serious gravity stoppages.

Green 1 had the Spitfire with eight guns and fared better. He trailed a fighter down towards the Thames, but it fooled him by flattening out and flying for Whitstable at an altitude of only 50 feet. On nearing the oyster beds, it turned towards the mouth of a river and flew off straight and level. Green 1 used the rest of his eight-gun ammunition on another enemy, which dived the short distance into the sea. Flt Sgt G.C. Unwin blew a port engine from an Me 110 out of its wing. Then his starboard guns jammed. Then the enemy's starboard engine toppled off. One of the aircrew baled out before it crashed south of Maldon. To offset the successes, one Hurricane was lost. Total losses for the day read: German sixteen, British sixteen.

Night-time now on 3 September. Raids on Merseyside, South Wales and Kent. They went for Liverpool via South Wales sometimes – a sort of back-door approach. The fires in the Liverpool docks were reflected in the waters of the Mersey near the Wallasey Ferry. Other bombs fell on or near Warrington, Chester, Waterloo and Sealand.

4 September

The worst civilian losses to date had to be conceded today. But first the sector stations escaped harm temporarily. Bradwell, Lympne and Eastchurch were less lucky. Short Brothers at Rochester were raided. So was Vickers at Brooklands. Nearly overhead the Weybridge factory, 253 Squadron of Hurricanes reached a stronger formation of Me 110s and sent six down over the Surrey landscape, complete with their trained crews. But some bombers got to Vickers and dropped six large high-explosives right on machine shops. There were eighty-six deaths out of the total casualties approaching ten times that number. The scant consolation was that more Me 110s were destroyed after the raid. Liverpool and Bristol received night-raids. More casualties up there, too. And over at Manchester, bombs found the Hope Hospital in the early hours. The day's losses: German twenty-five, British seventeen.

5 September

Nearing the end of this phase, over the desolate Romney Marshes thirty Dornier 17s plus twice the number of fighters were met by 501 Squadron. The bombers burst through them. Another force of comparable size followed the same path. This time, though, 41 and 234 Squadrons caught them at an altitude disadvantage and dispersed most of the attackers. Another punch at the hapless Biggin Hill resulted in 79 Squadron joining an affray against the invaders, who bombed hurriedly and wide of their main target. Detling was given another assault by masses of enemy. Remember

Antwerp was one of many centres where invasion barges were concentrated. RAF raids by Bomber Command and the Battle of Britain victory by Fighter Command ensured that they were never used.

that the twin forces over Romney Marshes numbered a combined 200, and there were others.

Two industrial targets were, first, a limited strike at Hawker's aircraft factory at Brooklands – just near the ill-fated Vickers plant. Unlike the latter attack, though, damage at Hawker's remained slight and casualties likewise. In the later afternoon bombers in the Thames Estuary hit the second of the day's non-airfield targets: the Thameshaven oil farm. It was not known whether this was a substitute goal for one or other of the airfields flanking the Estuary. This attack was repeated on the following day, too. The losses for 5 September were German twenty-three, British twenty. Then came the day that proved a surprise turning point, perhaps one of the worst tactical mistakes Hitler made. But first the RAF had to endure 6 September.

6 September

It was airfields again. Could they survive indefinitely? Could the fighters be produced in sufficient numbers? Could pilots be trained in time? Meanwhile, Biggin Hill and other south-east airfields heard the wail of the warning, the varying frequency throbs of fighters and bombers. The Surrey and Kent squadrons were short of their desired strength, both in men and machines. And the strain had been telling for some time now. On air and on ground crews alike.

The Luftwaffe stoked up the fires which had been more or less put out at Thameshaven oil storage tanks. Flames leapt into the Greater London sky after dark, too. Rochester and Weybridge were the other two industrial areas under threat during the day. As previously, the attack on Hawker's was intercepted by our fighters. Over fifty per cent of the entire Hurricane output came from the Weybridge plant, so it was crucial it should not be interrupted. The combats between the Ju 87s and the defenders took on climactic ferocity and included 303 (Polish) Squadron of Hurricanes from Northolt. These Poles were heroically reckless and seemed to count their lives cheaply. They scored victories and suffered losses. The figures for the day told the story: German twenty-five, British twenty-three.

At this stage, Hitler was still wedded to the idea of invading England. The date was yet to be decided. Throughout August the Royal Air Force had been making modest night-bombing raids on German targets: aircraft factories; airfields; oil plants; ports; shipping; marshalling yards and the like. Hitler had been especially annoyed by these raids and even more so by two specifically: the famous raid on the aqueduct of the Dortmund-Ems canal and the Berlin raid. By day the RAF somehow found forces to soften enemy airfields in occupied territory.

The Germans must have miscalculated the degree of damage they had done by their own raids: damage to airfields and to aircraft, whether in the air or on the ground. They thought that the RAF was weaker than it was and the British less resilient than they were. Hitler decided at this epochal stage to shift the focus of air attacks away from airfields and on to the capital of London. The Germans thought that the results of such attacks would be to cause terror and chaos among the population, as well as to make the continuation of effective government control less possible, even impossible. And then at the moment adjudged the optimum from the enemy's strategy, they would launch their invasion forces across the Channel on a broad front between Bognor and Margate. The main assault would take place on beaches between Brighton and Folkestone.

So sure were the enemy that they could invade successfully that in the forty-eight hours to 6 September, reconnaissance revealed additional barges still being added to those already waiting at Dunkirk and Calais. They threw

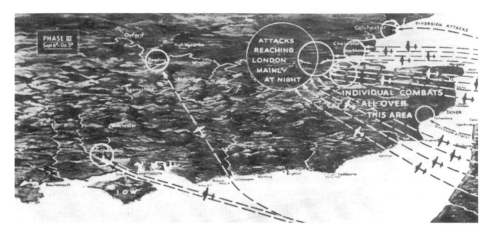

The climacteric: the whole strength of the Luftwaffe is hurled against London.

in thirty-four more at Dunkirk and fifty-three more at Calais. The British intelligence concluded that they must actually be considering invasion in the following three days. In fact Hitler had still ruled that the date should be 15 September – soon to be put back nearly a week to 21 September. Winston Churchill:

'In the fighting between August 24 and September 6 the scales had tilted against Fighter Command. During these crucial days the Germans had continuously applied powerful forces against the airfields of south and south-east England. Their object was to break down the day fighter defence of the capital, which they were impatient to attack. Far more important to us than the protection of London from terror-bombing was the functioning and articulation of these airfields and the squadrons working from them. In the life-or-death struggle of the two Air Forces this was a decisive phase. We never thought of the struggle in terms of the defence of London or any other place, but only who won in the air.

'There was much anxiety at Fighter Command Headquarters at Stanmore, and particularly at the headquarters of No. 11 Fighter Group at Uxbridge. Extensive damage had been done to five of the Group's forward airfields, and also to the six sector stations. Manston and Lympne on the Kentish coast were on several occasions and for days unfit for operating fighter aircraft. Biggin Hill sector station, to the south of London, was so severely damaged that for a week only one fighter squadron could operate from it.

'If the enemy had persisted in heavy attacks against the adjacent sectors and damaged their operations rooms or telephone communications the whole intricate organisation of Fighter Command might have been broken down. This would have meant not merely the maltreatment of London, but the loss to us of the perfected control of our own air in the decisive area ... I was led to visit several of these stations, particularly Manston (August 28) and Biggin Hill, which is quite near my home. They were getting terribly knocked about, and their runways were ruined by craters. It was therefore with a sense of relief that Fighter Command felt the German attack turn on London on September 7, and concluded that the enemy had changed his plan. Göring should certainly have persevered against the airfields, on whose organisation and combination the whole fighting power of our Air Force at this moment depended. By departing from the classical principles of war, as well as from the hitherto accepted dictates of humanity, he made a foolish mistake.

'This same period (August 24–September 6) had seriously drained the strength of Fighter Command as a whole. The Command had lost in this fortnight 103 pilots killed and 128 seriously wounded, while 466 Spitfires and Hurricanes had been destroyed or seriously damaged. Out of a total pilot strength of about a thousand nearly a quarter had been lost. Their places could only be filled by 260 new, ardent, but inexperienced pilots drawn from training units, in many cases before their full courses were complete. The night attacks on London for ten days after September 7 struck at the London docks and railway centres, and killed and wounded many civilians, but they were in effect for us a breathing-space of which we had the utmost need.

'During this period I usually managed to take two afternoons a week in the areas under attack in Kent or Sussex in order to see for myself what was happening. For this purpose I used my train, which was now most conveniently fitted and carried a bed, a bath, an office, a connectible telephone, and an effective staff. I was thus able to work continuously, apart from sleeping, and with almost all the facilities available at Downing Street.'

So to the ordeal of London – and the birth of the Duxford Wing.

CHAPTER FOURTEEN

London – and the Duxford Wing

7 September

By now the Germans either believed that they had struck sufficiently at the fighter airfields or else they were following a prearranged timetable to switch their attack again. For they opened the third phase of the Battle of Britain – to try to neutralize London. All this time, too, the threat of invasion persisted, but the British were gradually beginning to believe that this could not materialize without complete air superiority – which the enemy had so far patently failed to achieve.

After hammering away throughout 6 September against our inland fighter stations, next day the Luftwaffe launched an enormous effort to reach London and destroy the docks. These onslaughts aimed at the capital were to come in two or three distinct waves at intervals of about twenty minutes. It was another fine day and a quiet one until nearly 4 pm. Then a huge armada headed out from the Pas de Calais, watched by the strutting Göring and his senior staff. At this stage of an attack, it was always like a game of airborne chess. Neither side knew the intentions of their opponents. The enemy force fanned out into assigned groups and set their noses to cross the coastline at points ranging from Beachy Head, Sussex, in the west, to east Kent and even Essex.

Waves of twenty to forty bombers throbbed ominously overhead towards the capital, with fighter forces in close escort. Extra protection came from large groups of fighters flying at higher altitudes: up to about 26,000 feet. In a clear September sky, this made the task of the Observer Corps extremely difficult.

The RAF had to respond to the threat, though they did not yet know where it would develop in most strength. Some nine squadrons of 11 Group got the

The Luftwaffe inward-bound for London.

message to scramble at once: Nos 43; 253; 504; 249; 1; 303; 111; 79 and 501. They came from Northolt, North Weald, Hendon, Kenley, Gravesend, Croydon and inevitably, Biggin Hill.

Even from as far west as Tangmere. The pilots had been waiting in an assortment of chairs outside their dispersal huts and the scramble signal usually came through by telephone just inside the window. Some of the men now looked haggard under the eyes.

The enemy still shaped as if Kent, Sussex and Surrey would be their goals. Great waves of them as if undulating in the air. Almost mirage-like. Hundreds and hundreds. One RAF squadron saw the masses from the Surrey-Berkshire borders. Another one, miles above the Medway towns of Kent. Serried ranks of Dorniers and Heinkels, other rows above of Me 109s.

Somewhere between the English coast and the capital, usually in the Edenbridge–Tunbridge Wells area, but sometimes nearer the sea, the air forces met. Spitfires took the high-flying fighter screen; Hurricanes engaged the fighter escort; other Hurricanes flew hellbent for the bombers. Dogfights developed all over the Kent skies. For a few minutes at a time, the air was vibrant with distant machine-gun fire. At ground level, it sounded rather like the noise made by a small boy running a stick along a stretch of iron railings. And as background noise, the faint roar of hundreds of engines, sometimes swelling to a crescendo as some wounded aircraft screamed to earth.

Sometimes watchers like those on the keep of Hever Castle suddenly saw sprays of parachutes blossoming in the blue sky. The warm sun shone on more and more wrecks of the Luftwaffe's massed fleets, bearing on their jagged remnants 'the crooked cross of Nazi infamy' – to quote Churchill!

About an hour after the first reports from the other side of the Channel, it dawned on the defenders in charge of operations that the enemy were not after airfields. Their overall strength of about 1,000 aircraft had the main aim to bomb various targets in – London. As they flew over Kent they were met by 501 and 249 Squadrons of Hurricanes, numbering only one-tenth of the enemy force flying above the snaking Medway river. The RAF did all they could, but the great phalanx flew on.

The time was 4.55 pm when 350 bombers and fighters arrived in two waves. The time was also 4.55 pm when the newly formed Duxford Wing was finally scrambled. The enemy penetrated east of Croydon, up to the Thames Estuary. And eluding the defences over Kent and East Surrey, they threaded through them. They had the Thames to guide them and they dropped bombs on the military arsenal at Woolwich. The whole attack was followed by one on the shipping works of Harland and Wolffs. The enemy were already minus their escorting Me 109s, due to the latter's fuel shortage, so the post-bombing time would be the enemy's vulnerable one, its Achilles Heel. Nos. 1 and 303 (Polish) Squadrons flying from Hendon took off to rip them apart; so did 603 Squadron of Spitfires from Hornchurch; so did 73 Squadron from North Weald; and so did the Duxford Wing of 19, 66 and 242 Squadrons.

The battle now goes into suspense while it is seen against the whole background to the build-up of the Duxford Wing – and their first offensive action under Bader's leadership. Ever since 30 August, Bader had been thinking:

'Who the hell do these Huns think they are, flying like this in their bloody bombers covered with iron crosses and swastikas over our country?'

After the original idea and some discussion between Bader and the other two squadron leaders – Blackwood of 310 and Lane of 19 – they flew three or four practice sorties to test out the theory. Then the Duxford Wing reported ready for action. The method of operation was uncomplicated. Numbers 242 and 310 Squadrons of Hurricanes took off from Duxford. At the same time, 19 Squadron of Spitfires unrolled from the satellite station of Fowlmere. There was no joining up over the airfield. Bader turned straight on to course, climbing quickly, while the other squadrons took up position.

The Duxford Wing never took more than six minutes to get off the ground and on their way south – and frequently they did it in four minutes. The whole formation would arrive over the Thames Estuary at 20,000 feet just twenty minutes after take off.

There was no more difficulty in the control of the Wing in the air than of a squadron. The three squadrons were all on the same R/T frequency. An occasional word from Douglas Bader to the other two commanders and then finally his intentions when the enemy were sighted – that was all that was needed. Suggestions that the Big Wing was clumsy to operate are nonsense. Indeed they were disproved by the 1941 and subsequent fighter wing operations over France.

There was one fundamental problem, however: the frequent failure of the 11 Group operations room to get squadrons off the ground in time. Like everyone else, the 11 Group controllers were inexperienced when the battle started. They did not appreciate that in order for a pilot to be successful, he

Heinkel 111 over the familiar outline of the River Thames during the onslaught on London.

Hurricanes climbing to intercept enemy bombers.

needed height and position to dominate the battle. The vulnerable, indeed frequently fatal, position for a fighter pilot was to be climbing with the enemy above him. The German formations used to assemble in the Calais area when the bombers were at 15,000–17,000 feet.

Short-range Me 109s joined them and the whole lot proceeded across the Channel towards the London area. This initially precluded a successful interception by any of the 11 Group squadrons based at Manston, Hawkinge, Detling, Gravesend and Redhill, because they were too near the coast. A single incident confirms and clarifies this situation: on its very first operational sorties out of Kenley, 616 Squadron lost five out of twelve fighters on the climb without touching the enemy.

So far as the 12 Group Wing was concerned, it seemed to them at Duxford that most times they were sent for as an afterthought, or to do what used to be termed 'the lunch-time patrol' when there was no single aeroplane either German or British in the air at all.

For some reason, the 11 Group controllers would not call squadrons off the ground, and more particularly the 12 Group Wing, until the enemy were at operational height and leaving the French coast. If you look at the map and measure the distance to the 11 Group stations mentioned, the error of this thinking was self-evident. On several occasions, while the Duxford Wing was at readiness, Bader received telephone calls from the Duxford controller saying:

'Stand by, the Germans are building up over the Calais area.'

Every time, Bader asked: 'Can we take off *now*?'

Every time he received the inevitable answer: 'No, you must wait until 11 Group ask for you.' Duxford to Tilbury was, and still is, forty-three miles. If the Wing had taken off when the Germans were building up over the Pas de Calais area, Bader and his team could have been in the Ashford/Tonbridge area under favourable conditions to control a battle of their own seeking.

'Laddie' Lucas summed up Bader's views on this aspect of the Battle of Britain:

'Douglas's thinking was that he should be able to get these Wings into the air and into the right position to be able to attack the enemy aircraft as they were coming in to their targets, on the approaches to the targets. What he contended was that if you could get these aeroplanes up together, place them right, give them the right information, supply the right commentary, then it was up to Douglas as Wing leader to make the best use of it. His basic thinking was not only to get the aeroplanes off together and as quickly as possible, but that proper warning be given and proper decisions regarding control. The difficulty with the Duxford Wing was probably to get off the ground in time to discharge the tactics that Douglas believed to be necessary to fulfil his role. Too often he found himself climbing up as hard as he could bloody well go, while the enemy were already coming in – so he would have lost all the advantage of height and sun and so on.'

Bader disagreed with the attitude of fighting the Battle of Britain on a local level, rather as a private 11 Group affair, and an order from the AOC 11 Group subsequently available made it clear that in his mind his fears were fully justified. This was Park's peculiar instruction in force from 19 August 1940, which went against so much of what Bader felt to be the best approaches. It is worth quoting in full, so that Bader's reactions to it can be completely understood.

NO. 11 GROUP INSTRUCTIONS TO CONTROLLERS NO. 4
From: Air Officer Commanding, No 11 Group, Royal Air Force.
To: Group Controllers and Sector Commanders, for Sector Controllers.
Date: 19 August 1940.

The German Air Force has begun a new phase in air attacks, which have been switched from coastal shipping and ports on to inland objectives. The bombing attacks have for several days been concentrated against aerodromes, and especially fighter aerodromes, on the coast and inland. The following instructions are issued to meet the changed conditions:

(a) Despatch fighters to engage large enemy formations over land or within gliding distance of the coast. During the next two or three weeks, we cannot afford to lose pilots through forced landings in the sea;
(b) Avoid sending fighters out over the sea to chase reconnaissance aircraft or small formations of enemy fighters;
(c) Despatch a pair of fighters to intercept single reconnaissance aircraft that come inland. If clouds are favourable, put a patrol of one or two fighters over an aerodrome which enemy aircraft are approaching in clouds;
(d) Against mass attacks coming inland, despatch a minimum number of squadrons to engage enemy fighters. Our main object is to engage enemy bombers, particularly those approaching under the lowest cloud cover;
(e) If all our squadrons around London are off the ground engaging enemy mass attacks, ask No 12 Group or Command Controller to provide squadrons to patrol aerodromes Debden, North Weald, Hornchurch;
(f) If heavy attacks have crossed the coast and are proceeding towards aerodromes, put a squadron, or even the sector training flight, to patrol under clouds over each sector aerodrome;
(g) No 303 (Polish) Squadron can provide two sections for patrol of inland aerodromes, especially while the older squadrons are on the ground refuelling, when enemy formations are flying over land;
(h) No 1 (Canadian) Squadron can be used in the same manner by day as other fighter squadrons.

NOTE: Protection of all convoys and shipping in the Thames Estuary are excluded from this instruction (paragraph (a)).

sgd. K.R. Park
Air Vice-Marshal Commanding, No 11 Group, Royal Air Force.

In Bader's decided and considered view, these instructions revealed some serious errors of thinking in air warfare. Paragraph (e) was the fatal one, he maintained, as the best way to protect aerodromes was not to fly overhead waiting for an attack, but to go and intercept the enemy where he wanted. Stop them reaching our airfields. This same argument applied to paragraphs (c) and (f). Finally, paragraph (a) at one stroke precluded successful interception by any squadron south of the River Thames.

The following were Bader's views which should be borne in mind during the rest of the actions involving 12 Group. Lord Dowding made two vital contributions to the defeat of the Luftwaffe. During his pre-war command, he had laid down radar coverage of the south of England so that we had early warning of the Germans' intentions: secondly, he had persuaded the War Cabinet against sending more RAF fighters to a defeated France in May 1940.

Instead of assuming control and direction of the air defence of Britain, which was the C-in-C's job, Dowding left the conduct of the battle to a subordinate Group Commander, AVM Park of No 11 Group, making it the strongest in Fighter Command. Keith Park fought the Battle of Britain, not Dowding. He fought it under the disadvantage of being too near the enemy to deploy the strength which Dowding had given him. His problem was compounded by his operations room displaying a map of 11 Group territory only. In other words, Park was fighting an 11 Group battle which should have been a Fighter Command battle.

A map of the whole of England lay on the plotters' table at Fighter Command. It showed every fighter airfield, with the location and state of readiness of every squadron on the board above it. The difference was paramount. A controller at the Fighter Command operations room would have seen the enemy position as it was plotted. With the whole picture spread out in front of him, he would instantly have realized the need to scramble squadrons from the further away airfields *first* against the enemy. First, not last.

This would have provided the classic air defence in depth so desperately needed to make life easier for controllers and less costly for pilots. Eleven Group controllers, with their limited operations room facilities, would have given place to Fighter Command ones with the map of England in front of them. Eleven Group controllers were being harassed by enemy raiders almost overhead, which they were trying to intercept with only 11 Group squadrons available. The Fighter Command controllers would have had time to see the problem in its entirety. It was in this context that the Duxford Wing came into being, indeed for these very reasons. Leigh-Mallory saw the whole situation with clarity from his 12 Group headquarters. So did Bader.

Two Dornier 17s flying above fires started by bombs in the London Docks area on 7 September.

Easy for them, say the critics, they were not in the so-called front line. Quite right. But this highlights the great error: the front line should have embraced the whole of Fighter Command and not just 11 Group.

If ever Dowding should have seen the light, it was at the end of August, when the changing pattern of the German assault became clear beyond doubt. Vast enemy formations were to be seen congregating over the Pas-de-Calais. London must soon be the target. Surely the Commander-in-Chief, with his great reputation and the full resources of his headquarters and operations room, would now take over control of the battle from his 11 Group Commander?

In the event, he did not. A tired man was left to continue the struggle. It was as though General Montgomery left a Corps Commander to fight the Battle of Alamein and told him to call on other corps commanders for

The Operations Room at Fighter Command HQ. The officers on the dais look down on the plotters around the map table. The Battle scene changes almost from second to second.

assistance if necessary. The Battle of Britain was won by the efforts of tired but resolute controllers and the immense courage of 11 Group pilots. Properly exploited, the 12 Group Wing could have provided the spearhead against the enemy formations, creating havoc amongst them and giving the 11 Group pilots time to gain height and position to continue the destruction. To stress the irony of the 11 Group situation, squadrons sometimes had to climb northwards away from the enemy, to try and gain tactical advantage. At the top level of Fighter Command, there seemed an inability to grasp the basic and proved rules of air fighting. This is what Bader felt then and still felt for the rest of his life.

Twelve Group introduced its report on the first five Wing patrols with the following comments, setting the scene in the context of 7 September:

'Experience has shown that with the mass attacks on London and the South of England, the enemy has used not only larger formations of bombers but very considerably larger formations of protecting fighters. In view of this, when No 12 Group have been asked to protect North Weald and Hornchurch aerodromes, it was considered wholly inadequate to send up single squadrons for this purpose and therefore a

Wing has been employed. Up to the present, five such operations have taken place. Definite roles have been allotted to the squadrons on each occasion, with the general idea of having Spitfire Squadrons above the Hurricane Squadrons so that the former could attack enemy fighters and prevent their coming down to protect their bombers, whilst the remainder of the Wing break up and destroy the enemy bombers.'

Johnnie Johnson described the situation on 7 September rather more dramatically in his highly informed book, *Full Circle*:

'On 7 September, following Hitler's declaration that London would suffer as reprisals for Bomber Command raids against Berlin, Göring switched his bombers from RAF sector stations, and other airfields, to London and its sprawling docks. Towards five o'clock on that evening, more than three hundred bombers, and many hundreds of fighters, arose from their airfields across the Channel, swarmed into a dozen formations and, without feint or decoy, crossed the straits in two broad waves and headed for the capital. Because of their height, above 20,000 feet, and a stiff headwind, the bombers took a long time to reach London, but although RAF controllers found it easier than usual to intercept, the enemy fighter escorts seemed bigger than ever. There were so many enemy fighters, layered up to 30,000 feet, that a Spitfire pilot said it was like looking up the escalator at Piccadilly Circus.
    'Near Cambridge the Duxford Wing of two Hurricane and one Spitfire squadrons had been at readiness all day and Bader, anxious to lead thirty-six fighters into action for the first time, had been agitating for hours about getting into the air. At last they were scrambled ...'

Back to the main story. The Wing was ordered off from Duxford at about 4.55 pm to patrol North Weald. The altitude quoted was 10,000 feet. Control told Bader:

'100 bandits approaching you from the east.'

Arriving at North Weald on the 15,000 feet level, they noticed AA fire to the east and saw a quantity of enemy aircraft at 20,000 feet. Bader immediately advised Duxford of the sighting and obtained permission to engage the enemy.
    He took the decision to attack with 242, 310 and 19 Squadrons knowing that such a move must have been more successful had the Wing been at 25,000 feet. The element of surprise was lost to them and they endured the

added disadvantage of attacking the bombers knowing that there were Messerschmitt 109s above them and in the sun, so that while pressing home any attack they would have to try to keep an eye behind them at the same time – if they were to survive. No wonder Bader and other pilots of the Wing grew impatient at a policy which put precious aircrew at so substantial a hazard from the outset.

Bader opened his throttle and climbed for all he and the fighter were worth. The enemy aircraft were proceeding north over the Thames Estuary. The result of the full throttle climbing to get level with the enemy made the whole fighter force straggle out of necessity – so the attack could not be pressed home with the weight of the thirty-six aeroplanes at Bader's disposal. But he had to engage quickly or not at all.

He turned left to cut off the enemy and arrived on the beam slightly in front with only Red 2. Bader was flying Red 1, and Sub-Lt Cork flew Red 2. Bader opened with a very short beam squirt from 100 yards, aimed at enemy aircraft flying in sections of three line astern in a large rectangle. He turned with Cork, who also fired with him, and sat under the tails of the back section at 50 yards, pulling up the nose and giving short squirts at the middle back aeroplane. This was an Me 110 and it started smoking, preparatory to catching fire.

Even before attacking the enemy and whilst actually still climbing to meet them, Cork and Bader received a lot of crossfire from enemy bombers, which kept in perfect formation. At the same time, they were set on by enemy fighters, who had had the advantage of 3,000–4,000 feet in altitude. Cork broke away slightly to the right of Bader's section and fired at a Dornier 17 on the tail end of the group. It followed the usual destruction sequence of port engine afire and a vertical crash-dive.

Before Bader could see the result of his opening action, he made out the warning outline of a yellow nose in his mirror. The Me 109 was on his tail slightly above and as Bader turned there was suddenly a big bang in his cockpit from a bullet, presumably an explosive one. It came in through the right-hand side of the fuselge, touched the map case, knocked the corner off the undercarriage selector quadrant and finished up against the petrol priming pump.

Having executed a quick, steep, diving turn, Bader found an Me 110 alone just below him. He attacked this from dead astern and above. The enemy could not combat the accurate fire and went into a steepish straight dive, finishing up in flames in a field just north of a railway line west of Wickford and due north of Thameshaven. The first Me 110 attacked by Bader had been confirmed as diving down and crashing by another pilot, although Bader himself had not witnessed it. So that made a couple of Messerschmitts to the

Wing leader. Apart from the bullet in the cockpit, Bader's Hurricane also sustained hits in several places by bomber fire and twice by escorting Me 109s.

Just after Cork had destroyed the Dornier, he was set on from the rear by an enemy fighter and hit in the starboard mainplane. So he broke away downwards and backwards – and nearly collided with an Me 110. This was always a danger, and collisions did happen with fatal results to both parties. Cork pressed for a brief burst before pulling away to avoid the collision, and he saw the front of the Messerschmitt cabin break up and the aircraft take a vertical dive. Two of the crew baled out. Cork followed the machine down. It was stalling and then diving again alternately.

While Cork continued his vigil, an Me 109 went for his rear. One shot penetrated the side of his hood, hit the bottom of the reflector sight and then the bullet-proof windscreen. 'As I could not see very well, I broke away downwards in a half-roll and lost vision of the enemy machine.' Not really surprising with glass in his eyes … Somehow he kept on flying, having accounted for a Dornier 17 and an Me 110. When he landed, his Hurricane was so shattered with enemy fire that it was not considered flyable.

A great friend of Bader, Denis Crowley-Milling, was flying as his Red 3. The time was between 5.00 pm and 5.15 pm now and they were still in the thick of this dogfight, started from a poorly placed position.

Red 3 saw a lot of the crossfire from other bombers as he flew in to meet a force just above the AA fire. But he had to snap off due to a rear thrust by an Me 110. Red 3 banked left sharply and then came in again at the bombers. He spotted an Me 110 just behind the last bomber. He hit its port engine with a four-second burst and saw the starboard one smoking too. At that instant he was shot at from behind by an Me 109. His Hurricane received a shell in the radiator, another in the left aileron, and a third behind the pilot's seat. No one could deny he was lucky to be alive. He piloted the Hurricane down from 18,000–20,000 feet to a crash-landing near Chelmsford. In fact he had destroyed the Me 110.

Irrespective of individual actions, the rest of the engagement continued its weirdly beautiful pattern, as if moving to some predetermined choreography in an aerial ballet.

Flt Lt Ball as Yellow 1 positioned himself a few thousand feet higher than nearby enemy aircraft, and opened fire against an Me 110. But Me 109s caught him by the tail and he realised that by now he was utterly alone, with no friendly fighters in immediate sight. He saw a second 110 and closed from 330 to 80 yards. It caught fire soon after his running attack from above and behind. He fired on three or four other aircraft but they were impossible to engage for long, owing to the horde of fighters buzzing around their bombers.

Ball actually followed the formation out to sea, picking off a 110 en route. Both engines of the enemy were smoking, but a 109 got on his tail and he had to give up further pursuit. Although the enemy fired on him sporadically, Ball found their aim very wild and he was not hit.

Sergeant R. Lonsdale followed Ball in the original affray. As he flew into the attack level with the enemy bombers, Me 110s came down and broke up their particular formation. The enemy fighters kept good grouping but for that very reason were fairly easily avoided. Three 110s dived for Lonsdale but again he twisted out of trouble.

Then he went for the bombers by himself. The sun was on his starboard side as he selected a Dornier 17 to attack from line astern. After a diminishing range from 350 to 80 yards, the Hurricane's fire stopped the port engine and smouldered the starboard one. Lonsdale suddenly found his Hurricane being bounced about a lot by the slipstream of the bomber. He carried on his attack from slightly below to get out of its line. The Dornier gradually dropped back from the formation and started gliding down at about 120 mph. Lonsdale had given it a full fifteen seconds of firing and at this stage he ran out of ammunition. Despite this he followed the bomber down for some distance until it disappeared from his sight. Another Hurricane hit it as it glided on.

Flt Lt Powell-Sheddon led Blue Section and estimated the enemy forces at fifty bombers in tight grouping line astern with a strong guard of Me 110s and yellow-nosed Me 109s. The noses also had some silver on them as camouflage. He climbed to 22,000 feet to have a go at the fighters, having lost sight of Bader and the section in front. The other members of Blue Section had also become separated from him. But this was typical of the style and pattern of such a dogfight.

Powell-Sheddon chased several enemy aircraft but did not engage any for ten minutes. Volumes of jet black smoke were cascading up from Thameshaven oil refineries. Miles above, he saw a Hurricane being chased by an Me 109. They swerved right in front of him – a mere 100 yards ahead. He gave an instinctive deflection squirt at the Me 109 as it passed, and it then turned left and crossed his path at the same range. He repeated the squirt and got on his tail. As the Me 109 was firing at the Hurricane, Blue 1 was aiming at the German from a few feet above and only 50 yards. He could see his bullets finding their mark and saw pieces ripped from the Hurricane. He got in the enemy slipstream, ceased fire, eased slightly to one side, and fired again.

The Me 109 got the Hurricane, which went down with smoke streaming. Then the Me 109 itself hung in the air for a few seconds before falling

Half a dozen Heinkel He 111s on their flight path to England.

forward in a vertical dive. A trail of smoke etched its descent in the sky. It vanished into the dense blackness over Thameshaven. As it seemed to be in flames and out of control, the Me 109 could be claimed for Powell-Sheddon.

The speed with which the Wing went into action could be deduced from the time of these attacks: 5.10 pm to 5.15 pm. And only a quarter of an hour after actual take off. Blue 2 was P/O P. Bush. He went for a Heinkel but had to break off because of rear attacks from an Me 110. He executed an astern attack on another Me 110, which he damaged.

A few minutes later, P/O H. Tamblyn as Blue 3 destroyed an Me 110 at 5.20 pm. It became a total conflagration. Tamblyn next went after a 109 at 150 yards. Evidence suggested that he had hit it lethally, as it veered gently to the right and began to go down. It was one of the special yellow-nosed squadron. Tamblyn felt an effect of slipstream from both these encounters but managed to control his Hurricane somehow.

Green 1 now – and P/O D. Turner. A favourite of Douglas Bader. He was in the last section to attack and as he approached he saw an Me 110 already in flames. This was the result of one of the Red Section hits. While hitting a

110 and watching his bullets tear at the fuselage, Turner was in turn fired at by a 109. He outmanoeuvred the fighter and got a good burst into it. The enemy flicked into a dive. Turner went for some bombers next, and before being driven off by 109s, he got in a snap or two. Nothing for it after that but to head for Duxford.

Still 5.20 pm. Gardner was flying Green 4. He saw thirty Heinkels plus more bombers and many Me 109s. He noticed some Spitfires already in the fray. On entering the melee in sharp zig-zags, he found it very difficult to distinguish friend from foe – certainly in the instants available for decisions. But he did recognise a Dornier which started to circle and dive. Gardner went too and discovered he had another Hurricane along with him.

At 5,000 feet Gardner got in three short bursts from 250 to 50 yards, stopping the port engine and bursting the oil tank. The crew baled out and the Dornier crashed in a field about three miles north-east of Shell Haven. Gardner got a hole in his wing and engine cowling, but managed to land at 5.45 pm.

A Dornier singled out by Black 1, P/O M. Stansfield, loosed off about fifty rounds of machine-gun fire at him, but fortunately it missed his Hurricane. Coming up from below it, he caught the bomber in the port beam. The enemy went into a roll and then attempted a second one – but this was too low to be executed.

It dived into the ground, the pilot having misjudged the altitude.

So much for 242 Squadron. They took off at 4.55 pm. They landed at 5.55 pm. An hour to remember. They lost two Hurricanes, force-landed in Essex, but both pilots were safe. That was always the main thing. Five fighters became temporarily unserviceable through bullet holes.

The Czechs followed Bader and 242 in line astern. Flt Lt G. Sinclair was leading 310 (Czech) Squadron, A Flight, and wheeled into an up-sun position. He put A Flight into line astern to go for Me 110s behind the bombers. Having seen 242 attacking the bombers, Sinclair took as his target an Me 110 with a full deflection shot. He climbed into the sun and gave another one prolonged attention. The port engine on this Me 110 ceased to function, but then Sinclair ran out of ammunition so had to call off further acts.

Sinclair was Red 1, Pilot Sergeant B. Furst Red 2 and Sergeant Seda Red 3. Furst fired at one of the Me 110s attacked by Sinclair. Seda did the same. But Furst failed to find Sinclair again. Furst next hit a 110 and left it smoking from the port engine over Whitstable. A far cry from the days of peace and the famous oysters. The enemy glided down in turns towards the east, with both his engines failing to function. But Furst could only claim a probable success.

He was more definite a few minutes afterwards. He trailed a group of bombers north of Canterbury. Far below, the cathedral made its cross as it had done in plan view over the centuries. Furst found himself 50 yards behind an Me 109. One burst hit the Messerschmitt. But not before the pilot baled out. Furst was waylaid by two Me 110s and had to beat a hasty retreat.

Sergeant Seda followed Sinclair as he led their section in a curve towards the bombers. Next moment, he saw an Me 110 only 50 yards ahead. He fired. White smoke made parallel trails from the engines but Seda did not see the enemy crash.

Again in the five-minute spell from 5.15 to 5.20 pm, P/O S. Janouch was leading Yellow Section, A Flight, at 25,000 feet over Grays Thurrock. He took the section towards enemy fighters, level out of the sun. Then they had to transfer efforts to a bomber force. But the fighters wedged between the bombers and themselves. An Me 110 appeared just in front of Janouch's windscreen and tried desperately to escape by going into a glide. Janouch fired five bursts at 400 to 50 yards, the middle burst producing smoke from both engines. Yellow 2 and 3 also went for this one, but only Yellow 3 got in a burst. These other two of Yellow Section saw two men bale out of the aircraft. Janouch climbed to regain an operational height and joined another squadron of Hurricanes, before being called on to land.

Flt Lt J. Jeffries led B Flight of 310 Squadron. He climbed into the sun, fired all his rounds at one fighter, and saw scraps of metal careering off it. But he was slightly out of range and just unable to get any closer – so could not clinch his attack. Jeffries was flying Blue 1, P/O V. Goth came in behind as

Typical sight over all areas of southern England during the historic summer of 1940.

Blue 2, with F/O J.F. Boulton as Blue 3. Goth had an adventurous few minutes, surviving to tell about it.

Jeffries told them to attack singly some scattered enemy. An Me 110 selected by Goth joined the bombers and was insisting on orbiting above. Goth delivered his fire from the sun and the rear. He dived on the Me 110 from the port, opening fire at 200 yards. By 50 yards' range, the enemy was emitting a heavy smoke pall and Goth saw the cockpit break up in the air. The machine fell vertically towards the Thames Estuary between Southend and Foulness Island.

As Goth broke away, however, he felt that his Hurricane had been hit. Then another enemy was upon him. A fight started. Enemy fire ceased and he saw that their port engine was badly struck. The enemy lurched right and then dramatically left, apparently set for a spin. Goth saw the air-gunner hit as the port engine flamed. They were both over the sea by this stage.

Goth could not see anything more as his cockpit was oozing with oil. His engine started cutting off. The glycol tank was pouring forth white smoke. Then the engine cut off completely. Goth shut the throttle and dived towards the coast. Somehow he saw through all the usual obstacles, set against an invasion. He landed with his undercarriage up about two miles south-east of Maldon in Essex. A lucky denouement.

Blue 3 had a less dramatic outcome. Boulton made his attacks between 5.15 and 5.35 pm. He fired at an Me 110 over the Estuary from below and behind. No results. Then he espied a Heinkel heading south-east over Kent. After crossing the coast, he carried out a couple of stern attacks at 15,000 feet. He fired all his remaining rounds at the Heinkel and the port engine smoked. It lost height remorselessly and never recovered composure, crashing into the Channel not far from the notorious Goodwin Sands. The pilot of another Hurricane confirmed this gain.

Green 1 and 2 were the last two Czechs reporting. P/O E. Fechtner as Green 1 fired at a force of bombers from below. He caused the middle of a bomber engine to smoulder. An Me 110 appeared and he fired at this one. The enemy gave a little climb, lurched into a wounded spin, and descended into the mass of dense smoke over the oil refineries. A bullet hit Fechtner's main tank but did not explode, so he was not hurt.

While P/O S. Zimprich at Green 2 was en route for Dornier 17s, he diverted to an Me 110 below him. Firing from 300 to 50 yards, he hit the port engine and the machine glided groundwards. He followed another Me 110 just above the beachline, only 400 yards over the blackness rising from the bombed oil tanks. The aircraft folded up on the left, crumpled, and crashed into the inferno. An enemy bullet struck the 'footstep' of Zimprich's Hurricane, but he survived.

Eight Spitfires of 19 Squadron accompanied 242 and 310 Squadrons. They saw a force of twenty bombers escorted by fifty fighters flying east at 15,000 feet. Number 19 Squadron was the last of the trio of the Duxford Wing to attack, being 5,000 feet lower than this enemy formation.

While still on the climb to attack, they met an Me 110 diving past them at a substantial speed with Red Leader, A Flight, after it. Two Hurricanes were also in tow. All five members of A Flight fired at this enemy which met its end a mile or so east of Hornchurch and south of a railway line. The crew of two baled out but one parachute failed to open … The other man landed in a field and appeared to be taken prisoner by two women from a nearby house.

Sqn Ldr Lane was Red 1, with Sergeant Jennings Red 2 and Flt Sgt Unwin Red 3. Red 1 and 2 plus Yellow 1 returned to base as the main combat had literally vanished. Red 3 mislaid the others but on climbing to 25,000 feet found and joined a Hurricane squadron. Someone else's group even. He was led into a force of some sixty enemy machines, bombers and fighters mixed about equally. The Hurricanes were busy with the bombers, while Red 3 suddenly found himself surrounded by Me 109s. He fired at five. Two went down. He then extricated his Spitfire, shadowing an enemy group from a great height. This force was at 20,000 feet and being attacked accurately by AA fire which scored two strikes. Red 3 used up his ammunition on a batch of unescorted bombers.

Yellow 2, P/O Cunningham, also lost the rest of the squadron and joined up with the Hurricanes. They flew east and aimed for twenty-four Heinkels. Yellow 2 selected and fired at one of them, set it ablaze, attacked again from below and finally saw it die some ten miles inland from Deal or Ramsgate – he was not sure which at that moment and it did not really matter.

B Flight of 19 Squadron were out of range of the enemy by the time they had staggered up to the level required and Blue 1 and 2 had to return to base without firing. Blue 3 cottoned on to another squadron and shot down an Me 110 into the sea off Margate. Blue 1, 2 and 3 were, respectively, Flt Lt Clouston, Flt Sgt Steere and P/O Dolezal.

So summarizing the results of the first Wing action in adverse conditions, the three squadrons under Bader inflicted claimed damage of twenty destroyed (perhaps fewer) for the loss of four; plus one damaged; with one pilot killed and one wounded. The pilot lost was P/O Benzie.

While this non-stop set piece was developing, another enemy group hit Thameshaven again, while a third went for the West Ham docks area. Warehouses burned; oil tanks flared; houses crumbled. As the exposed enemy bombers and fighter bombers – Me 110s – turned to get away, the same scenes were re-enacted. The fighters picked them off.

Then as these first waves fought and flew their rearguard retreat back across the Channel and the North Sea, fresh formations darkened the already-evening skyline. The total number of RAF squadrons scrambled was twenty-three. All but two managed to find and intercept some of the swarms. The RAF had some trouble in not being overwhelmed. A dozen Hurricanes of 249 Squadron took off from North Weald. Five failed to return there. With massed raids like these, there was something to be said for Big Wings. The enemy losses proved to be fighters rather than bombers. They believed the figures worthwhile in view of the damage inflicted. And it could not be denied that this was quite vast.

London docks burned vividly in the dusk. The fires came from warehouses and ships berthed in that veritable warren of waterways. Lighting, communications and other public services were all badly struck. Water mains burst and gushed over the back streets in the East End. Those living in the defence zone of London had watched some of the air battles clawing the skies on that Saturday evening. In the gathering dusk, a red glow appeared in the clouds over eastern London. The warehouses went on blazing. London itself became an easy target for the massed raid that followed as darkness fell.

Heinkels crossed the white Sussex cliffs at nearly half past eight. Other groups headed for London from routes over Kent and the Thames Estuary. All converging on the London fires. For the next six hours or so, from 9 pm to 3 am, 250 bombers maintained a comparatively uninterrupted aerial highway progress to and from London. They dropped over 300 tons of high explosives plus an estimated 13,000 incendiary bombs. The anti-aircraft defences were pitifully lacking, claiming only one aircraft shot down.

The damage spread far beyond the earlier targets of the docks. Bombs ripped into central London, causing fatalities and injuries; roads and railway lines were made impassable; enemy action blocked the Rotherhithe tunnel under the Thames. Havoc ran along the banks of the river as it wound around the historic Pool of London. People were made homeless in a second by wrecked houses, but emergency services gave them food and shelter. The following were hit: a utility plant; docks of the Port of London Authority; warehouses tightly packed beside the waterline; barges; and two schools. Fortunately the last premises were empty. In the lower Thames, fires melted many of the oil installations there. The casualty figures announced after these raids were 306 killed and 1,337 seriously injured. The Blitz had began – unofficially at any rate.

Invasion was still an hourly possibility and the armed forces were shifted up a gear to maximum readiness. As for the Londoners who had virtually their first taste of total warfare, next day's newspapers told their readers what they really already knew. London had been bombed for the first time. The aircraft losses for 7 September read: German forty, British twenty-eight.

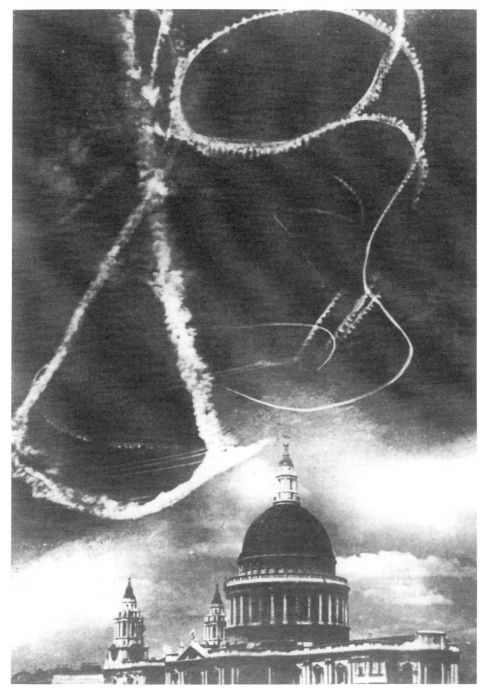

Famous composite of St Paul's Cathedral surmounted by vapour trails – purporting to show a scene during the Battle of Britain.

CHAPTER FIFTEEN

Day and Night Raids on Capital

8 September

The enemy plan seemed clearer now. Bomb London at night and accept some small losses; bomb London by day covered by big fighter numbers which would further neutralize the rest of Fighter Command resources; and then invade. The authorities here knew this, even if the public did not really appreciate it. What happened was a week more of night raids on the capital and other metropolitan centres. Or taking the longer view beyond the Battle of Britain, fifty-seven nights altogether. The raids on London and other cities in fact went on through the winter until May 1941, when as we now know the Germans were preparing to turn their ground and aerial attention eastward towards the forthcoming and ill-advised struggle against Soviet Russia.

Meanwhile, on 8 September, London heard the wailing and howling of the warnings soon after dark. The bombers again had the benefit of the River Thames with its highly individual curves to guide them. As before, bombs were broadcast over many regions indiscriminately. Fires occurred mainly in the Thames-side districts, but with others elsewhere. Small houses were damaged or demolished; public and mercantile buildings crashed down; and there was especially bad damage to the railway network emanating from the main line termini hubs both north and south of the river.

The official communique put it like this:

'London has once more been the main objective of the enemy, and its citizens have met the blind savagery of these latest night attacks with admirable courage and resource.'

Some 286 people were killed and about 1,400 seriously injured in the raids on this single night. The aircraft losses for the 24-hour period were fairly light in comparison to these horrifying figures: German fifteen, British two.

9 September

The daylight battle went on, too. This time early twin targets were the Thames Estuary and also Southampton. Then ensued a 200-bomber effort to reach and pulverize London by day. Both 11 and 12 Groups were summoned to assist, so belatedly perhaps Park was appreciating that he and his courageous pilots were not engaged in an exclusive grudge fight between 11 Group and the Luftwaffe. This was a full-scale air international, Germany versus Britain.

Eleven Group were of course called on first. The raids by the 200 bombers, plus as many or more fighters, resulted in lethal actions killing aircrew on both sides. Ultimately many enemy bombers decided to dispose of their loads anywhere, as fast as they could be released. One result of this was that southern and eastern suburbs of the capital were the recipients. It seemed that there could be no winners without losers in this grappling fight over the ribbon development of Greater London. The anti-aircraft defences had been doubled around the capital since the previous shattering nights of 7 and 8 September, but today it would be left to Fighter Command to stop even more massacre. Both 11 and 12 Groups succeeded. But as the battle so far has concentrated on 11 Group, the rest of the day's actions describe how 12 Group were coming increasingly into the reckoning.

Once more, Johnnie Johnson set the scene for the second Duxford Wing action that afternoon:

> 'On 9 September the Luftwaffe repeated their tactics of the 7th, sending over two waves in quick succession, with fighter forces ranging ahead and on the flanks of the main formations. The Germans were after London and aeroplane factories at Brooklands, Weybridge, but had little success, for one raid was met, as Park intended, well forward, and the bombs were scattered through much cloud near Canterbury.'

As usual Bader ventilated his feelings to his sector commander, Wing Commander Woodhall, about getting into the air – or not getting into it. Woodhall pressed the 12 Group controller who, in turn, enquired of his opposite number at 11 Group whether the Duxford Wing was required.

Eventually they were scrambled, and once radio contact was established between controller and Wing Leader, Woodhall said:

'Will you patrol between North Weald and Hornchurch, Angels Twenty?'

Never one at the best of times for blind obediency to orders, Bader noted Woodhall's 'Will you'. It was not lost on him. This intimacy between the two men was important, because it had wide repercussions on the authority of Wing Leaders in the future.

Woodhall, affectionately known as Woodie, was a veteran of the Kaiser's War, and was one of the best and most trusted controllers in Fighter Command. His calm and measured tones seemed full of confidence and assurance, and he was fully aware of the limitations of radar, which, at this time, was often distorted by enemy jamming. Woodhall knew that his Wing Leader was in the best position to judge how and when to attack, and therefore his controlling technique was to advise rather than to instruct.

Bader, climbing hard to the south, figured that once again the Germans would come out of the evening sun, so he forgot about Hornchurch and the

Suburban cinema receives a direct hit in the first night raid on London.

height and climbed high over Staines, 30 miles from Hornchurch and well within 11 Group's preserves. He was just in time to position his Wing between the sun and two big shoals of bombers accompanied by the usual pack of 109s.

It was at about 5.40 pm that Bader saw the enemy coming from about 15 miles south-west of them and at the same height of 22,000 feet. Leading the same three squadrons as two days earlier, thirty-three fighters this time instead of thirty-four, he turned to head the enemy off, while climbing all the time to gain advantage of altitude. The enemy were in two large rectangular formations; one of approximately sixty, then a space of about a quarter mile of sky, followed by a further sixty, with a 500- feet step-up between the two groups.

Bader radioed Duxford to tell 19 Squadron of Spitfires to climb up and protect their tails and then he turned 242 and 310 in above the front bomber formation – nearly down-sun and 1,000 feet above them. Bader had told 242 to attack in loose line-astern and to try to break up the enemy formation. He was aiming at the leader, who was slightly in front of the first section.

As he turned 242 directly above the bombers, Bader noticed some fighters diving out of the sun between the twin enemy bomber forces, but he dismissed them as friendly fighters. Actually they turned out to be Me 109s which went for 242 on its turn. The squadron retaliated, though, so Bader was not really worried by them.

Dornier 215 bomber.

Bader followed his plan by diving on the leader with a two-seconds' burst at point-blank distance. He continued his dive past the enemy, through and under the formation. He pulled up underneath them, intending to give his victim another squirt from below, but saw white smoke misting from both wings. Then he saw the machine roll over on its back in a dive. He did not bother to watch it further, but Sgt Brimble and P/O Bush both saw at least one person bale out as it descended in a flame-trail. Bader could not be sure at that second whether it was a Dornier 17 or not – he admitted to finding it hard to tell the difference between Dornier 17s and 215s.

P/O Willie McKnight was Bader's faithful Red 2. At 5.45 pm they were south of the Thames now. McKnight flew into the enemy from 1,000 feet above and on his left beam. He broke to the left to go for the protecting enemy fighters. He got behind one of them and sent it down in flames. Next he got between two enemy attacking his Hurricane. He opened up at once on one of them, and the machine shed metallic fragments as it dived to earth. But the German at Willie's rear also opened up and blew off the Canadian's left aileron. McKnight saw his second Me 109 quite out of control. He survived with his missing aileron.

While Bader manoeuvred into the sun and did his dive on the leading enemy section, Flt Lt Ball leading Yellow Section took his Hurricane at the second enemy section. He dived right through the enemy, pulled up, and did a frontal attack on the leading section, hoping to split them up. He saw no effect from his plan, but he did see an Me 109 buzzing on his tail. He wriggled around to reverse their relative positions and, firing from 300 to 100 yards, witnessed the spectacle of the 109 literally blowing up in mid-air. Satisfying yet sobering. Ball got only one bullet in his Hurricane.

Blue Leader was by now a veteran of 242: Flt Lt Powell-Sheddon. Even before the attack, the sections became open and irregular, with Bader still out in front. Powell-Sheddon, Blue 1, saw Bader drop his nose and head ram-like for the first thirty enemy aircraft. Blue 1 admitted to making a mess of his first attempt. He tried to get the leader but overshot and could not open fire. Then he made a steep climb, turned swiftly, and roared at the bombers again – aiming this time at the second leader. Three seconds at 50 yards and he saw the bullets striking the engine nacelle and the wing. He passed over the enemy about 20 feet from it and broke away in another steep climb. Glancing back, he saw the port engine afire. The bomber lagged behind and fell out of the formation, like a runner dropping behind with cramp.

Powell-Sheddon then lost sight of it for a very good and immediate reason. He lost control of his Hurricane. His starboard aileron control cable had been shot clean through and broken. By a bit of superior piloting, he managed to regain some semblance of control and set his nose towards home, with the enemy lost amid a mixture of haze and cloud. But he was credited with the destruction of one Dornier. The dogfight went on.

Bader remained under the formation he was attacking – some 300 feet below them. He pulled up periodically, squirting various aeroplanes at very close range. But although he damaged them, he saw no definite results. He did see another Dornier in the front diving slowly in a left-handed shallow spiral, obviously out of action and smoking. This was the second leader shot down by Powell-Sheddon.

Suddenly Bader discovered salvoes of bombs falling all around his Hurricane, so he decided to ease his stick away to the side. The bomber formation veered to the right and made off south-east. They were still in formation, about twenty of them, but they had left a lot of stragglers all over the sky some damaged and others going slowly, even for bombers.

It was obvious that their bombing was absolutely indiscriminate. London was covered by a 3,000-foot layer of broken-cloud thick haze up to 9,000 feet and clear above. They were bombing from 20,000 feet and so far as Bader could see, south of the Thames – around London Bridge and in the Battersea area. Bader went on with his plan of chasing the stragglers and firing close-range bursts at them to conserve ammunition. But finally it was all gone. Before he left, he saw a very large bomber with a single rudder flying home quite slowly and sedately. He attacked it by flying very close and then turning across it to put it off its stride. But it took no notice and did not even fire at him. There was nothing more he could do. His tally was one Dornier claimed destroyed and several damaged.

Flying close to Powell-Sheddon as Blue 2, P/O R Bush sighted the enemy first over the Thames near London Bridge. He took part in a line-astern attack from the sun on these bombers. Evading an Me 109, he found a 110 and shot it down, the aircraft breaking up like some miniature toy machine. But this was not child's play. Fire from behind by another 110 prompted Bush to execute a neat half-roll and call it a day.

Blue 3 was P/O F. Tamblyn. He saw some 200 enemy, a daunting experience on its own. This was 5.35 pm. As he approached, he observed five Me 110s detach themselves and turn in a right-hand circle towards the rear of the enemy formation. Their altitude measured 22,000 feet. Tamblyn turned into an astern assault and noticed a Hurricane set a 110 on fire. And in turn, on the tail of the Hurricane another 110 dogged it. A long burst at the Hurricane did not seem to do any damage. Tamblyn opened at the 110 whenever it straightened up – and after one of these bursts both engines lit up. Meanwhile, Tamblyn also noticed a Hurricane with its port wing folding up and another fighter in a similar predicament.

Tamblyn flew to the far side of the formation and climbed again. He saw a 110 making across at him in a steep turn, so gave a brief burst. From dead astern he then devoted several seconds to the same aircraft which crumpled into a fairly steep dive. The Hurricane Blue 3 followed it down and watched it actually crash in front of a cricket clubhouse within a hundred yards or so of another crashed aircraft. There were many star-like spots on the ground, which could have been the results of incendiary bombs.

Sergeant E. Richardson as Green 1 found a Dornier. He brought smoke to its starboard engine and main-plane. The sergeant pilot broke away at 200 yards. Regaining position 300 yards behind it, he closed to 100 yards – seeing smoke from the port engine after his second burst. Richardson then experienced a long return fire from the Dornier. This seemed to be tracer, but had no apparent effect on his Hurricane. After a third onslaught from 100 yards astern, flames sprang from the starboard main-plane. It seemed clear that the Dornier was doomed.

Both Green 1 and 2 had already been singled out by a group of eight to ten Me 109s. P/O Latta as Green 2 engaged one and fired for six to eight seconds – a long time in terms of aerial combat. The only evasive tactic taken by the German was a steep climbing turn left. He then instantly lit up in the cockpit, like a struck match, and spun off the climb – and continued spinning. The fighter would not recover from such a situation. Latta was then attacked and a bullet jammed his port aileron. He dived steeply to get a second to think. Luckily he was not followed and he got back to base. But it was a near thing, like everything else in the air. A few feet or semi-seconds could make all the difference between survival or perishing.

As Bader had gone into his own attack, Sergeant RW. Lonsdale in Yellow 4 saw three Me 109s speeding towards the rear of 242 Squadron and about 1,000 feet below. He made a quick turn but could not catch them. Then he found himself on the tail of Dorniers. He attacked the rearmost one which swung across the rest. Lonsdale found he was virtually touching the tail of another Dornier, slightly to one side of it. His Hurricane was being hit by heavy crossfire from the reargunners of the bombers, but he managed to dispose of the balance of his ammunition into the Dornier – or towards it.

While carrying out this second attack, he was being hit repeatedly in the engine and the controls. Smoke began to seep into his cockpit – as well as streams of glycol mixture and oil. His controls were practically useless except for the elevator. As he broke away from the attack, the enemy had smoke wisping from the fuselage and an engine stuttered to a halt.

Lonsdale baled out at about 19,000 feet and came to earth in a pine tree at Caterham. His Hurricane took its own course down, crashing rather symbolically on Kenley aerodrome about 200 yards from the main guardroom. While he was dropping to ground, a Spitfire pilot flew around Lonsdale all the time to protect him till he touched down.

The time: 5.40 pm. The squadron: 310. Flt Lt G.L. Sinclair was Yellow Leader as he turned to attack the bombers. But he saw Me 109s hurtling down on them from port. The squadron was turning to starboard and he turned slightly to port to see what the enemy were doing. Without any further warning, Sinclair received a hard blow across the shoulders. This was accompanied by a loud noise and followed by three more distant bangs. He then found his Hurricane in an inverted spin. He was thrown hard against the roof of the cockpit. He was apparently without any starboard wing, though he found it very difficult to discern anything in that position. He had to think quickly. He decided to get out. He had most trouble in opening the canopy and undoing the straps, due to the pressure in the cockpit. But he knew he had to – if he were to live. At last he did it and just shot out into space without any further effort on his part.

The parachute descent took nearly thirteen minutes and Sinclair landed in a wood just off the Purley Way at Coulsdon. He was picked up by Lieutenant G.D. Cooper of the Irish Guards from Caterham. Cooper had been watching the whole action through his field glasses and told Sinclair what had happened. Flying Officer Boulton, also flying a Hurricane, had collided with Sinclair and Boulton's machine had afterwards collided with a Dornier. Both machines crashed in flames. Boulton was lost. Sinclair survived. So a Dornier had been destroyed, but at a cost of one pilot and two Hurricanes.

Pilot Officer Fejar flew as No. 3 to Sinclair's section. After some preliminary skirmishing, Fejar found an Me 110. It tried to wriggle free from him by a series of twists, turns, climbs and dives, but Fejar hit it with a trio of attacks. Smoke from the port engine encouraged him to make one more attempt whereupon flames licked the whole port side of the Me 110.

But at that precise second in time, 22,000 feet over south-west London, Fejar noticed the starboard leading edge fairings of his Hurricane were loosened. The fighter began to vibrate badly and head towards the ground. He slowly pulled up the nose. He reckoned that the Hurricane had been hit not by the enemy but by a splinter from an anti-aircraft shell. He left the battle and landed safely.

After the disturbing sight of the two Hurricanes colliding in front of him, P/O Bergman saw an Me 110 trailing another Hurricane. He increased the boost and followed the enemy. The Hurricane broke away safely. Bergman hit the Me 110 with a determined burst. Both engines blazed with a blackness that turned into a red glow. He felt it was a victory for sure.

Sergeant Hubacek also saw the collision. He had a brush with a Heinkel. Next he found a quartet of Me 110s and set about them from the side out of the sun. The last one retaliated but Hubacek did likewise. The fuselage and rudder of the Me 110 were both fragmented and he saw several splinters fall away from the machine, wafting into airspace. It was to be hoped they did not hit anyone on the ground. The enemy dived into a cloud and counted as a probable for Hubacek, who had fought hard from 20,000 feet right down to 8,000 feet.

Again at 20,000 feet over east London, P/O Rypl made several turns. Above his head he saw enemy fighters not yet in action. When he realized that some of them were on to his section, flying below, he chased one. He got in a shot or two at this Me 109 and saw grey smoke gushing out of the engine. His altitude at this stage of the proceedings read as 23,208 feet! This must take any award as the most accurate height reading made during the entire Battle of Britain.

Rypl flew on. He chased bombers, eluded fighters, and at length saw that he was over hilly and partly wooded countryside. As he was by then flying with the reserve petrol tank open, he did not have much time for orientation and as he could find no aerodrome he decided to make an emergency landing to save the aircraft. He did his very best and landed in a long field with the undercarriage down. Unfortunately, the field was obstructed with anti-invasion glider-wire fixed on wooden poles, which Rypl could not possibly see from above. So his Hurricane was damaged after all, though he was safe. Visibility by that time of the September evening had grown rather poor as well.

Back aloft, the battle was approaching its latter stages. Sergeant Rechka had to cope with three Me 110s who all chose to fly at him. He gamely fired at the first one and hit its port engine. Diving away in distress, the Me 110 could easily have come to grief over the suburbs of south-east London.

P/O Zimprich wanted to make a really typical Czech dash at Dorniers together with the leader of his section. But he lost his number 1 in a sharp turn. This was all too easy to do. So he tried to go for the first Dornier alone. Then he saw an Me 110 so transferred to this adversary. He scored on the port engine before having to evade other Me 110s seen in his mirror.

That was not the end of Zimprich's sortie. He picked up another Dornier and decided to destroy it at any price. Closing from above and from starboard at 300 to 50 yards, he sent him spinning down. He saw both engines stopped, the gunner cease firing, and the bombs jettisoned. The Dornier landed near Westerham without its undercarriage down. Zimprich circled and saw the Army approaching the Luftwaffe crew. He himself landed at Biggin Hill. It should be remembered that the Czech pilots were not familiar with the general terrain of southern England.

Nine Spitfires of 19 Squadron saw the enemy initially as they were flying north-west. The fighters wove and searched above the bombers. It had been arranged by Bader for 19 Squadron to take the enemy fighters. Flt Lt W.G. Clouston as Blue 1 put them in line astern and clambered up to 23,000 feet for an attack on half-a-dozen Me 110s also on the climb. Just then a pair of Me 109s cut across their bows and Blue 1 loosed a burst before them. The second of the pair started a downward glide, possibly evasive.

The squadron went on to tackle the 110s. But Blue 1 had used all his ammunition so could not participate further. He had had his moment. Blue 2, Flt Sgt H. Steere cut across in front and Blue 3 Flt Lt E. Burgoyne took a full deflection shot. The enemy was then slipping inwards and Blue 1 saw it fade into a left-hand spiral out of control. Blue 2 chased another 110 out over the Channel but failed to get in range. Blue 3 stayed with Blue 1 and so did not take part in the main attack; he preferred to protect his leader, which he did successfully.

Red 1, Flt Lt W.J. Lawson, opened fire on the tail of an Me 110 at long range, scoring a starboard strike. With bits of wing blown off, the Messerschmitt finally crashed five miles east of Biggin Hill. Red 2, Sub-Lt A.G. Blake, did not fire in the first fight, but followed the main enemy formation out to sea, and stumbled on a straggling Heinkel. He left it dropping, flaming, towards the water. Red 2's windscreen was pierced by a bullet which ended in his petrol tank. Not the best place. Red 3 got on to an Me 109. Some of the enemy's engine flew out in a rather surrealist manner and P/O W. Cunningham left the 109 flame-enveloped. Red 3 got a bullet in his mainspar. Bullets could be harmless or lethal depending on where they struck.

Lastly, Yellow Section. Yellow 1 attacked one of two 109s with a deflection burst. No hits. He was F /0 FM. Brinsden and he saw a Hurricane going for a Heinkel, so he joined in from dead astern until he could fire no more. By that time, around 6 pm, Red 3 had landed at Detling and the Heinkel was down to 1,000 feet, with both engines stopped and his flaps and undercarriage down. He was gliding east, aiming to make a forced-landing a little south of Detling, too.

Yellow 2, P/O A.F Vokes, dived to attack one of six Dorniers straggling and with its wheels down. He fired all he had and then left it to another Spitfire. Yellow 3, Sergeant D.G. Cox, shot down an Me 109. But Cox's Spitfire was hit during the exchange in the mainplane and airscrew. He also had a bullet through the petrol tank. He was lucky to live.

Bader could not see a single other British fighter in the sky by this time and he maintained that the fleeing Germans could have been broken up still more severely and savagely if two fresh squadrons had arrived – five instead

Six Spitfires in starboard echelon.

of three. The enemy adopted tactics as with previous interceptions made by 242 Squadron. They had approached from the south, flying north over the west side of London, before turning south-east for home. The 12 Group Wing was instructed to patrol North Weald and Hornchurch, a useless procedure in Bader's very experienced view, because he could see 50 to 80 miles to the east but no distance to the west – up-sun. In his considered opinion, quite unshaken and in fact substantiated by 9 September, they should have been patrolling many miles south-west, where they would have been up-sun from the enemy and could have attacked before the Germans got to the Thames. Bader was convinced that they would have shot down at least twice the number which they did. If senior controllers had confined themselves to telling formation leaders where the enemy were supposed to be and left them to choose height and place to patrol, much better results would have been achieved.

Bader insisted that if aerodromes like North Weald and Hornchurch wanted protection, the patrol line should have been somewhere west of the Thames in the evening and south-east in the morning, because of the sun. The Battle of Britain was being fought not at ground level or on some plotting table, but five miles high above the Thames Estuary, London, and Kent. That was his view.

The results claimed by the three-squadron Wing on 9 September were twenty-one aircraft destroyed, plus probables and damaged. Our casualties were four aircraft destroyed or missing, three damaged and two pilots killed or missing. Let us leave the postscript to 9 September once again to Johnnie Johnson:

'Fortunately for Bader neither North Weald nor Hornchurch was attacked, otherwise Park might have lodged an official complaint with Dowding who, however, would have taken into account the tremendous results of this engagement – twenty enemy aeroplanes destroyed before bombing, for the loss of four Hurricanes and two pilots. And Leigh-Mallory must have thought a bit of occasional poaching like this was well justified, for he was so delighted with the results that he offered Bader two more squadrons, making five in all, for the next show. So it was in 12 Group, if not in 11 Group, that a leader could interpret instructions from the ground as he thought fit.'

The complete air losses for the day read: German twenty-eight, British nineteen.

London newsvendor with an excusably exaggerated scoreline.

Then came the evening and night raids again. Once more the official communiqué put it starkly without embellishment. The facts were sufficient, all the more telling for their soberness:

'The enemy has now thrown off all pretence of confining himself to military targets. Bombs have been scattered at random over London without any distinction of objective. They have fallen in the City and caused fires in the immediate vicinity of St Paul's Cathedral and the Guildhall; they have fallen on a large maternity hospital which was twice attacked, a number of casualties being caused; they have fallen on a poor law institution for the aged, on an L.C.C. housing estate, and on a large number of workmen's cottages, especially in the East End of London, which were heavily and repeatedly attacked; and they have also fallen in the residential districts of west and north London.

'The majority of the casualties occurred when an elementary school in the East End of London, which was affording temporary shelter to families whose homes had been destroyed, was hit and collapsed.'

It was announced subsequently that the number of casualties in London on this night totalled about 400 killed and 1,000 injured. Someone coined the phrase 'London can take it'. The capital and its citizens would have to prove this from now on.

CHAPTER SIXTEEN

The Climax Approaches

10 September

The rains returned, restricting Luftwaffe actions to slighter daytime raids. After dark they went for London again, South Wales and Merseyside, the respective aircraft losses signifying the limited contact made by night fighters and anti-aircraft: German four, British one.

The most heartening event of the twenty-four hours was the announcement of a night raid on an enemy airfield at Eindhoven. The bombers used were Blenheims and the gains made on the ground were nine or ten Heinkel 111s. This determined punch at the Luftwaffe-occupied Dutch airfield counted as a major strike in the continuing sub-plot of the battle: the counterattacks on both enemy-held airfields from which raids were being made, and enemy-held ports where invasion preparations continued. Both of these series of operations made their contributions towards the final outcome, now approaching daily.

While these Blenheims were destroying their counterpart bombers on the ground in Holland, others were over the Channel coastline and pounding the invasion paraphernalia – from Calais docks to Boulogne waterfront. Flames, flares, flashes, glares. Flying Officer R.S. Gilmour was piloting a Blenheim with Ostend as their target. He made his approach and dived for the Dutch port:

'Then came the great surging kick on the stick as the bombs left the plane. A second later the bomb-aimer was through to me on the phones: "Bombs gone." My waiting hand threw open the throttle levers in a flash. The motors thundered out. Hauling back on the stick, kicking at the rudder, we went up in a great banking climb. As we went I stared down and out through the windows. There they were! One, two, three, four vast flashes as my bombs struck. In the light of the last one, just as lightning will suddenly paint a whole landscape, I saw the outline of the jetties in vivid relief. Between them the water boiled with their black shapes. They were barges flung upend and fragments turning slowly over and over in the air.

'Then came a most gigantic crash. We were nearly 2,000 feet up now and well away from the jetties, but the whole aircraft pitched over as if a giant blow had struck us underneath. A vivid flash enveloped us and lingered as the sound burst round our ears. It was a blinding white flash like a great sheet of daylight stuck in between the dark. While all hell broke loose round us, I fought like mad to get control of the bomber. But all the time my mind was blankly wondering – half-stunned as I was – what the devil we had hit. Afterwards I learned that the last bomb had struck a group of mines stacked on a jetty waiting to be loaded aboard the minelayers. Photographs taken the next morning showed two stone jetties blown away to the water's edge; all barges vanished from the inner basins; and devastation over a mile radius.'

On the same day as these raids, the German Naval Staff wrote in their diary:

'There is no sign of the defeat of the enemy's Air Force over southern England and in the Channel area, and this is vital to a further judgment of the situation. The preliminary attacks by the Luftwaffe have indeed achieved a noticeable weakening of the enemy's fighter defences, so that considerable German fighter superiority can be assumed over the English area. However … we have not yet attained the operational conditions which the Naval Staff stipulated to the Supreme Command as being essential for the enterprise, namely, undisputed air superiority in the Channel area and the elimination of the enemy's air activity in the assembly area of the German naval forces and ancillary shipping … It would be in conformity with the timetable preparations for Sealion if the Luftwaffe now concentrated less on London and more on Portsmouth and Dover, as well as on the naval ports in and near the operational area …'

11 September
Unknown to Britain at the time, 11 September was the date when Hitler put back the projected start of the enemy invasion again: first from 15 to 21 September and now to 24 September. Otherwise, the day was marked as the one registering the most nerve-breaking air fights and the maximum combined losses of the whole week. The bare history recorded: four airfields attacked, also London, Southampton, Portsmouth. And by night: London and Merseyside.

Dover: half past three. Mid-afternoon. Three hundred enemy aircraft in two bomber-and-fighter formations crossed the coast, just as thousands had now done previously. Eleven Group scrambled eleven squadrons. Twelve Group scrambled squadrons of the Duxford Wing. The enemy fighters were double their Dorniers and Heinkels. The confused fighter scraps trailed above vast tracts of Kent. Time was on the RAF's side, because the Messerschmitts always had limited fuel, certainly the 109s.

Now the 109s had to turn for home. By this time many bombers had pressed through to the three overlapping, interwoven London areas of East End homesteads, the docklands, and the commercial city. But once they had bombed, they were as usual open to fighter blows on the return route. Heinkels and Dorniers fell over London, Horsham and Hornchurch, to cite the scale of territory covered. Each loss usually meant several men – undeniably brave. One squadron of Spitfires, No. 92, suffered five shot down. The traditional lighthearted buoyancy of the RAF pilots was beginning to be put to its extreme test. Somehow they had to accept the losses. There was nothing else they could do. They had already become fatalistic about their personal destinies. But they could have been forgiven if they did wonder: how much longer can we go on?

Wreckage of German aircraft which crashed in south-east England town.

Patrolling Spitfires with their powerful Merlin engines and guns capable of firing 1200 rounds per minute.

Meanwhile, this could only be England. Her Royal Highness the Duchess of Gloucester visited 12 Group headquarters. Hitler and the Luftwaffe notwithstanding sherry was served formally in the large ante-room before lunch on Wednesday, 11 September. Air Vice-Marshal Leigh-Mallory was there too. The Duchess left at about 2.10 pm.

One hour later at 3.20 pm a Wing took off from Duxford under the command of Squadron Leader Lane. This comprised half of 19 and 266 Squadrons and the whole of 74 and 611 Squadrons. They had the by-now-familiar notice to patrol the Hornchurch/North Weald area at 23,000 feet. At least the altitude was getting more realistic.

Between London and Gravesend, AA fire drew their attention to an enemy force of some 150 aircraft flying generally north at 20,000 feet. The Germans were flying in waves of tight formations of Dorniers, Heinkels and Junkers 88s, with protecting fighters. Me 110s were behind the bombers and a formidable force of Me 109s behind them at about 24,000 feet. It had been arranged that the two Spitfire squadrons in the lead (composite 19/266 and 611) were to attack the fighter escort, while 74 Squadron aimed at the bombers. As 74 Squadron went for the force of Junkers 88s, they met fighters diving on them, but they gamely continued their policy of striking for the main formation. For once, Douglas Bader was not in the scrap!

Eight aircraft of 19 Squadron and six of 266 Squadron were leading the Wing. They dived in line astern for a head-on attack on the leading Heinkel 111s and their screening Messerschmitt 110s. After this first insurgence, Red 1, Sqn Ldr B.E. Lane, broke off to port and saw the enemy turning south-east over Sittingbourne in Kent. He went for the nearer of two 110s, blowing bits off its starboard engine and then setting it alight. The other Me 110 opened its throttle and left.

Discretion being the better part ... Red 1 tried for the Heinkels and saw some flames emerging jaggedly from one, but nothing more.

Sergeant Jennings as Red 2 finished off a Heinkel, and moved on to the end one of fifteen Me 110s. It fell out of the force and crashed in a wood somewhere remote between Sittingbourne and Maidstone. Red 3 was Sergeant H.AC. Roden. He took on thirty Me110s, endeavouring to form a circle. Pieces flew from the port mainplane of one and it took a shallow dive – inconclusively.

Flt Sgt Hawin at Red 4 knocked lumps off both engines of a Heinkel III from a mere 50 yards. The bomber went into a tell-tale spiral. Then a Dornier decided to go for him – unlikely but true. It shattered his windscreen and registered a hit on his engine. The Spitfire was not in good shape. Hawin switched off his engine and forced-landed in Kent with no drastic damage to either the fighter or himself.

Green 1, F/O L.A. Haines, climbed to engage forty Me 110s slightly higher than the Heinkels. They formed a defensive circle but he penetrated to one, which he hit from 200 yards. As he was in the midst of this, Me 109s swooped down on him and hit his Spitfire in both mainplanes. Haines hurriedly made for ground-level and crash-landed, both tyres being punctured during the combat. He was not hurt. Green 2, P/O Dolezal, hit an Me 109. As he followed its belching trail, he was also hit from behind and wounded in his right knee. His engine got a strike, too, but between them they got back to base.

Blue Section had to interrupt their main attack as Me 109s roared up from the rear. Blue 1, Flt Sgt H. Steere, fired at two of them. Blue 2, Sgt D.G. Cox, took Me 110s instead. Then he stopped the starboard engine of a straggling Dornier.

It was after 4 pm by now. The AA fire which had originally drawn attention to the enemy was proving troublesome and downright dangerous during the widespread melee. Despite hampering the plan of attack, 74 Squadron stuck to their task and inflicted considerable losses on enemy bombers. Number 611 Squadron went for both bombers and fighters.

Number 611 Squadron encountered the enemy over the Thames Estuary – a favourite locale for 12 Group – at altitudes from 18,000-24,000 feet. The squadron was formed up in three sections of four Spitfires in line astern. At 20,000 feet their gaze was met by the rather daunting aerial spectacle of fifteen to thirty Dorniers and some Heinkel 111s at 18,000 feet; a mass of Messerschmitt 110s stepped up behind at 20,000 feet; and the Me 109s behind them at 24,000 feet. A spread of 6,000 feet. The squadron split up.

Flt Sgt H.S. Sadler, Yellow 4, gave an Me 110 long bursts, using nearly all his ammunition in his enthuslasm. The enemy fuselage caught fire and the machine lost height. P/O J.W. Lund, Blue 4, dived on to an Me 109 and fired a burst. Another enemy hove into his mirror so he climbed, only to run into five Me 110s. He hit the starboard one with an astern attack. Sergeant A.D. Burt caught a Heinkel 111 from 300 feet above it. The enemy rear-gunner ceased abruptly. Other tracer fire caused Burt to invoke a steep climbing turn. The Heinkel seemed to have gone.

Sergeant S.A. Levenson was really outclimbed by the rest of his section when they started pursuing the bombers. As he flew around fifty Junkers 88s, he met a pair of Me 109s circling in the opposite direction. The three of them made quite a pretty pattern. Turning on to them, he made a 60-degree deflection attack from the rear and allowed both aircraft to pass through his sights while he fired from 200 yards. One of them turned on its back and began to spin. Levenson lost sight of it and climbed back above the Junkers.

The bombers flew in a tight shape. He attacked the starboard line of bandits from the front quarter, allowing the whole lot to pass through his sights while firing from 100 yards. Two of them broke away below. He hit an engine of one of them and the aircraft glided down 10,000 feet in ten miles. Levenson flew actually alongside for some time until the AA guns opened up. He broke away as black smoke suddenly sooted out from underneath his instrument panel. He tried to make Kenley aerodrome – the nearest one – but before he got close enough his engine stopped. It was a matter of skill to survive. He dared not panic. He glided down with wheels up and brought the Spitfire to a reasonable landfall in a field not far from the aerodrome. A nearby searchlight post crew told him that the enemy aircraft he had been trailing down had crashed six to ten miles south of Kenley. Levenson returned to his base by train on the following day. Rather a prosaic means of transport compared with his Spitfire.

F/O D.H. Watkins climbed towards the sun and at 4.15 pm sighted forty Dorniers under AA fire. As he was about to attack them, two anti-aircraft bursts upset his Spitfire in its dive and the engine stopped. He had no option but to forceland at Hornchurch and later returned to Duxford thence to Digby – the same airfield as Levenson.

Sqn Ldr H.E. McComb followed by P/O T.D. Williams were about to take on an Me 110 when a 109 attacked them instead. They did not manage to locate any other enemy. Flight Lieutenant K.M. Stoddart fired 1748 (!) rounds at an Me 109 without any result. Flying Officer I.B. de Hay covered Stoddart's rear so never got within range of the Me 109. P/O D.H. O'Neil and P/O D.A. Adams both fired at a Dornier but then the AA got in their way. Sergeant F.E.R. Shepherd and his Spitfire No. 07298 were both missing...

The outcome of this third Wing patrol was that the thirty-six aircraft involved claimed to have destroyed twelve, with fourteen probables and seven damaged. Our casualties were three aircraft lost and three damaged. One pilot was killed and one wounded.

The total losses for that day were not good: German twenty-five, British twenty-nine.

Winston Churchill made the following broadcast to Britain on this very day:

'Whenever the weather is favourable waves of German bombers, protected by fighters, often three or four hundred at a time, surge over this Island, especially the promontory of Kent, in the hope of attacking military and other objectives by daylight. However they are met by our fighter squadrons and nearly always broken up, and their losses average three to one in machines and six to one in pilots.

'This effort of the Germans to secure daylight mastery of the air over England is of course the crux of the whole war. So far it has failed conspicuously. It has cost them very dear, and we have felt stronger, and actually are relatively a good deal stronger, than when the hard fighting began in July. There is no doubt that Herr Hitler is using up his fighter force at a very high rate, and that if he goes on for many more weeks he will wear down and ruin this vital part of his Air Force. That will give us a great advantage.

'On the other hand, for him to try to invade this country without having secured mastery in the air would be a very hazardous undertaking. Nevertheless, all his preparations for invasion on a great scale are steadily going forward. Several hundreds of self-propelled barges are moving down the coasts of Europe, from the German and Dutch harbours to the ports of Northern France, from Dunkirk to Brest, and beyond Brest to the French harbours in the Bay of Biscay.

'Besides this, convoys of merchant ships in tens and dozens are being moved through the Straits of Dover into the Channel, dodging along from port to port under the protection of the new batteries which the Germans have built on the French shore. There are now considerable gatherings of shipping in the German, Dutch, Belgian and French harbours, all the way from Hamburg to Brest. Finally, there are some preparations made of ships to carry an invading force from Norwegian waters.

'Behind these clusters of ships or barges there stand large numbers of German troops, awaiting the order to go on board and set out on their very dangerous and uncertain voyage across the seas. We cannot tell when they will try to come; we cannot be sure that in fact they will try at all; but no-one should blind himself to the fact that a heavy full-scale invasion of this Island is being prepared with all the usual German thoroughness and method, and that it may be launched now – upon England, upon Scotland, or upon Ireland, or upon all three.

'If this invasion to going to be tried at all, it does not seem that it can be long delayed. The weather may break at any time. Besides this, it is difficult for the enemy to keep these gatherings of ships waiting about indefinitely while they are bombed every night by our bombers, and very often shelled by our warships which are waiting for them outside.

'Therefore we must regard the next week or so as a very important period in our history. It ranks with the days when the Spanish Armada was approaching the Channel, and Drake was finishing his game of bowls; or when Nelson stood between us and Napoleon's Grand Army at Boulogne. We have read all about this in the history books; but what is happening now is on a far greater scale and of far more consequence to the life and future of the world and its civilization than those brave old days.'

After the first four days and nights of raids on London, the anti-aircraft barrage in and around the capital was strengthened still further. On the night of 11 September, the enemy raiders were met by a ground defence which seemed for a time to surprise and stagger them. Nevertheless, they continued to fly over the capital and the extreme altitude they adopted made it difficult for the searchlight crews and gunners to hold the aircraft in their sights and score hits. The bombers were thus still able to drop their missiles more or less at random. They made no attempt to aim at military or even strategic targets. More precautions were being taken now for civilian safety, yet casualties remained heavy. They tended to decrease slightly, but the figures reflected the tragic losses to civilians. Whether people lived or died in these raids became a matter of mere chance, when a bomb-aimer pressed his release button. Three-quarters of all the nation's air-raid casualties were now being suffered in London.

On the night of 11 September, too, raiders roamed further than London. The Liverpool-Crewe railway line was blocked by bombing while the important Liverpool–Bala water pipeline was fractured. The Humber, Hull, Lincoln, Grantham, Wolverhampton, St Helen's, Warrington, Digby, Ely, Mildenhall and Stoke were also visited.

12 September

The intention to invade remained. Royal Air Force reconnaissance showed that the enemy build-up of barges still proceeded. The reconnaissance aircraft managed to photograph the evidence despite poor weather. The Luftwaffe made a few day sorties scattered over England and the cloud conditions allowed the odd raider to reach central London undetected or undeterred. They actually hit the War Office, the Admiralty and Buckingham Palace itself.

The attack by a lone Heinkel 111 on Buckingham Palace was memorable because of its immediate sequel – and the RAF pilot responsible. Unfortunately for the German, a single experienced Hurricane pilot shot him down. This pilot was Flight Sergeant J.H. Lacey – nicknamed 'Ginger' because of his colouring. The weather was so poor that after his victory Lacey could not make his way home. He climbed up in the copious cloud and baled out – landing safely to fight many more duels.

National Fire Service personnel at an incident in the City of London.

'Ginger' Lacey had been an unqualified chemist's dispenser before he joined the ranks in the Royal Air Force. He soon qualified as a pilot, and although almost still a boy at the time, he had a remarkable record in the Battle of Britain. He destroyed eighteen enemy aircraft during the battle as a whole, none more memorably than the Heinkel 111 that bombed Buckingham Palace. His name remains as one of the leading fighter aces in the Royal Air Force.

Then the enemy resorted to night bombing as usual: London and the Midlands, Merseyside, and South Wales. The losses were minimal: German four, British zero. A welcome pause. Douglas Bader was awarded the Distinguished Service Order.

13 September

The only incident of unusual note was the very first enemy activity to be reported over Northern Ireland. So now all four parts of the United Kingdom had been enmeshed at first-hand in the raids. Otherwise, small scattered attacks were the pattern. The persistent raids on London were becoming an irritation to all its citizens, as well as far worse to those numbered among the volume of casualties. German air losses four, British one. To try to offset the big build-up of German barges and other craft, Bomber Command made widespread onslaughts on several of the ports harbouring them.

14 September

Rather random day raids featured on south London. Heinkels and Junkers were releasing their loads literally anywhere. And random loss of life was worst in such suburban areas as Croydon. Equally indiscriminate forays caused comparable casualties on the two South Coast resorts of Brighton and Eastbourne. There seemed to be scant intelligence for such a policy. Then came the wearing night raids on London and South Wales. Losses were not negligible in men and machines. German fourteen, British fourteen.

The momentous week ended when Hitler had changed emphasis from RAF fighter airfields to London and other civilian targets. The reason for the switch to night raids was obviously because the daylight ones had become too costly. This same week marked the point in the battle when the number of RAF fighters in reserve started to rise from the figure of only 125 on 7 September. However, Dowding's more critical concern was the continuing shortage of pilots to go on flying and fighting for an unforeseeable time into the future. As it happened, this would be shorter than he feared. Meanwhile the strain was not only being felt by fighter pilots. It stretched to all Service personnel of both sexes and a considerable proportion of the British population. So dawned 15 September.

'Ginger' Lacey and his Hurricane: one of the highest-scoring aces.

CHAPTER SEVENTEEN

The Decisive Day – Morning

15 September

This was the day when the Battle of Britain was won. Over the south-east of England, that Sunday dawned a little misty, but it cleared by 8 am to disclose light cumulus cloud at 2,000 to 3,000 feet. The extent of the cloud varied, and in places it was heavy enough to yield light local showers. But visibility remained good on the whole, with a slight westerly wind shifting towards north-west as the day advanced. Later on, too, it merged into one of those typical September days with a soft light spread over the scene.

The first enemy patrols arrived soon after 9 am. They were reported over the Straits of Dover, the Thames Estuary, off Harwich, and between Lympne and Dungeness. At about 11.30 am, Göring imperiously launched the first wave of the morning attack, consisting of 100 or more aircraft, soon followed by 150 more. These crossed the English coast at three main points – near Ramsgate, between Dover and Folkestone, and a mile or two north of Dungeness. Their common goal was London.

This force comprised Dornier 17s and 215s escorted by Me 109s. They flew at various heights between 15,000 and 26,000 feet. From the ground, the enemy aircraft looked like black dots at the head of long streamers of white vapour; from the air like model aeroplanes from childhood and then, as the range closed, as full-scale aircraft. One controller said: 'This looks like the biggest show yet.'

The 11 Group controller not only had sufficient time to couple ten squadrons into wings, he was able to bring in reinforcements from the adjacent Groups before the first German force crossed the coast. Two Biggin Hill Squadrons got off the ground at 11.05; two from Northolt at 11.15; two from Kenley also at 11.15; and two from Debden at the same time. These were closely followed five minutes later by single squadrons from Hendon, Hornchurch, and Middle Wallop. The one squadron at Martlesham clocked in at this time, too, while the second Hornchurch squadron was about 20 minutes later at 11.40. Add to all these 11 Group squadrons the Duxford Wing of five squadrons, airborne roughly as the enemy were crossing the English coast. Not too bad, for once. Bringing up the rear came a trio of squadrons from Croydon, Gravesend and finally the third one based at Northolt. That made over twenty squadrons actually in the air.

First in action were a score of Biggin Hill Spitfires, which made the short flight of some fifty miles to encounter the enemy roughly above the coastline. Their task successfully carried out was to occupy the Me 109s and so prevent this screen from defending their bomber charges. Hurricanes of 253 and 504 approached to go for the bomber masses. As the aerial scene moved rapidly towards London, the 11 Group fighters had already shot down enough of the bombers and escorts to crumble the intended raid into a variety of disorganized sections. Then the Duxford Wing under Bader arrived fresh on the scene. We will deal with them later.

Battle was soon joined and it raged for about three-quarters of an hour over East Kent and London. A hundred bombers or so burst through our ground and air defences to reach the eastern and southern quarters of the capital. A number of them were intercepted above the centre of the city itself, just as Big Ben was striking the hour of noon. A symbolic moment indeed.

Close-up of Spitfires on patrol.

The sky over south-east England was like one colossal aerial battlefield – from the Thames Estuary down to Dover, from London to the coast. Individual and collective fights erupted all over these skies. To understand the nature of this battle, it must be made clear that it was really a concentration of attacking and defending aircraft flying and fighting anywhere over an area of England south of a straight line drawn from Norwich in Norfolk to Portland in Dorset, in the early stages perhaps compressed into a space mainly in the south-east. The aeroplanes involved were flying at anything from 200 to 300 mph and 400 mph in a dive. Once the enemy was intercepted and a large formation scattered, running battles between two or more aircraft continued all over the sky. At those speeds, place names became almost meaningless. The enemy, for example, might have been met over Maidstone, but not destroyed on the return route until within a few miles of Calais. Combat reports of British pilots might read:

'Place attack was delivered – Hammersmith to Dungeness.'

'Attacked enemy – London to the French coast.'

These phrases in the reports forcibly illustrate the size of the area over which the battle was conducted. Such attacks might start and be pressed home at any height from 25,000 feet down to near the ground or the sea. There could be as many as 140 separate fights going on if you could cut a cross-section across the skies. One moment the sky was full; the next, no one else could be seen in the heavens. That is how it seemed to the pilots involved.

As suggested, this particular phase of the battle was taking place in rather less extensive space than the Norwich-Portland line indicated. It was roughly a cuboid about eighty miles long, thirty-eight miles broad, and up to five or six miles high. It was in this vast space between noon and half past twelve that the individual combats occurred: even more than 140 now, perhaps up to 200. Many of these developed into stern chases only broken off within a mile or two of the French coast – and enemy-held territory. It could be compared to some life-or-death game of three-dimensional chess, played out by dozens and dozens of players always at great speed and with no time to think. And also with no limitation on the direction the pieces might be moved.

That morning, sixteen squadrons of 11 Group, followed by five from 12 Group, were in action. All but one of them came face to face with the Luftwaffe very soon after taking to the sky. Five squadrons of Spitfires opened their own attack against the oncoming aerial hordes over the Maidstone–Canterbury– Dover–Dungeness area. These were in action marginally before the Hurricane squadrons, which clashed further back, between Maidstone– Tunbridge Wells–London.

The RAF found the enemy flying in various types of formation. The bombers were usually some thousands of feet below fighters, but sometimes this position was reversed. The bombers flew in either vics – a V-shaped formation – of from four to seven aircraft; or in lines of five aircraft abreast; or in a diamond pattern. The Me 109s were usually in vics. One RAF pilot saw the enemy as attacking in little groups of nine, arranged in threes like a sergeant's stripes. Each group of nine was supported by nine Me 110 fighters with the single-seater Me 109s circling high above.

The enemy soon realised that the defences were awake and active. On ground radios, German pilots could be heard calling out to each other over their own wireless phones:

'Achtung! Schpitfeuer!'

With good cause, too, for our pilots opened fire at an average range of from 250 to 200 yards, closing sometimes to less than fifty yards. The length of a couple of cricket pitches in the sky. Many of the enemy fighters belonged to the readily-identifiable yellow-nose squadrons. British pilots always thought that they were supposed to be special, until others appeared with different-coloured noses – blue, red, white or even two colours together. Then they realized the Luftwaffe aircraft were just different squadron identification colours. Once the battle was joined, pilots lost formation utterly, and each one chose individual enemy aircraft.

It was as usual a fast-flying, fast-moving, ever-changing affair, demanding the utmost alertness – if survival were to be achieved. One particular pilot dived out of the sun on to an Me 109, which blew up after one burst. By this time, he found that another Me 109 was on his tail. He turned, got it in his sights, and set it on fire after several bursts this time. As he had become parted from his comrades, he started to return to base. Just as he was coming down, he received a message saying that the enemy were above. He looked up, saw a bevy of Dorniers at 14,000 feet, climbed, and attacked them. He got in a burst at one of them, which crashed into a wood and exploded amid all the afforestation. Just one incident among hundreds, all happening simultaneously.

While Spitfires and Hurricanes were very much in action over Kent, other Hurricanes were dealing with those of the enemy which had broken through to the London outskirts by sheer strength of numbers. An amazing fourteen squadrons of Hurricanes took up this challenge, almost at once reinforced by three more of Spitfires. All of them came into action between noon and twenty past twelve. Then followed an engagement extending all the way from London to the coast – and beyond. In it, the tactics so carefully conceived, so assiduously practised, helped to secure victory. A squadron leader described the morning fighting and the results achieved:

'The day dawned bright and clear at Croydon. It never seemed to do anything else during those exciting weeks of August and September. But to us it was just another day. We weren't interested in Hitler's entry into London; most of us were wondering whether we should have time to finish breakfast before the first blitz started. We were lucky.

'It wasn't till 9.30 that the sirens started wailing and the order came through to rendezvous base at 20,000 feet. As we were climbing in a southerly direction at 15,000 feet, we saw thirty Heinkels supported by fifty Me 109s 4,000 feet above them, and twenty Me 110s to the flank, approaching us from above. We turned and climbed, flying in the same direction as the bombers, with the whole squadron strung out in echelon to port up-sun, so that each man had a view of the enemy.

'A Flight timed their attack to perfection, coming down-sun in a power dive on the enemy's left flank. As each was selecting his own man, the Me 110 escort roared in to intercept with cannons blazing at 1,000 yards' range, but they were two seconds too late. Too late to engage our fighters, but just in time to make them hesitate long enough to miss the bomber leader. Two Heinkels keeled out of the formation.

'Meanwhile, the Me 110s had flashed out of sight, leaving the way clear for B Flight, as long as the Me 109s stayed above. B Flight leader knew how to bide his time, but just as he was about to launch his attack the Heinkels did the unbelievable thing. They turned south, into the sun, and into him.

'With his first burst the leader destroyed the leading bomber, which blew up with such force that it knocked a wing off the left-hand bomber. A little bank and a burst from his guns sent the right-hand Heinkel out of the formation with smoke pouring from both engines. Before returning home, he knocked down an Me 109. Four aircraft destroyed for an expenditure of 1,200 rounds was the best justification of our new tactics.'

This great battle at midday consisted of squadron attacks followed by those personal combats, all being forged and fought to some sort of conclusion. Squadrons flying in pairs, or wings of three units, or even a five-squadron wing, went into action against an enemy similarly disposed though perhaps not five squadrons together. After each first attack, delivered whenever possible out of the sun, the formations broke up, and individual combats ensued.

But there were exceptions: there were the dive attacks carried out by one squadron of Spitfires, which passed through a large enemy bomber force not once but twice, each time blasting off beam attacks as they did so. These tactics threw the Luftwaffe into extreme confusion. The bombers turned almost blindly it seemed, aircraft dropping in flames or in uncontrolled dives every few miles of the long return route. It was a fantastic scene. One of the enemy aircraft had its cowling and cabin-top blown off. Then it shed its crew. They all baled out except the rear-gunner, seen hanging from the lower escape hatch until the aircraft dived into a wood, ten miles east of Canterbury.

One pilot twice sped for an Me 109 which each time strove to escape in an almost vertical dive. The first of these from 20,000 feet proved successful, for the German pilot straightened out – but only to find that his opponent had followed him down and was still close on his heels. 'By that time,' said the RAF pilot, 'I was going faster than the enemy aircraft and I continued firing until I had to pull away to the right to avoid a collision.'

His burst of fire had taken effect, for the German never managed to rally, but plunged down until he encountered and entered cloud about 6,000 feet below. The British pilot then had to recover from the dive as his aircraft was going at nearly 480 mph. For 1940 that was certainly straining an aeroplane.

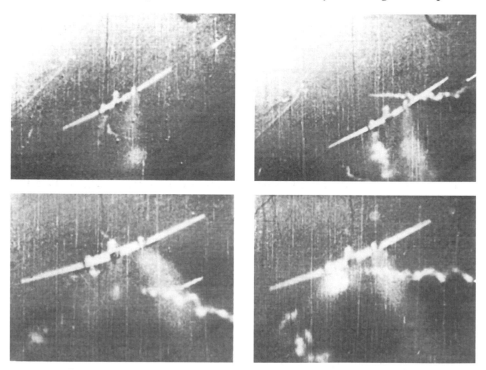

Sequence showing the destruction of an Me 110: the enemy tries to escape, tracer a trifle high, a hit on the port engine, further hits and it bursts into flame.

He reported,

'I then made my way through the cloud at a reasonable speed, and saw the wreckage of the enemy aircraft burning furiously. I climbed up through the cloud and narrowly missed colliding with a Junkers 88 which was on fire and being attacked by numerous Hurricanes.'

George Barclay was flying a Hurricane of 249 Squadron down from North Weald. The squadron went for Dorniers already dispersed and also disheartened. The view of the developing battle, as on all other days, could be seen either in long shot – embracing literally hundreds of aircraft- or in close-up through the windscreen and the eyes of a single fighter. Richard Hough and Denis Richards reported that George Barclay fired at one bomber 'and let the Dornier fly into the bullets like a partridge'. Number 609 Squadron of Spitfires from Middle Wallop and 504 Squadron of Hurricanes from Northolt were others trying to shield London at all costs. One bomber retreating home jettisoned the last of its load beside that famous stretch of straight railway line from Tonbridge to Ashford. The pond-craters are still visible from trains some seventy years later ...

A glimpse of another part of the battle at noon comes from Squadron Leader John Sample, leading his Hurricane at the foes:

'The bombers were coming in towards London from the south-east and at first we could not tell how many there were. We opened our throttles and started to climb up towards them, aiming for a point well ahead, where we expected to contact them at their own height. As we converged, I saw that there were about twenty of them, and it looked as though it was going to be a nice party, for the other squadrons of Hurricanes and Spitfires also turned to join in. By the time we reached a position near the bombers, we were over London – central London, I should say. We had gained a little height on them, too, so when I gave the order to attack we were able to dive on them from their right.

'Each of us selected his own target. Our first attack broke them up pretty nicely. The Dornier I attacked with a burst lasting several seconds began to turn to the left away from his friends. I gave him five seconds, and he went away with white smoke streaming behind him. As I broke away and started to make a steep climbing turn, I looked over the side. I recognised the river immediately below me through a hole in the clouds. I saw the bends and the bridges and idly wondered where I was. Then I saw Kennington Oval, and I thought to myself, "That is where they play cricket".

'I found myself soon below another Dornier which had white smoke coming from it. It was being attacked by two Hurricanes and a Spitfire and was travelling north and turning slightly to the right. As I could not see anything else to attack at that moment, I climbed above him and did a diving attack. Coming in to the attack, I noticed what appeared to be a red light shining in the rear-gunner's cockpit, but when I got closer I realized I was looking right through the gunner's cockpit into the pilot and observer's cockpit beyond. The red light was fire. I gave it a quick burst and as I passed him on the right I looked in through the big glass nose of the Dornier. It was like a furnace inside.

'He began to go down and we watched. In a few seconds, the tail came off, and the bomber did a forward somersault and then went into a spin. After he had done two turns in his spin, his wings broke off outboard of the engines, so that all that was left, as the blazing aircraft fell, was half a fuselage and the wing-roots with the engines on their ends. This dived straight down, just past the edge of a cloud, and then the cloud got in the way, and I could see no more of him.

'For me, the battle was over by then. I couldn't see anything else to shoot at, so I flew home. Our squadron's score was five certainties, including one by a sergeant pilot, and was a remarkable episode.'

A flight sergeant of 504 Squadron attacked three Dorniers. From the first, which he hit, he got a spray of enemy oil over his windscreen, practically blacking out his vision. Then he went for a second Dornier, which he set on fire. And the third time he went one better, for he suddenly saw a parachute flapping out of the aeroplane. Suddenly his Hurricane went out of control and into a spin, caused either by colliding with an enemy or for some other reason. All he knew was that the fighter was spinning at a terrifying speed into the clouds and he was trapped in his cockpit. Once through the clouds, he somehow struggled against all the various strains acting on his body, and flung himself into what seemed like a solid sheet of wind.

No sooner had he felt the parachute check his fall than he landed – bumping via a low roof into a neat Chelsea garden. The Dornier he had hit spun down only a mile or so away, crashing through a shop and on to the pavement at the very entrance to – Victoria Station. And some of its crew floated safely to earth across the Thames and right in the middle of Kennington Oval! But to no purpose, for the Germans never did play cricket ...

The enemy bomber, minus its tail, actually dived into a small tobacconist shop just outside the railway station. The newspapers printed a picture of it some 200 feet from the ground. Someone obviously must have taken the shot while watching its descent. And a subsequent photo depicted the shop in ruins and the grinning proprietor standing outside. In front of him on the pavement was a trestle table with some packets of cigarettes on it, together with a cardboard notice bearing the information 'Business as usual'. That same notice was scrawled many times across London. It was the sort of spirit which won the Battle of Britain.

By this stage of the struggle, it was becoming clear to the British pilots that the tide was turning. It was a feeling that was crystallizing daily. The enemy bomber crews were not pressing home their attacks. As soon as our pilots went into the fight, and sometimes even before, they were jettisoning their bombs, breaking formation and heading for home.

Twenty Dorniers were met over the London docks in a diamond pattern and escorted by Me 109s stepped up to 22,000 feet. A level quarter-attack broke up the bombers from their neat grouping, enabling intercepting fighters to pursue them towards the coast and shoot down many of them. One exploded in a peaceful field in south-east England, to the genuine surprise of a flock of sheep grazing there. The whole battle was a contrast between the skies and the ground.

In the confused combat, British squadrons sometimes found themselves outnumbering the enemy, an unusual and highly satisfactory state of affairs.

The collapse of No. 23 Queen Victoria Street, London.

When the mixed forces of Hurricanes and Spitfires ran into a smaller group of the enemy, they disposed of them with some ease.

But it was seldom that we had such an advantage in actual numbers. Yet the enemy seemed incapable of profiting from their numerical superiority. It was quality that was beginning to tell. A single Hurricane met twelve Me 109s flying straight at it. The pilot dived under them, but swooped upwards and shot down the rear aircraft from directly underneath. As he still had plenty of speed, the RAF pilot half-rolled off the top of his loop and followed the formation, which had not noticed the fate of their friend in the rear rank. The Hurricane destroyed a second aircraft from the rear, and damaged a third before the enemy awoke to what was happening. He was forced to break off, however, still being in the inferiority of nine to one.

The first phase of the great battle of 15 September was all over by 12.30 pm. By the time that people were ready to sit down to their Sunday lunch, the routed air armada was in full flight back to its bases. Mr Churchill had spent the morning in one of the operations rooms of 11 Group. It was noticed that for once his cigar remained unlit all the time, as he followed the bewilderingly swift shifts of the battle being depicted on the large table-map before them. For a fleeting moment, some of the enemy had succeeded in penetrating into the centre of the capital, but they dropped comparatively few bombs. The firing was too hot, the defence too strong. That was how 11 Group saw the battle. This was how it appeared to 12 Group. For once they were working in unison. Turning the clock back an hour or so, it was precisely 11.22 am when 242 Squadron were ordered off. The Wing comprised 242, 310, and 302 in that order, plus 19 and 611 Spitfires. The five squadrons formed up according to plan over Duxford and at once proceeded south towards the action. For once, too, they had been scrambled in time. They were speeding towards the Luftwaffe at height, at the very time the enemy were over the Channel. The Wing sped south to patrol a flexible area beyond the Thames in the Gravesend region. Bader made sure he had the sun behind them as 242, 310 and 302 reached Angels two five, with 19 and 611 stepped up behind them to an altitude varying between 26,000 and 27,000 feet. The Hurricanes had the task of harrying the bombers, while the Spitfires kept fighters at bay. So much for the theory. The practice was about to begin again.

Bader saw two squadrons passing right underneath them in formation flying north-west in purposeful manner. The enemy looked like Dornier 17s and Junkers 88s. AA bursts caused Bader to turn the Wing. He saw the enemy again now 3,000 feet below. He managed to perfect the approach with 19 and 611 Squadrons between the Hurricanes and the sun. The enemy were still below and down-sun. Next he noticed Me 109s diving out of the sun, so he warned the Spitfires to look out for these and also to watch for friendly fighters. The Me 109s broke away and climbed south-east.

Bader was about to attack the bombers which were turning left to west and south when he noticed Spitfires and Hurricanes of 11 Group presumably already engaging them. He was compelled to wait in case of a collision. Then he dived down with his leading section in formation on to the last section of three bombers.

'Leader calling – prepare to break – line-astern.'

As P/O N.N. Campbell took the left-hand Dornier 17, Bader went for the middle one, while Sub-U R.J. Cork took the right-hand one. Bader opened fire at 100 yards in a steep dive and saw a sudden large flash behind the starboard motor of the Dornier as its wing caught fire. The shots must have hit its petrol pipe or tank. Bader overshot and pulled up steeply. Then he carried on to attack another Dornier 17 but had to break away to avoid an oncoming Spitfire. The sky seemed full of both Spitfires and Hurricanes queueing up. They were metaphorically pushing and jostling each other out of the way to get at the Dorniers, which were for once really outnumbered.

Bader squirted at odd Dorniers from close range as they silhouetted into his sights, but he could not hold them there for long for fear of collision with the friendly fighters. Bader was flying as Red 1. He saw a collision between a Spitfire and a Dornier 17, which wrecked both aeroplanes instantaneously. He finally ran out of ammunition while chasing a crippled and smoking Dornier 17 into clouds. Bader realized even in the midst of the mêlée that for the first time the 12 Group Wing had position, height and numbers.

This is an extract from how Bader himself described those minutes around 12.15 somewhere over Hammersmith:

'At one time you could see planes all over the place, and the sky seemed full of parachutes. It was sudden death that morning, for our fighters shot them to blazes.

'One unfortunate German rear-gunner baled out of the Dornier 17 I attacked, but his parachute caught on the tail. There he was swinging helplessly, with the aircraft swooping and diving and staggering all over the sky, being pulled about by the man hanging by his parachute from the tail. That bomber went crashing into the Thames Estuary, with the swinging gunner still there.

'About the same time, one of my boys saw a similar thing in another Dornier, though this time the gunner who tried to bale out had his parachute caught in the hood before it opened. Our pilot saw the other two members of the crew crawl up and struggle to set him free. He was swinging from his packed parachute until they pushed him clear. Then they jumped off after him, and their plane went into the water with a terrific smack.

'I've always thought it was a pretty stout effort on the part of those two Huns who refused to leave their pal fastened to the doomed aircraft.'

But Bader was only the leader of fifty-six aircraft. What happened to the other fifty-five? We left Sub-Lt R.J. Cork nosing for the starboard Dornier 17 of the rear section. After the first sally, he dived to the right, climbed again, and saw the starboard engine of the bomber groaning and flaming. The Dornier did a steep diving turn to port and down. It was also being fired on by four other Hurricanes and a Spitfire, so Cork decided not to pursue. Instead he fired at another bomber. It was last seen steeply falling into the clouds and must have failed to recover. Cork contributed a completely unsolicited testimonial to the Wing Leader:

'The success of the whole attack was definitely due to the good positioning and perfect timing of the CO of 242 Squadron, who was leading the Wing formation.'

So even if Bader did not account for more than one definite Dornier plus others damaged, the final figures soon to emerge would be because of his shrewd skill in the air.

P/O N.N. Campbell was Bader's Red 3, and he attacked a Dornier 17 from astern and below. The lower gun of the bomber fired close to his Hurricane, but ceased soon after Campbell fired back. Smoke billowed and blew from the lower part of the enemy fuselage, so he could claim one Dornier damaged.

Successful as this engagement was proving, the element of risk remained present for the RAF just as for the Luftwaffe. Yellow 1, Flt Lt Ball, poured all his fire towards a Dornier 17 without noticeable result. But then he sustained a hit in his own fuel tank. The Hurricane caught fire quickly but Ball contrived to lose height while still in control and bring down the fighter in a field a few miles from Detling. Great presence of mind.

Yellow 2 was P/O N.K. Stansfield. During a stern attack on another Dornier 17 the rear-gunner fired at him steadily. But Stansfield silenced the enemy which dived for cloud protection with smoke streaming in ragged parallels from both engines. He followed it through the clouds to make sure of the outcome. The Dornier crashed directly on top of a house, but

Stansfield had no time to wonder about either the Germans or the occupants of the unlucky house.

Blue 1 was to have an adventurous day, only he did not know it yet. Flt Lt Powell-Sheddon made several stabs at Dornier 17s. While setting an engine on fire at one stage he nearly collided with a Hurricane, also after the same quarry. Three of the enemy aircrew baled out as the Dornier descended and crashed into a small wood near a house. The bomber exploded on impact and the whole tree area appeared enveloped in a sheet of flame. Powell-Sheddon landed at Duxford to find he had a bullet hole through his oil tank. But the afternoon was still to come…

Meanwhile, behind Blue 1 came P/O Tamblyn as Blue 2. He fired on a Dornier 17 at 150 yards and turned away till friendly fighters had completed their attacks. He remembered Bader's advice about watching for our own fighters. Next time at the Dornier, he noticed slight smoke from the enemy engines, which decreased a little. The damage had been inflicted in company with no fewer than five other friendly fighters. They followed the Dornier down to 2,000 feet when the crew baled out. The bomber crashed near West Malling in a field. Tamblyn thought that one of the crew failed to survive. Blue 3, P/O Latta, for once could make no definite claims, though he did engage the enemy more than once. That was the way things went. Sometimes it was skill, sometimes luck.

On to Green Section. Green 1, P/O P.S. Turner, chose a struggling Dornier to attack three times. The last close-range pressure hit home and burst the enemy's oil tanks. Three crew managed to get out before it began its final unpiloted plunge into the inevitable field, where it blew up. Turner thought there seemed to be an acceptance of their fate on the part of the Germans from the moment his Hurricane opened up. In different circumstances, he might have felt sorry for them.

Seeing that the enemy bombers were well engaged and on equal terms, P/O Hart at Green 3 veered to go for the next best thing – an Me 109. It was flying at 15,000 feet in the general direction of France. Hart proceeded to dive on him, forcing the enemy down to 11,000 feet. This put the Messerschmitt right on top of the cloud layer which had built up a little since early morning. Hart continued his gentle dive on the enemy till he was directly above it. Then he instigated a steep dive and opened fire. The bullets smashed the pilot's enclosure and the engine cowling. Flames spurted. Hart flew on after him and saw the Me 109 disturb the surface of the Channel some eight miles off the English coast.

All the 242 pilots managed to get back to Duxford except Ball, but at least they had not lost anyone. Would the other four squadrons fare so well? How many men would survive this day? These questions still remained to be resolved. They were always at the back of pilots' minds.

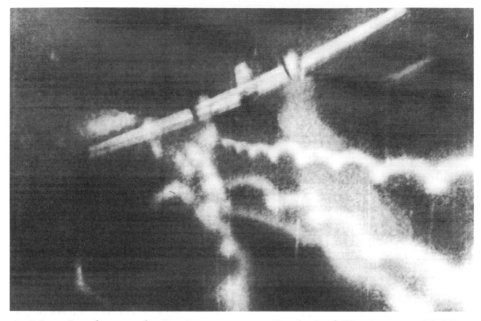

Aerial combat photograph taken by camera guns fitted to both Hurricanes and Spitfires shows concentrated fire into the port engine of an Me 110.

Flt Lt J. Jeffries was leading B Flight of 310 Squadron when they saw the enemy first. The Luftwaffe were west of London and flying north, but as the Wing turned south to attack, they also took a turn southwards. The B Flight dived on the enemy and Jeffries fastened his sights on one machine. He caused its port engine to catch fire, whereupon it was taken over by some other Hurricanes. That was a Dornier. Jeffries attacked another one and its occupants baled out almost at once. He did the same thing again and a second Dornier crew also deserted their bomber. A Spitfire then dived straight through the fuselage of this Dornier and the RAF fighter went down out of control. Losses as well as gains.

P/Sgt Kominek started an attack with Jeffries, but at 15,000 feet he lost sight of his leader. Probably because Jeffries was four miles above Kingston on Thames while Kominek had by then reached Tunbridge Wells! Kominek and three other Hurricanes fought a Dornier which made the clouds. The other Hurricanes went elsewhere but Kominek persevered with three more bursts. After the last one, some sheets started to fall off the bomber and smoke signals appeared. The crew just dumped their bombs over the Kent countryside and baled out not far behind their missiles. The Dornier ploughed into an already furrowed field some three miles south-west of Tunbridge Wells.

P/Sgt Kaucky shared a Dornier. He delivered his effort over London at 12.05–12.10 pm. Two other Hurricanes were also in this scrap. Kaucky used up all his ammunition and between the three fighters they saw the Dornier going groundwards – minus its crew. There would be a lot of Luftwaffe prisoners of war.

At about the same time and place, F/Sgt Hubacek had an exchange of fire with a Dornier. He made his run from the port and rear, and the enemy soon started to glide. Another Hurricane helped in the conflict. The enemy glide steepened to a dive as several more Hurricanes and Spitfires joined in to seal the agony of the stricken bomber. At 8,000 feet part of the Dornier's rudder broke off. Two men got out. One did not. The Dornier crashed somewhere south of London. As Bader said: 'It was sudden death this morning.'

Finally in 310 Squadron, Sgt Puda challenged a pair of Dorniers. He opened fire and the aim must have been impeccable, for the bomber fell with both engines streaming. Puda broke away to prepare for finishing it off. But just then a Spitfire did it for him from fifty yards.

The Poles followed the Czechs. P/O J. Chalupa of 302 Squadron saw the bombers through puffs of our anti-aircraft fire. He got in three bursts at the leader of the second vic in an enemy Dornier formation. The range was shortened dramatically from 250 to thirty yards. The bomber dived violently. Then Chalupa saw a second Dornier and attacked it from 100 yards. Smoke and flames from the port engine signified success. Two airmen jumped from the burning bomber. Meanwhile one of the other Polish pilots cut off the tail of this burning aircraft with his own wing – tearing it in the process.

The Poles were going in irrespective of survival. Flt Lt Chlopik went for the hindmost section of Dorniers. He hit one and saw its port engine smoking heavily, with blue wisps also emitting from the starboard. The Dornier dived on its back. The three crew jumped out in time and three parachutes brought them down safely.

Chlopik was over south-east London now. He hit a Dornier from behind and above. With its port engine faltering, the bomber became the focus for a whole group of Hurricanes and a couple of Spitfires. The sun was on his beam during his first fight and later behind him. Chlopik was flying at 14,000–17,000 feet over the southern suburbs of London.

The report ended with the poignant words:

'This pilot could not sign, as he was killed …'

The Poles knew what freedom meant – and the lack of it. They were willing to risk everything in their passionate nature to try to restore it to Europe. Bader did not forget Chlopik. Nor should we.

302 Squadron had height advantage as they flew their Hurricanes in at 300 mph. F/O Czerwinski met a Dornier above and in front of him. He went in alone with three bursts. The port engine sparked into fire and the bomber dived. Three other Hurricanes also attacked this one, so that by the time Czerwinski had gone in again the bomber was written off by the crew, who had jumped.

Flt Lt Jastrzebski flew down-sun, gave a Dornier some brief bursts, and paused to consider the situation. The Dornier did not return the fire, but wiggled sharply to left and then right. Another Hurricane went for it, too. The Pole turned 180 degrees to the right of the Dornier and did not see it again. But on climbing he was confronted by five parachutists. Owing to loss of position he landed at Henlow and refuelled before returning to Duxford. Again a case of lack of geographical knowledge.

F/O Kowalski fired at the last Dornier of a group. Two bursts and the bomber took to the clouds, but he was sure it must have crashed. Below the clouds he saw two more Dorniers already being set on effectively by Hurricanes. After a few seconds, both bombers plummeted.

F/O Palak was one of three Hurricanes sharing a Dornier. It crashed. Palak climbed again to notice a more formidable and perhaps worthier opponent – an Me 109. It was diving towards another Hurricane, so Palak turned towards him at full throttle, squirting twice. Bits spun off the Me 109 as it took the vertical dive. Palak could only claim a probable although the aspect of the enemy machine made it unlikely that any recovery would be possible. Palak landed at Maidstone at 12.35 pm. Quite a way from Duxford!

Sgt Paterek encountered Heinkel 111s flying in a formation of five close together at a measured speed of 270 mph. He made a beam attack. The enemy rear gunner ceased to reply. That left Paterek free to aim a long burst at very short range. He could scarcely miss and the bomber took the inexorable course downwards, out of any semblance of control. The altitude at the start of the dive was 5,000 feet. It never recovered and fell the remaining mile to earth. Paterek was not exactly familiar with England yet, and so he, too, landed at the likeliest looking aerodrome he could find. It turned out to be Wattisham (from where I flew in my first Lightning a quarter of a century later!).

Sqn Ldr W. Satchell was leading 302 Squadron. As Bader had headed for the most westerly of the three formations of bombers, Satchell took the middle group which were flying in vics. He attacked the left leader and saw him go down straight. In this attack, Satchell followed Bader's advice and dived from above the enemy almost vertically, giving a full deflection shot.

This strategy presents a fairly easy shot and does not give much of an aiming mark for any enemy gunners. But Satchell did in fact get scratches from a few stray bullets. His Hurricane got the marks, not himself. Then as he commenced to attack another Dornier, he was hit by an Me 109 but survived. Next he spotted a dozen Dorniers east of London flying east-south-east. Satchell made a beam and quarter attack from either side and saw one of them falling. It might have landed between Rochester and the coast.

Sgt Wedzik got on the tail of a Dornier 17. At the end of his burst, he observed the bomber in dire distress. Smoke from the port engine, flames from the port mainplane. The bomber banked steeply to the left. He did not see the end of it, as he returned over London trying to find his leader. But being unable to do so, he headed back to Duxford – and found it. Seventy minutes after take off.

Last in the Polish squadrons was Sgt Sindak. He paced a Dornier 17 at 240 mph before firing. The usual black smoke, this time from the cockpit and port mainplane. The enemy rear-gunner fired at him spiritedly. Sindak lost the machine-gun panel of his port mainplane, while the whole mainplane looked to be badly torn. The Dornier spun down, as a second Hurricane finished it off. A large piece flew off the underbelly of its fuselage. Number 302 Squadron had done well.

So to the two Spitfire squadrons ranged higher than the original 25,000 feet of the Hurricanes. Flt Lt Lawson led 19 Squadron as they spotted a score of Dornier 17s escorted by Me 109s. The enemy were 10,000 feet lower down. He hurried on ahead of the bombers and turned to deliver frontal fire. He dived past the left-hand Dornier of the rear vic. Then he turned and attacked the same aircraft from its rear – 300 down to fifty yards. Fragments fell off the starboard wing and the starboard engine started streaming glycol. The enemy waffled away from the rest and glided down with glycol still pouring. The result: one probable Dornier 17.

'Tally ho! Tally ho! Bandits ahead and below me.'

The air rang with such typical pilot jargon. The RAF might be mixing its vocabulary. The quarry was human.

Sqn Ldr Lane, Sub-Lt Blake and P/O Cunningham were flying in one section of Flight A. Cunningham attacked behind the other two but did not really get a chance to fire. Then veering off on a solo he fired at a solitary Me 110. Its starboard engine was hit and stuttered after this attack. Cunningham turned in from port to deliver another squirt from that side. The Me 110 was already as good as done for – when a pair of Hurricanes shot it from the sky. The three of them had shared this success at Angels 16.

F/Sgt Unwin took on an Me 109 with a yellow nose at 20,000 feet over Westerham. A six-second burst was enough and the pilot baled out. His machine came down between Redhill and Westerham – around the Surrey–Kent border country.

F/Sgt Steere too saw 109s bearing on them. He fired one burst from a good position, then chose an even better one. His first deflection fire from 350 yards soon diminished to a mere fifty yards. As near as safety allowed – if there were such a thing as safety. Thick bluish smoke swirled around the Me 109 as it spiralled into the clouds. Steere chased another 109, came into range, but only to find that he had no ammunition left – so no point in hanging about longer.

F/O Haines was south of London and near Biggin Hill when he too went for an Me 109. It half-rolled and dived to 12,000 feet but then straightened out again. Haines was flying faster than the 109 and had to pull away rapidly right to avoid a collision. Smoke seemed to be pouring from underneath the 109 pilot's seat.

Haines went down with it to 6,000 feet and had to be careful to recover from this drastic dive, as the enemy was by then touching 480 mph. Haines made his way more slowly through a bundle of low cloud and as he emerged he saw the wreckage of the – or a – Messerschmitt burning on the ground. It had been painted yellow from spinner to cockpit, so was certainly his. Haines climbed through clouds and narrowly missed hitting a Junkers 88. This bomber was actually on fire and being pounded by other Hurricanes.

The locale: Tunbridge Wells. The height: 15,000 feet. Sgt D.C. Cox had one or two abortive brushes before finding an Me 109 about to attack him head on. As the enemy passed over Cox, the Spitfire pilot turned and climbed steeply. He came up underneath the 109 with a couple of bursts, stalling as he did so. The Me 109 hit the earth five miles east of Crowborough.

Bader's strategy of five squadrons was working. The second Spitfire squadron was 611. Red 1 saw the bombers at about 18,000 feet with their screen of fighters at 28,000 feet. But Bader's perspicacity had put the Spitfires almost up to them. Red 1 was 5,000 feet above and to one side of the main Wing Hurricanes. They were flying north-west with the sun more or less on their left.

As the Wing went into attack, the 611 Spitfires kept company with 30 Me 109s, who were further west and slightly higher. They did not descend. After the Wing had broken up, the bombers turned round through 180 degrees to south-east. Red 1 waited for five to seven minutes before he told Bader he was coming down.

'Red 1: Echelon port.'

They were then going south-east, still up-sun of both the Wing and the enemy. They made a head-on ramrod thrust on to ten Dorniers. Red 1 took one head-on. Next an Me 110 turned over and went down in a death-throe. Red 2 behind him could not follow. Red 1 tried to pick up any enemy lame ducks along the coast but saw none.

Number 611 Squadron attacked in three sections of four Spitfires: Red, Yellow and Blue. Yellow 1 was around Angels 18 as he sped some ten miles west of Canterbury. He first tried a trio of Dorniers. Then he picked out a single one and fired all he had into this. Its port engine literally exploded. Red 2 saw the crew bale out. Other Spitfires seemed to be going for this same unfortunate Dornier but Yellow 1 got the credit and it crashed seven to ten miles south-east of Canterbury.

Yellow 2 was in the same area: a moving triangle that at the time of his main action was bounded by London/Rochester/Herne Bay. Rochester with its memories of Dickens and Great Expectations and the marshes. Another century. Another world.

'Bandits at Angels 18.'

Yellow 2 heard the phrase and acted on it. He dived on thirty Dorniers from about 4,000 feet above them. Next he chased one towards Rochester. The enemy's altitude began to dwindle as it neared the Herne Bay zone. Smoke from port engine. Crew baled out. The familiar story. The Dornier crashed on the edge of a wood or thicket four or five miles south of Herne Bay. Four attacks had to be completed before this final chalk-up. Yellow 2 was not exactly unscathed or fully fuelled. He landed at Detling owning up to being slightly lost. It was 1 pm. He was hungry.

Last of the morning's mammoth Wing action was Blue Section 611 Squadron. Blue 4 caught a Dornier by itself at 14,000 feet. Blue 4 rolled over and demonstrated an old astern attack by diving on to the bomber. One long burst and both enemy motors began to smoke. Blue 4 climbed and carried out the same drill again. By this time, though, the Dornier had both its engines obscured by smoke and fire. Flames tongued from both mainplanes behind the engines. The result: one more destroyed.

The Duxford Wing of fifty-six aircraft claimed twenty-six aircraft destroyed in a little over an hour, with eight probables and two damaged. It might have been exaggerated, but it was still a spectacular success. Despite the sound and fury of battle, the citizens of London had their lunch in peace. A lull fell over the skies and the ground for about an hour and a half … till two o'clock.

CHAPTER EIGHTEEN

The Decisive Day – Afternoon

15 September

Shortly after 2 pm, fresh enemy forces returned to the onslaught in about the same strength as in the morning. They flew from France in three main groups – with later and smaller ones heading for Southampton and Portland. The three-pronged assault crossed the Kent and Sussex coasts at 2.15 pm, 2.30 pm, and 2.40 pm. They comprised the usual Heinkels and Dorniers estimated at between 150 to 200. The fighter force of Me 109s and fewer 110s could well have been as numerous as 300 to 400. This made a total epic aggregate of 500 to 600 aircraft. These formations spread out over the south-east and south-west of Kent like so many flocks of migrating birds all following a lead.

With our early-warning system developed more efficiently than appreciated by the Germans, all three RAF Fighter Groups were scrambled. Eleven Group to meet the anticipated continuation of the desperate lunges against London; and 12 Group, about to be in full cry south from the Duxford starting line; and even 10 Group.

Before the enemy could get much further, 11 Group flew into them. Twenty-one squadrons were sent into the air and everyone of these eventually made contact with the mass intruders. Unlike some previous raids, however, when the Messerschmitts had abandoned their bombers in early stages through fuel shortage, this time they were still there, clustered above and around them like hens with their chicks. But this time numbers were nearer parity on the two sides, and the fighting edge of the RAF forces became clear. Although our fighters experienced a hard time getting through to the bombers, they managed it.

Our fighters tore at them. There is no other term. The sky was patterned with the criss-cross of condensation trails in the Sunday afternoon sky. Every now and then the blue was stained by the dark plume of a dying aeroplane, German or British. So determined was the defence that the enemy started to

Armourer rearms Spitfire for further action while the pilot has a word with the mechanic on serviceability.

crack. And their fighters could not hang on for long and had to turn for home. At the psychological second, each RAF pilot picked out an enemy and the sky was transformed once more into an aerial battlefield. There had never been anything like it in history before this day.

More fighter squadrons flew on to the developing drama, to add to the original ones airborne first: six from 11 Group, five from 12 Group, and a couple from 10 Group.

Throughout the vast volume of airspace from the Thames Estuary down to Dover, from London to the coastline, dogfights flared furiously. Squadrons swiftly scattered, so that two which took off from their base together were scrapping fifty miles apart in just quarter of an hour. There was nothing haphazard, hit-or-miss, about the plan. It was only feasible on such a scale because details had been honed down in the fighting of the previous weeks and months. As reports reached operations rooms of the German approach, the RAF had been able to send enough squadrons up to achieve, ensure, maximum results. But it had taken the past seventeen days for Fighter Command to ease round rather reluctantly towards the view that 11 Group could not win the Battle of Britain on its own. They needed all the help they could get from 12 Group, too.

Trying to relax prior to take-off.

Meanwhile, some squadrons of 11 Group were detailed to deal with the enemy screen of highflying fighters halfway between London and the coast. Those enemy fighters still with fuel for the fight, and the stomach for it. This left others free to attack the big bomber clusters and close escorts before they could reach the line of airfields east and south of London. Some seventy of the enemy eventually managed to pierce this elaborate defence system, only to be tackled and mauled by squadrons of Hurricanes who hurtled into the fray actually over London. They also chased any stragglers. Just as in the morning raids, some 200 individual combats were going on, each in their own little moving patch of sky, and although no two were quite alike, the general pattern remained similar. Sometimes the duels overlapped, too. Reports of typical pilots told the same story of impending victory – at least on this day!

'I engaged the enemy in formation, causing them to scatter in all directions.'
'We sighted a strong formation of enemy aircraft and carried out a head-on attack. The enemy scattered, jettisoned their bombs, and turned for home. We encountered heavy cannon fire.'

'The whole of the nose, including the pilot's cockpit, was shot away …

'I saw tracer flying past my left wing and saw an Me 109 attack me …

'I did not consider it worth while to waste any more ammunition upon it …'

'I then looked for more trouble and saw an He 111. I attacked and closed to about ten feet …'

'I gave him everything I had …'

'Aircraft became uncontrollable. I baled out, coming down with my left arm paralysed (afterwards learned dislocated) …'

Bob Stanford Tuck was one of the great air aces. He had had outstanding successes over Dunkirk and during the battle. Now he was leading an 11 Group Wing of three squadrons from Debden. In theory he should have had thirty-two aircraft with him, but as he closed on the bombers, his total fighter force amounted to only eight. The rest were still straggling below for various reasons. Needless to say, Stanford Tuck was in the thickest of the air fray on this crucial afternoon. He ended the war with an incredibly impressive twenty-nine victories to his credit.

Back to the heat of the afternoon four miles high. Although claims were inevitably exaggerated amid this heat of battle, many of the enemy's losses could hardly be contradicted. C.A.W. Bodie, for instance, was one pilot with

Grassy take-off – Spitfire at Duxford.

Bob Stanford Tuck: fighter ace par excellence.

four aircraft put down against his record. Bobby Oxspring of the same squadron claimed a Dornier. These two were typical of the myriad fighters of 11 Group up at that time. Then Oxspring suddenly saw the Duxford Wing bearing down on the scene ...

Hardly had the Wing landed earlier and refuelled when they were ordered up again – and again vindicating the strategy conceived by Leigh-Mallory and Bader. The take-off time was 2.12 pm. The clouds were eight-tenths at 5,000 feet. The Wing now consisted of forty-nine fighters instead of the fifty-six in the morning/midday combat. But the same five squadrons were involved. The same men. Bader led them up through a gap in the clouds and hurried south still climbing. The three Hurricane squadrons – 242, 310 and 302 were in line-astern with the pair of Spitfire squadrons on the right.

The Hurricane formations climbed slightly the quicker of the two types of fighter. Douglas and 242 were at 16,000 feet and still rising when they sighted quantities of enemy bombers punctuated by the dark clusters of anti-aircraft shells. The enemy were at 20,000 feet, still three or four thousand feet higher. This was just the sort of situation that tended to annoy Bader. Those precious extra minutes of warning to get airborne might have enabled them to gain the additional altitude, so that they could have been plus 4,000 feet instead of minus it. And it could mean literally – life or death. Perhaps the powers-that-be did not always remember this. It was The Few who flew.

Hurricane hurry: pilots of 601 Squadron run to their aircraft.

Bader endeavoured to climb and catch the enemy, but 242 were set on by Me 109s from above and behind. Bader told the Spitfires to come on and get the bombers, while he and his fellow Hurricane pilots broke up and engaged the enemy fighters. Bader was nothing if not decisive. Then things started to happen all over that particular patch of sky over the Kenley / Maidstone ground area.

After ordering the break-up, Bader himself pulled up and around quite violently. Coming off his back, he partially blacked out and actually almost collided with Yellow 2, P/O Denis Crowley-Milling. That could have been the end of a glorious friendship. Bader spun off Yellow 2's slipstream and straightened out at only 5,000 feet. He had not fired a shot yet.

However, he climbed back and got in a brief burst at a twin-engined bomber flying westwards. He was just in the enemy's range and fired a three-second squirt from a completely stalled position. He then had to spin off again and lost still more height. Eventually he went through the clouds near Ashford, Kent, to try and trace enemy stragglers but it was no use. Bader was furious at the whole situation. They were all too low. They had to seize whatever opportunities they could. He had to admit that his lead was not as effective as it could have been in better circumstances. They were up-sun, too low, and he had spun out of position.

He turned his mind once more to the inescapable truth: if they had managed to get off ten minutes earlier and reached their height, then the whole story could have been better. That was perfectionist thinking, of course, but had a distinct grain of truth and reason in it. The reality of the situation was rather different, at least in that the Wing did manage to do phenomenally well given their abysmal location.

Bader did not mind missing his personal victories on this occasion and was pleased later to hear how well things had gone after all. The faithful Sub-Lt Cork as Red 2 made height at the maximum speed – as per instructions. As soon as Bader had told them to break formation, Cork went sharply to the right, accompanied closely by an Me 109. He was now in a dive and found himself flying right through the second squadron, thereby losing his quarry. But he spotted a Dornier 17 to the starboard.

Cork dived 6,000 feet into the attack and concentrated a long squirt at its port engine, which started to smoke. His next thrust was a beam one, large lumps of the Dornier tracing crazy angles in the sky as they tumbled away with gravity. The starboard wing also flushed with fire near its tip. The Dornier dived gallantly for cloud-cover but Cork waited till it emerged. Then he simply put in a head-on assault and the Dornier died. Cork climbed one thousand feet and was stung by a vicious pair of yellow-nosed Me 109s from above. They flew rather like twin insects. He tilted steeply to the left and got on the tail of one, trying to reverse the situation. But in the midst of a promising burst of firing he ran out of ammunition. The other fighter-insect was then on his tail, so he put his stick into a virtually vertical dive down to 2,000 feet and got away unscathed. Red 3, Campbell, fired a couple of thousand rounds at divers enemy but could make no claim. 'You can't win them all,' he sighed.

Yellow Section got up to 21,000 feet: nearer the height that Bader would have preferred. P/O Stansfield saw a Heinkel flying below cloud and under attack from two other Hurricanes. He joined in and stopped the enemy's port motor. By then both the bomber's engines were in dire mechanical trouble. Other aircraft also fired on this unfortunate Heinkel, which eventually pancaked on to an aerodrome south-east of London. The aircraft carried a crew of five – quite a complement. On its tailplane were painted three pinkish stripes, presumably to imitate similar markings being painted on RAF aircraft and to confuse any potential attackers.

Denis Crowley-Milling, having survived the near-miss with Bader, picked out an Me 109. The enemy performed a veritable series of barrel rolls and aileron turns before he finally hit it. No amount of writhing seemed to make any difference. The machine caught fire around the cockpit and Crowley-Milling followed it down according to instructions. He saw it crash several miles south of Maidstone. While the midday battle had been above London, this afternoon's encounter moved south-east into central Kent. P/O Hart engaged the enemy but modestly refused to make any claims for success.

The time was around 3 pm now. Forty-eight minutes since the slick take-off. Blue 1 was Bader's friend Powell-Sheddon. He reported 200 enemy aircraft. One other pilot put it more succinctly:

'The whole bloody Luftwaffe!'

He was probably one of Bader's Canadians. Powell-Sheddon saw swarms of 109s mostly higher than 242 Squadron; swarms of fighters plus shoals of bombers. All approaching London. Two hundred plus. Me 109s flashed out of the sun and from behind. One came head-on and he fired at it. Then he saw some thirty bombers flying north-west for the capital. They were not being attacked by any of our fighters – from 11 or 12 Groups. Blue 1 broke away from the dogfight after them. Before he caught up with them, these bombers had turned round and were heading SSE.

Flt Lt Powell-Sheddon got between them and the sun – and 1,000 feet above. He picked off a Dornier 17 flying a few spans away from the rest and fired. Heavy smoke and fire followed his second and third go at it. All his efforts came from the sun. After the last one, he climbed back into position and saw the Dornier disappear into 7/10ths cloud in a tight spiral, with volumes of smoke as signals of impending impact with the ground. He reckoned the bomber was bound to crash somewhere near Rye on that Kent/Sussex border.

Powell-Sheddon set off for Duxford in a gradual dive for low cloud at low speed to economize on his dwindling fuel. The gauge was hovering perilously close to empty. Almost at once he was pounced on by an Me 109 which must have scored a hit on his Hurricane. The fighter became quite out of hand. Powell-Sheddon felt shaken up and baled out. He landed safely though his left arm felt temporarily paralysed. The reason was that he had dislocated it. He was soon in the little Rye Hospital, credited with one Dornier 17 destroyed. A typical sort of day.

The afternoon was turning into a slightly more golden tone. The time: 3.15 pm. P/O P.S. Turner in Blue 2 sent an Me 109 into a spin. He could not be sure that it crashed, but he believed the pilot was dead – hence the lack of attempt to correct the spin. He could not cogitate about it for long.

A gun shell exploded in the side of his Hurricane under its tail and hurled Turner into a spin. Or rather the fighter. He retained consciousness, however, and recovered control. He found he was below the clouds. The sorties went on. He was still airborne. It was still the Battle of Britain. These solitary dramas were being played out in hundreds of cockpits. He attacked a Dornier and its starboard engine smouldered. The Dornier took a gentle dive and hit the ground, exploding between some houses and a river bank east of Hornchurch. None of the crew got out of that one.

Stan Turner accounted for two enemy aircraft after his own fighter had been hit by a cannon shell: 15 September.

P/O Latta was another old chum of Bader. As Blue 3, he was under attack from Me 109s. Not the best prospect to face all alone. One of them overshot him, so that he was able to get in a burst at it from fifty yards or so dead astern. The enemy was still on fire as it entered cloud at 5,000 feet. Latta was over Maidstone at this phase and he could not really visualize any recovery for the damaged 109.

As usual now, 310 Squadron followed Bader and 242. Flt Lt Jeffries was leading them when they sighted the black-bomber blocks above and ahead. Then 310 was jumped on by Me 109s and the Wing as such broke up. Jeffries rose rapidly to 24,000 feet into the sun – as if by levitation. It was as planned. The enemy fighters turned west. Jeffries waited till they had done this manoeuvre to aim a head-on attack at them with the sun behind him. He started and dived straight through their first formation. They were east of London. He fired at one of the leading Me 109 sections, whose starboard engine caught alight. It broke away in anguish and went down.

Behind Jeffries came Sergeant Rechka. He and two other Hurricanes took a Heinkel so utterly by surprise that Rechka saw it crash-land on the beach near Foulness. Impassively he watched two of the crew get out safely. P/Sgt Jan

Kaucky was also in the vicinity at the equivalent time of 2.40–2.50–3.00 pm. He and two Spitfires from another squadron shot down a Dornier between them.

Sqn Ldr Hess and P/O Fejfar plus three other Hurricanes and a pair of Spitfires encountered a dozen Dornier 17s. One aircraft attacked by Fejfar had a stream of what looked like petrol colouring its wake. He went back for more Dorniers. As one of them flew hide and seek in and out of the clouds, the 310 Squadron pilot fired at him twice very effectively. Fejfar followed it down to see it make an emergency landing near the Isle of Grain in the Thames Estuary zone. He flew over it until he was quite sure that civilians had approached it and taken the crew prisoners. Then he nosed back to Duxford. The Czechs had done well once more.

But the day had yet to take its final toll of Allied airmen.

Seven of the Polish 302 Squadron were told to scramble at 2.10 pm and gain Angels 20 as soon as humanly possible. The instructions were to fly due south where enemy aircraft over a hundred strong were about to cross the coast at Dover.

'Will you patrol Canterbury?' the controller Woodhall had asked Bader. The rest was up to him. One thing was sure none of the Wing would be circling around Canterbury waiting for something to happen. It was his philosophy to make things happen.

302 Squadron were the rear of the trio of Hurricane formations. When the drones of Dorniers dotted into view, Me 109s were encircling them. Blue 1 veered to go for fifteen enemy aiming east. Just before getting into position, Blue 1 – Sqn Ldr Satchell – spied a 109 in his mirror, flying above him. He waited until the enemy dived to attack and then pulled up sharply, letting it pass below him. Satchell then got on its tail and pressed several long bursts. The 109 groaned on to its back with smoke issuing, gave up, and spun to the Kentish ground.

Seeing that Blue 1 was busy, Blue 2, P/O Pilch, dived for the bombers. He found that Red 1 had done the same thing. The enemy collection fanned out for cloud cover, so Blue 2 waited underneath until they emerged blinking. Then he took a Dornier 17. At the same second, a Spitfire spat at it, too. Blue 2 made a double-quick turn and attacked from its tail, getting in bursts down to almost zero feet from it. Smoke signalled hits and the downward direction signified the rest. From 6,000 feet the Dornier turned towards the Thames Estuary, losing height the worse it burned.

Just then, Blue 2 saw another Dornier taking a peep out of the clouds. He actually saw its rear-gunner take aim and fire briefly – but after Blue 2's response nothing more was seen or heard. Smoke had started from the Dornier's port engine but the usual end was interrupted by heavy AA fire bursting all around the Hurricane. He waited for it to stop and went in for the kill. This is what the battle was about – killing. The Dornier dived into shallow waters not far from Margate.

Blue 3, P/O Kaiwowski was preparing to attack about this same moment, but as he did so his port machine-gun panel became loose. It did not fly off completely, but caused very strong drag and prevented proper control of the machine: the Hurricane, that is. Blue 3 was uttering Polish oaths, but he had no choice but to dive away and find a field safe for landing. His left undercarriage wheel got in a rut and broke away, the fighter finally coming to rest with a broken undercarriage. The pilot was safe. Blue 4 also had the misfortune to be forced to break off his intended offensive owing to engine failure. He got back to Duxford all in one piece – pilot and aeroplane. He was F/O Czerwinski.

Red Section of 302 had a tragic time.

Flt Lt Chlopik was attacking Dorniers before Blue 2 arrived. He caused one to break up. Chlopik was compelled to bale out later during a particularly violent exchange with the Luftwaffe and for some reason unknown was not able to pull his parachute ripcord. He was killed.

P/O Lapka dived for a Dornier 17 from the beam. At this moment, his starboard machine-gun panel blew up, causing a heavy drag. Lapka was hit by firing from the Dornier 17 rear-gunner and smoke filled his cockpit. At an altitude of 15,000 feet, he dived away and things looked bad for him. But after a few frantic instants he baled out, pulled cord, and sailed to earth. His total damage personally was a minor foot injury.

F/O Kowalski swooped down on a lone Dornier 17. He did not open fire till he was within thirty yards. He could actually discern the small lettering on the Dornier's tail flank. The tailplane disintegrated and chunks of wing also careered from the bomber. It dived at about 45 degrees for the ground. What was its fate?

Kowalski then saw another Dornier ahead of him. He noticed its rear-gunner calmly firing tracer at him, but he shot this one down, too. When he finally landed and examined his fighter at Duxford, Kowalski found that his flap and undercarriage were not working properly and one of his wheels was punctured.

So to the Spitfires. Sqn Ldr Lane was leading 19 Squadron. Just as he sighted thirty Dorniers, he glimpsed higher up the fighter screen at about 30,000 feet. Three Me 109s dived on Lane and his men. Lane lunged to starboard and a loose dogfight ensued, with more 109s coming down as if sensing an advantage. Lane could not get near any of the immediate enemy, so climbed to take on a collection of 110s. No result, though, this time.

Suddenly his second sight became aware of a couple of Me 109s just above him. He manoeuvred round on the tail of one and fired. The 109 seemed a determined type and took positive and violent evasive action. While screeching for cloud cover, the 109 received a burst of five seconds from Lane. The enemy flicked over, inverted, and entered a cloud doing a shallow dive and inverted. It seemed to all intents beyond pilot control.

Flt Sgt Unwin saw the German bombers in vics of three, line-astern. Above, there seemed to Unwin to be 'thousands of Messerschmitt 109s'. He was somewhere over Kent at Angels 25+. He engaged one of them at close quarters and it half-rolled into the clouds. He followed keenly but during the descent amid the clouds his windscreen froze up at 6,000 feet and he lost it.

Clambering all the way back to 25,000 feet, Unwin saw another pair of 109s passing over his head. He chased and caught them up at Lydd. He shot down the first, which went into earth, beach, or water near this rather remote coastline – he could not say for sure where it fell. The second venture was equally devastating. The other 109 took a vertical thrust waterwards and ended up just off the Kent coast.

Flt Lt Clouston took both Blue and Green Sections into an assault on Dornier 17s. After setting the starboard engine of one afire, he watched while some ten feet of the bomber's wing snapped off. This was many miles distant from Kent, between Southend and Burnham on Crouch. One of the Germans tumbled out over a convoy fifteen miles east of Burnham. Clouston continued pressing home hundreds of bullets towards the depleted bomber until it rolled over and over to port. A definite destruction. As he had used all his ammunition, Clouston headed for the Essex coast. He reached this after flying for some nine minutes at 260 mph. So he reckoned he must have been about thirty miles out to sea.

Flt Sgt Steere followed Clouston towards the Dornier 17s and singled out one. Closing to fifty yards and firing all the time, he saw chunks and lumps flying off the bomber, whose port engine trailed fire. The crew baled out and then the bomber 'waffled' into the clouds. Three bombs had been jettisoned before the crew had abandoned aircraft – and in fact they dropped close to P/O Vokes who was bringing up the rear of this particular scrap of the whole jigsaw.

Vokes confirmed that the Germans had baled out of the stricken Dornier. He climbed back into the ring and was surprised by an Me 110 sneaking in from astern. Always remember to look in your mirror, Bader had said. Tracer fire flashed past the starboard wing of the Spitfire, one bullet hitting the main spar. Vokes climbed still more steeply and after two or three minutes of aerial ballet, he finished on the 110's tail. Vokes fired and the enemy's wing started streaming forth. The machine seemed out of control as it struck the clouds. What could be worse than being in an uncontrollable aeroplane diving vertically through blinding clouds? Equally awful for German or British alike.

F/O Haines had already claimed an Me 109 at midday. Now at 2.40 pm over the Thames Estuary he noted a quintet of 109s forming a defensive ring. One rolled off so Haines peeled off too. He took aim and closed to fifty yards. The Messerschmitt lasted only a few seconds. Sometimes the life expectancy.

Haines re-climbed to 25,000 feet and patrolled the coast near Beachy Head. He saw bombers being attacked by Hurricanes. He also saw numerous 110s, fired at one, and hit the starboard motor. Although he was on the receiving end of fire from other 110s, he followed the original one diving badly now. Bits were being hurled from it as it fell. Haines was the persistent type of pilot and followed it to the bitter end. The enemy managed to scrape through the air till it got to the French coast (near Deauville?), where it crashed on the beach. Haines did not hang about there, but scampered for home!

Flt Lt Lawson and P/O Cunningham were attacked by 109s. Then Sergeant Roden was hit and Cunningham broke off to try and help him. After a dogfight with a 109, Cunningham lost the main party but saw three other 109s. With a Hurricane for moral support he went for them. Cunningham chivvied one through the altitude belt of 16,000–14,000 feet. He saw the enemy reeling ablaze into clouds and claimed its destruction. He reckoned reasonably that it would have gone down somewhere towards the Dover area.

Red 1 Leading 611 Squadron of Spitfires ran into whole groups of bombers before gaining enough height. They ignored these tempting targets as they rose westwards to keep the 109s off the Wing. There were only eight Spitfires in 611 and they could not outclimb the Me 109s in time.

As twenty-five Dornier 17s seemed to be flying south unmolested, and the squadron had got away from the Wing anyway, Red 1 then ordered sections 'Echelon Right' and they dived. Red 1 took the rear Dornier. Smoke from port engine. Enemy on the descent. Smoky flame wake. It seemed all over for the Dornier. Then Red 1 blacked-out badly in the clouds but survived.

P/O Williams found a Heinkel 111. But he did not manage to hit it. In fact the enemy had the temerity to be firing back! Williams was then at 18,000 feet to the south of London when he saw a score of Dorniers flying west. They turned north and he went for one. He was only 100 yards astern as he observed one of its engines stopped. He did a slight right-hand gliding turn in the haze, then 2,000 feet thick. He could not see the enemy aircraft but did spot one airman dropping by parachute. The German landed safely on the edge of a wood near Hawkshurst Golf Club some five or six miles north of Hastings – near where another battle had been waged a mere 874 years earlier.

Flt Lt Heather followed Red 1 into the attack. He fired every single round of his ammunition at one Dornier, which bore all the evidence of numerous hits. Me 110s then swooped on Heather but he swerved clear in time. The claim was one Dornier destroyed. Heather took off from Duxford at 2.15 pm but landed at Croydon at 3.40 pm. Probably fuel shortage after eighty-five minutes' flying.

P/O Brown followed Red 1's punch at the Dornier which had put an engine out of action. But Brown had flown rather close to the scene of this episode and oil or glycol from the enemy aircraft spattered the intervening airspace and covered up his windscreen. He had to break off as the fluid oozed down the screen. But he was not finished with the fight. He caught a straggler and fired a deflection burst. The enemy spiralled. Brown noticed that the escape hatch above the pilot's seat was hanging and flapping open, due either to his firing or the crew escaping. He did not see anyone bale out, but this could have been because a swarm of 109s darkened a segment of sky and he decided it prudent to become scarce in the clouds. The aircraft he shot down was a Heinkel 111K.

P/O Lund took on twenty-five Dorniers. But especially one 'drop-out'. Flashes of fire. But three or four other Spitfires were also after this Dornier, so the damage caused could have been by them, he conceded. Lund climbed to 19,000 feet. He was deterred by the presence of six Me 110s – not good odds. One of these was coming at him anyway, so he fired a brief burst head-on and then turned. The 110 flashed by on Lund's port side. He saw a smoke trail from an engine and Lund's own starboard wing was punctured by at least one bullet hole.

The extent of the battle can be gauged by the towns quoted. Having fruitlessly attacked an Me 109 and a Dornier, Blue 3 found himself approaching Brooklands Aerodrome at 10,000 feet. Dorniers and Messerschmitts were winging above him – all after the aerodrome as a prime target. Blue 3 climbed with the sun behind him until he was 1,000 feet beneath them and 1,000 yards to the port and front. He opened fire and saw his stuff hitting the leading aircraft. The effect was that the leading vic of four broke away to port with white smoke in parallel lines from engines 1 and 2. Before the incident closed, Blue 3 glimpsed the banking of the old motor race track surrounding the aerodrome.

Flt Lt Sadler made two pokes at a Dornier over the London zone at 18,000 feet. A Hurricane also attacked the bomber from line-astern after Sadler had finished. Although Sadler did not see the Dornier go down, it was behaving in a very disabled manner, eventually fading below cloud at a mere 3,000 feet. Not a height from which to recover and return to the Continent. Sadler simply claimed it as sharing destruction. The time was 2.45-2.50 pm. The clash was nearly over.

During the afternoon, the Duxford Wing of forty-nine aircraft had claimed destruction of a further twenty-six enemy, with eight probables. But whereas the Wing had virtually no losses in the earlier sortie, the first signs showed Wing losses as follows: three RAF aircraft destroyed, two RAF aircraft damaged, two pilots killed or missing, three pilots wounded. That day, the Wing claimed a total of fifty-two enemy aircraft destroyed. Even allowing for the inevitable exaggeration, the results were good. Statistically, the figures for the first five Duxford Wing patrols were: enemy aircraft destroyed 105, RAF aircraft lost fourteen. Again, even scaled down, these successes justified the Wing.

But the battle was not yet done. It was 3 pm. Churchill was still in front of the map in the operations room of 11 Group. He asked Air Vice Marshal Keith Park:

'What other fighter reserves have we available?'

Enemy attacks were widespread – from southern England to Scotland.

Park replied:

'There are none.'
The stakes were immensely high; the margin incredibly narrow. Then minutes after Churchill's question and the memorable reply, the last main action ended. The long note of the 'all-clear' sounded, level and reassuring. Britain had risked all and won. By teatime on Sunday, 15 September 1940, the tide of the enemy offensive had been triumphantly turned.

While the Luftwaffe limped away, like a retreating aerial army, they left copious evidence of their losses spreadeagled over the landscape of Surrey, Sussex and Kent, like bodies on a battlefield. Which in many cases they were.

Then came the two later raids of the day on the west country. Thirty bombers reached the Portland Bill promontory, but achieved success limited partly by their lack of numbers. Then at 5.55 pm, came another assault by fighter-bombers on the hard-pressed Supermarine Spitfire factory at Woolston near Southampton. With 10 Group fighters still engaged or returning from the actions to their north-east, the local anti-aircraft batteries went to full stretch in a frantic bid to staunch the low-level attack from hitting home on the still-crucial works where much of the Spitfire production was based. Somehow they attained higher degrees of accuracy and intensity than ever, to such effect that the raiders failed to strike home even once. By the time the raid ended, the day had already been won elsewhere. The aircraft losses for the day told the overall story: German sixty, British twenty-six.

In the ten weeks of all-out aerial combat, the enemy had failed to achieve superiority. And Hitler knew this to be vital to launching his invasion, although the barges were still collected along the Channel ports. After 15 September, Hitler had to admit, if only to himself, that the Luftwaffe could never win such supremacy in the air. The enemy never came in force in daylight over London. The projected invasion had to be postponed. Our photographic reconnaissance aeroplanes had continually reported the build-up of the barges in the ports of northern France and Belgium. But after 15 September they observed that these were reluctantly being dispersed. This date is regarded as Battle of Britain day because the greatest number of enemy aircraft were shot down during its course.

Yet that was not really the end of the battle – nor even the end of this special day. Night raids followed on London and the Midlands and would drag on for many months. And on the night of 15 September the RAF offensive against those very invasion barges went on, too. Hampdens attacked them at Antwerp. The particular reason for this raid to be remembered was because of one man among many – John Hannah. He was only eighteen but he was about to win the Victoria Cross.

Sergeant John Hannah was both wireless operator and air-gunner in the Hampden, flown by a Canadian, Pilot Officer Connor. After bombing the port of Antwerp, they left the barges there burning, the flames reflected in the dark surrounding harbour. But then a holocaust hit the Hampden as intense anti-aircraft fire poured into the sky around their small formation of twin-engine bombers. Not all of them would get home. At the zenith of the opposition, one of the Hampdens went down to the Belgian waterline.

Then the next moment their own Hampden had a direct hit from a projectile of explosive and incendiary kind. It seemed to burst inside their bomb compartment, and at once started a fire which quickly enveloped the wireless operator's and rear-gunner's cockpits. A fire in an aircraft can be a terrible experience, and as if this were not enough, both the port and starboard petrol tanks were pierced by the explosion or shrapnel. It seemed certain that the fire must soon spread and engulf the whole bomber. Decisions would have to be taken very shortly.

Hannah forced and fought his way through to get two extinguishers, to try to cope with the fire. He found that the rear-gunner had already had to bale out. Hannah could have done, too, through the bottom escape-hatch or forward through the navigator's hatch. He did not. Instead he stayed and fought the fire for ten minutes that must have seemed like ten hours. He sprayed the flames with both extinguishers until they were empty, and then he beat the bare flames with his logbook.

Hannah had every justification for leaving the blazing bomber. The rear cockpit became an inferno. The whole of the bomb compartment was turned into a sort of blow-lamp – with the forced draught coming through the hole caused by the hit.

All the aluminium on the floor of Hannah's cockpit was melted away after those ten minutes, leaving only a grid formed by the cross-bearers. The draught blew the molten metal backward causing it to plate in great smears on the rear bulkhead. The electrical leads and all other inflammable equipment inside the cockpit were alight. Drums of ammunition were blown open, and rounds went off in all directions in this dangerously confined space. The outer layer of the sheet metal on the door and the bulkhead of the rear compartment had also melted. Almost blinded by the choking heat and fumes, Hannah had the astounding presence of mind to turn on his oxygen supply. This was the only way in which he could have carried on. Wearing his mask, he went on tackling the flames, literally licking all around him now.

Luckily the flying-suit he was wearing was to some extent fireproof, but when exposed to prolonged heat it had been known to burn. If that had happened, Hannah knew he would have been burnt to death in a very few moments. But by now he was in a desperate plight. His parachute became hopelessly burned as he struggled to control the conflagration. The cords of the parachute lay, charred and shrivelled, as he continued to combat the fire in the bomb bay. He realised that he had delayed too long if he wanted to escape by parachute.

But could the fire be controlled? Must they perish? Burned and blackened on his face, eyes and hands, he fought on with his pitiful little logbook, beating back the yellow heat. And all the time Connor continued to pilot the Hampden home towards Scampton. Would they ever see Lincolnshire again?

Somehow Hannah got the flames under control. Through his action he probably saved Connor's life. And he certainly saved the aircraft. Connor, in his turn, rose to the desperation of the occasion and flew the badly hit Hampden home to a bumpy landing on the airstrip at Scampton. The commanding officer of the Hampden bomber group said: 'I can only add that no one who has seen the condition of the aircraft can be otherwise than amazed at the extraordinary presence of mind and extreme courage which Sergeant Hannah displayed in remaining in it.' John Hannah received the Victoria Cross and Connor the Distinguished Flying Cross. So ended 15 September 1940.

CHAPTER NINETEEN

Invasion Postponed

16 September

The Royal Air Force had originally organized the boundaries of its Groups imagining that air attack would come from Germany, not occupied countries. In the event, the burden should have been shared by two groups, not one main and two ancillary groups. And did 11 Group's airfields have to be situated so vulnerably? What were they protecting? The more sheltered and distant they were, the better for air defence. But it was not yet time for rational retrospective thought. The battle was still in progress. And certainly the war as a whole was not yet won.

So the story must be told to its eventual end. Cloud and drizzle on 16 September resulted in minimal enemy day activity, restricted to East Anglia and south-east England – followed by night raids on the usual south-central-north targets of London, Midlands and Merseyside. The losses: German nine, British one.

17 September

Another similar day this one, with fighter sweeps, followed by night sorties to London and Merseyside. Not the Midlands. The day's score: German eight, British five. But perhaps the achievement of the day was that bombing raids on Dunkirk sank masses of invasion barges – a turnround from the great withdrawal in May-June – plus the unknown news that the invasion was put off *sine die* by Hitler.

18 September

Better weather meant more raids. Abundantly protected by fighters, Junkers 88s came across in an attempt to destroy the oil installations dotting the banks of the Thames and the adjoining terrain. Number 92 Squadron of Spitfires and other formations put down nine of the Junkers in record time. The Duxford Wing tore into other bombers, claiming a similar number

Aircrew at readiness. Soon they could be engaged in aerial draughts on a three-dimensional scale.

destroyed. Remembering that they represented every single pilot in every single squadron of Fighter Command, this was how the latter action went.

The Wing was despatched twice to patrol the North Weald airspace once at 9 am and then again at 12.50 pm. But at neither time did they glimpse the Germans. Then came the third take off at 4.16 p.m. The usual five squadrons started to patrol the zone from the centre of London to Thameshaven. Their height was 24,000 feet. At 20,000 feet the cloud reading was $^{10}/_{10}$ths, with a lower layer at 6,000 feet, $^{8}/_{10}$ths upper. The higher level was spreading from the south. This top layer was only about 100 feet thick, so Bader decided it was no good patrolling above it and chose instead immediately below at 19,000 to 20,000 feet.

Suddenly he saw AA bursts to the south-west, coming eerily through the clouds, so he proceeded north-west and found two enemy groups. There were about twenty to thirty in each and they seemed to be entirely unescorted. Flying along at 15,000–17,000 feet, the Germans were approaching the first bend of the Thames, west of the Estuary, near Gravesend. They were actually south of the river when Bader went for them.

Number 242 Squadron dived from east to west, turning north on to the enemy. Conditions seemed rather favourable to the Wing, with their targets set against the white cloud base. Never one to try and hide his few errors, Bader insisted he rather misjudged the lead-in, owing to a desire to get at them before they crossed the river. As a result, he had to resort to diving into the middle to break them up.

He fired in the dive. It was a quarter attack turning astern at the leading three enemy aircraft – Junkers 88s. His bullets scored on the left-hand one of the leading section, and as Bader arrived right in amongst them, this Junkers swung away in a leftish dive, its port engine hit. It zoomed down and out of the fight towards the north bank of the Estuary, somewhere west of Thameshaven. Sergeant Brimble as Yellow 3 confirmed the crash.

Bader's initial dive broke up the front of the formation and he found himself shortly afterwards among another hostile group. He gave a couple of quick squirts and then got out of this collection. He nearly collided with two of the enemy before extricating himself – and also nearly collided with at least one Hurricane. He spun off someone's slipstream and lost about 3,000 feet altitude in next to no time. Regaining control, he set for the south-east. Bader discovered a Dornier 17 rather detached, so he closed to shortest range and fired. The immediate result startled him. He got no return fire but the rear-gunner at once baled out and in so doing wrapped his parachute around the tailplane of the bomber. The Dornier started doing aerobatics in the shape of steep dives followed by zooms on to its back. It was losing height as Bader watched.

After the second or third performance like this, two members of the crew baled out from in front and the Dornier was left doing its aerobatics alone with the rear-gunner. Bader tried to kill him to put him out of his misery, but he was unsuccessful. The last Bader saw of this aircraft was in a vertical dive into cloud at 4,000-6,000 feet, where he decided to leave it. He thought that it crashed either into the Estuary or south of it, not far from Sheerness.

The faithful P/O Willie McKnight was Bader's Red 2. South-east of Hornchurch about the 17,000 feet line he scored a direct blow on a Dornier 17. The starboard engine blazed and the surest guide to the degree of damage was, as usual, that the crew baled out. McKnight plus a Spitfire found a Junkers 88 and left it without either engine running. The crew again baled out and McKnight actually saw the pilot land in a field a little north of the Thames. The bomber itself crashed north of the river.

P/O Campbell, Red 3, followed 1 and 2 on the German group. He overshot his target but then drew off to the left and sought a fresh one. A Junkers 88 had got left behind on the turn, so he positioned himself astern and to the left of this bomber. Campbell could hardly miss it. A short burst. Short range. The Junkers just fell out of the sky. Another Junkers 88. Another short-range burst. Both engines gave up.

By this time, the sky was spreadeagled with friend and foe. Some of the enemy were still grouped but well ahead of Campbell. At full throttle, he set out to overtake them. When he got in range he opened fire. He damaged a Junkers 88, but at this second he was caught in a nasty bout of crossfire from the enemy. One machine-gun bullet hit his port mainplane. As his position was not advantageous, he broke off. Later he saw a Spitfire cause wisps of smoke to gasp out of a Junkers' starboard engine. Red 3 went in and hit the other engine, so the Junkers fell with flames issuing from both.

Flt Lt Ball was Yellow 1. The time was then shortly before 5.15 pm and the general area ten miles south of London. Ball saw Junkers 88s in a box formation and also Dornier 17s. But no fighters. Ball followed Bader into a diving astern attack and only effected a very short burst though the idea of breaking up the enemy box seemed to have worked. Ball broke away, gained height, and turned into a favourable position as the altimeter rose. He saw a Ju 88 on its own and went for it from dead astern. He opened up and at 100 yards he was suddenly covered in oil. He was naturally alarmed but saw the starboard engine of the Junkers afire. At the time Ball thought he must have collected a bullet in his oil tank but on landing at Gravesend as quickly as he could, he discovered that the oil had come from the Junkers, as his own oil tank was quite undamaged. That is how near some of these combats were fought.

Yellow 2 engaged without much luck. Yellow 3, Sergeant Brimble, saw Bader's Ju 88 go down. Brimble found a Dornier 17 out of its rightful place in the box. He despatched it with four bursts and saw it go down to earth a little north of the Thames. Still in their own territory.

F/O Stan Turner was a favourite of Bader's. Turner must have muttered some curses as engine trouble forced him to turn back to Duxford before sighting the enemy at all. He was Blue 1. P/O Tamblyn at Blue 2 found himself right in the middle of the enemy formation he had attacked. He shot at a Dornier 17 before turning to get out of this slight predicament. He did not notice any outcome of the firing, but Willie McKnight did. One Dornier shot down by a pilot who did not know he had done so.

P/O Hart at Blue 3 opened at a Ju 88 and could clearly see the bits cascading off the pilot's enclosure. Hart pulled up for another attack. As he flew in, he saw smoke from the enclosure. He gave another short burst, causing the enclosure to catch alight. The bomber dived down with all its crew. Hart followed it down until the crash came north of the Thames some fifty yards from a railway line.

Then Hart turned south to see another Junkers also southbound at only 5,000 feet. Very low. He saw that the enemy port engine was already dead, though otherwise it was all right. Hart stole up underneath it in a vertical climb, firing about thirty yards in front and hitting the wings and fuselage. The other motor gave out. The Junkers rolled over and crashed down the mile to earth.

Green Leader, Sub-Lt Gardner, was already a veteran. He found a few stragglers and made a good quarter attack on one. Port wing and motor flame, this Dornier 17 dived to its doom somewhere in the Thames Estuary – graveyard of so many bombers.

Turning in pursuit of six or eight bombers heading back for France, Gardner caught them up. One was flying 100 yards behind the rest, so he fired at its port engine. The propeller slowed to a halt. He pulled away and went for the other side. Its second engine also gave the fatal smoke signal. The Dornier glided down from about 10,000 feet over Canvey Island. Bader confirmed the destruction of Gardner's first Dornier, and thought the other one probably went down, too. The claim: a probable.

P/O Bush at Green 2 followed Gardner on the rear of twelve bombers. He got in a shot at one of them. But he did not see any more, as he was set on by a Spitfire! The Spit did not actually fire at the Hurricane but would not get off his tail. A slight case of mistaken identity – very easy in the stratified emotions several miles over the Home Counties with cloud and evening both coming up fast. P/O Denis Crowley-Milling, at Green 3, for once could not claim anything.

Flt Lt Jeffries was leading the Czechs. Number 310 Squadron saw fifteen Dorniers over London at about 19,000 feet. He drew level with them but they turned towards him, so he had to break away to avoid passing too close.

Hurricane of 85 Squadron towards the end of the Battle.

Jeffries hit both engines of a Dornier which went down. Sergeant Kominek behind him saw it crash. The leader then followed the bombers out along the south bank of the Thames, his machine guns barking at them all the way. Fierce AA fire forced him to stop at one stage. As the enemy passed over the Kent coast, the Dornier which Jeffries had been firing at seemed to have engine trouble and may not have reached France.

P/O Zimprich also went after a Dornier. He hit it and heavy smoke obscured much of the machine. Zimprich was already well out over the sea, near North Foreland. The Dornier glided seawards and Zimprich fervently wanted to finish it off. But his ammunition was expended so he never saw it in contact with the sea. Claim: one probable.

P/O Janouch was leading Red Section. They were south of London at the 20,000 feet mark. Janouch went in with two other Hurricanes. Two attacks on a Dornier and he saw the whole crew bale out. No doubt about that one. A Dornier could not be expected to find its own way back to base without any guidance. P/O Fejfar shared the early attacks with Janouch. As another bomber started a display of aerobatics, the reason became clear. Again the crew had left it. There was a strange visual sense about an aeroplane with no human beings aboard. Uncanny.

P/Sgt Jirovdek at Red 3 hit both engines of a Dornier, which was obviously in direst distress. Two other Hurricanes hit it as well and P/Sgt Puda saw it 'burn down' on the ground until there seemed nothing left of it at all. The two Czechs claimed a share of the bomber. Puda saw at least one of the crew bale out. The Dornier had dived and crashed not far from Stanford-le-Hope.

P/O Fechtner fired a burst at a Dornier from 800 yards! No luck! But he later hit it. Both engines ended on fire, but before the final moments the enemy gunner fired at his Hurricane and actually made a hole in a blade of his airscrew. Fechtner later found he had four bullet holes in his aircraft, the one in the propeller plus three in the elevator. But he was unhurt.

P/O Bergman aimed for the whole of the Dorniers, then took one especially. The usual story. The usual end. One engine. Both engines. One bomber destroyed. F/Sgt Prchal forced yet another Dornier to spin down and drill into the ground. Minus its crew.

There was still time for some courtesy, even amid this battle. An enemy pilot baled out. A Czech pilot reported afterwards:

'It is a matter of regret that his parachute did not open …'

The Poles, too, had a field day that afternoon. Ordered to scramble at 4.50 pm, the instruction was 'Patrol Hornchurch Angels Twenty'. Number

302 was the third of the Hurricanes squadrons, with the Spitfires on flank above. Thirty-plus bombers were in vics of five. Red 1, Sqn Ldr Satchell, closed to eighty yards. His target bomber was then enveloped by a mixture of smoke and flame and was never seen again. Before breaking away, Red 1 had his Perspex covered with oil from the burning aircraft, showing just how near he was. Then Red 1 saw two enemy crash, one in the sea off Sheerness, the other on the peninsula between the Medway and the Thames.

Red 2, Wg Cdr Mumler, chose a different bomber on the port side. He fired but then had to break away to make room for another aircraft attacking. As he did so, he saw flames from the turret of the enemy rear-gunner. Red 3, F/O0 Kowalski, went for one Dornier, then another. At his last burst, he saw a parachute open from the rear-gunner's turret. It became entangled in the mainplane. Bits of the aircraft flew off this mainplane, causing Red 3 to break off the combat temporarily. He never saw what happened to the unfortunate rear-gunner. That seemed to be an increasing hazard for German aircrew.

Yellow Section went in behind Red. Flt Lt Farmer at Yellow 1 chased a Dornier and then a Ju 88. Pieces peeled off the Junkers before it vanished into a convenient cloud, by which time Farmer had used all his ammo. Yellow 2, Flt Lt Laguna, had trouble in that he could not focus his sights properly and rather than risk hitting a Hurricane, he could do little but fly along for the ride. Sergeant Wedzik, at Yellow 3, chased a Ju 88 out to sea, forcing it down to a dangerous altitude of only 1,000 feet. He and another Hurricane pilot attacked alternately, with pieces flaking off it regularly. But no certain success.

P/O Pilch was leading Green Section, which caused a good break-up of an enemy group. Green 1 went right for the middle – Bader-like – and saw metal careering about the sky. Next he found a Ju 88 whose rear-gunner fired at him the whole time he was making five attacks on it. By the fourth attempt, the port engine was out of action. At the fifth, the bomber fired a red light, clearly a signal of some sort. One man at least out of it.

Sergeant Peterek was Green 2. He also had a Junkers 88 as target from 100 yards. With one engine afire, the Junkers was attacked again. The crew of three called it a day and jumped – their parachutes all opening at once. But as they did so, a few fragments of the Junkers flew off and hit Green 2's propeller. The Hurricane fluttered violently. Something hit the radiator – and the reserve petrol tank broke – spattering Peterek with petrol. Green 2 wisely switched off his engine at once and glided southwards. He saw the enemy crash and then made a forced-landing himself, sustaining no further damage. Green 3 was P/O Karwowski. He destroyed a bomber with great accompanying violence. The number of parachutes emerging from it: one.

Blue Section now. Flt Lt Riley as Blue 1 put paid to two Ju 88s. Flt Lt Jastrzebski had shots at several enemy. Then he noticed seven bombers hurrying in formation across the Channel for France. They had already lost the other five or so of their formation.

P/O Wapniarek at Blue 3 was going for a Ju 88 a second time when he saw the rear-gunner jump out near Southend-on-Sea. The Polish pilot wondered momentarily what would happen to the man. He caught another Junkers about to be dimmed by cloud. The bomber fired at him from two or three guns, using tracer bullets. Blue 3 was not deterred and used all the rest of his own ammunition on it. He saw it break up utterly on striking the sea. Blue 3 flew for eight minutes over the water before reaching the home coast again. By then he was virtually out of fuel, as well as ammunition, so had to make a rapid landing at the nearest possible place, which turned out to be Rochford, Essex.

As there was cloud-cover at 20,000 feet, the Spitfire squadrons – 19 and 611 – started their patrol above it. No enemy were met but the AA fire burst through the cloud with exciting if alarming effect. So 19 Squadron followed the Hurricanes below the cloud, where they encountered the enemy. Number 611 Squadron remained on patrol overhead. By the time that 19 Squadron commenced to attack, there seemed to be only one of the original two enemy groups left. A score of bombers and some scattered Me 110s. The bombers were mainly Ju 88s and Heinkel 111s.

Flt Lt Clouston fired almost all his ammunition at a single Ju 88 with devastating effect. The crew leapt out even more urgently than usual and the bomber crashed behind some houses to the west of Deal, on the Kent coast. The indefatigable Flt Sgt Steere closed with a Heinkel 111, hit it, and watched while it struck the waters at the mouth of the Thames. Steere then finished off a Ju 88 already on the dive from a Green 1 burst. Flt Sgt Unwin set an Me 110 on fire; the pilot got out; the aeroplane came down near Eastchurch – that much-bombed airfield.

F/O Haines met a pair of 109s and observed firing coming laterally from one of them. It seemed to be from a fixed gun below and behind the pilot's seat. Undeterred, he closed to fifty yards and sent the 109 diving vertically.

P/O Dolezal was next to Haines. He took on a Heinkel. Jet black smoke. Spinning aircraft. The pilot saw the Heinkel spin right down into the sea. The Spitfire next to Dolezal picked up another Heinkel. By the end of his third round of bursts, the crew saw no reason to stay longer. They escaped. The Heinkel hit ground near Gillingham, Kent.

Flt Lt Lawson led the last section on nine Ju 88s, which turned desperately south-east. He fired at the rear one and looked set for a success when he got a bad glycol leak and had to land at Eastchurch. Lawson was Red 1. Red 2 aimed at the same Junkers. Red 3 joined in until it was finally seen to crash at Sandwich, near the famous golf course. They all shared the credit for this one with P/O Cunningham and Sergeant Lloyd.

The next time the Duxford Wing were actually in action was 27 September, although they went up several times before then. Meanwhile, they had scored remarkable success on 18 September, with scarcely a scratch on their own fighters. The claims of course had to be modified later and the day's figures went down as German nineteen, British twelve, including 11 Group sorties.

Neither London nor Merseyside were spared night raids. These were now worse than the air battles themselves. Casualties came to frightening figures. High explosive, incendiaries, chandelier flares, and shrapnel from our strengthened anti-aircraft fire, all combined to make London and Liverpool highly dangerous places for the population of these tight-packed conurbations. In danger, too, were the half-forgotten emergency services such as air-raid wardens, ambulance and hospital staff, firemen and all the rest.

19 September
Overcast conditions cut enemy day sorties, but the London and Liverpool raids were kept up. For the first time since 4 August, the scoreline for aircraft losses read German 0, British 0. In fact, these dates were two of only three in the entire battle when neither side lost an aircraft.

20 September
London formed the focus of attention, both by day and night. Luftwaffe fighter sweeps were stepped up and in the opposition put up by 11 Group, Spitfires came off not worse but with about comparable losses. Number 222 Squadron from Hornchurch had three shot down, and 40 Squadron from Rochford lost the Spitfire belonging to George Bennions, but not the pilot. He was one of The Few with a charmed life, having already been faced with forced-landings three separate times in the recent past. Aircraft losses: German seven, British seven.

21–23 September
The next day, 21 September, was the third one of the battle when neither air force lost any aeroplanes, despite some typical sweeps in the Manston and other regions. Then on 22 September, during a foggy day, the enemy lost one without British loss. Clearer weather returned on 23 September, when the rare and unwelcome losses had to be admitted of German nine, British eleven. The enemy were still sweeping north-west from Kent crossing-points, but all the time the invasion threat was receding. By now the British

forces had been stood down from No. 1 to No. 2 state of readiness. Reflecting a conclusion that an attack was possible though improbable.

24 September

Now it was more a case of random raids, isolated tragedies. On 24 September such an event occurred in one of the two raids by enemy fighter-bombers – on Tilbury and Southampton. The latter was on the Supermarine Spitfire factory at Woolston, near the port. The tragedy here: one bomb by chance scored a direct hit on a shelter where up to 150 staff hoped to be safe. Nearly two-thirds of them were killed and the rest injured. By comparison with such poignant figures, the aircraft losses seemed less relevant than usual, German eleven, British four.

25 September

Unbroken fine weather enabled the enemy to keep up this sort of raid. The bombers used had the supported resources of large fighter formations. Portland, Plymouth, Bristol were three goals – all in 10 Group territory. The sector at Middle Wallop sent up interceptors, but by switching direction late in the flight over the west country, the force of sixty enemy bombers attacked the Filton factory, near Bristol. Like the losses the day before at Woolston, the

Pilots' rest room of a Spitfire squadron.

raid killed eighty-two and injured 170. The factory and its rail links were both badly hit, though the high-level bombers did lose five afterwards.

26 September

The aircraft production industry was sustaining a shattering few days. On 26 September the Germans went for the Spitfire factory again at Woolston. For some reason they were able to get through to Southampton Water without much trouble and to score gutting strikes on workshops. Fortunately, much Spitfire output had been dispersed from this vulnerable Hampshire environment. Unfortunately, the fatalities of the raid amounted to more than thirty workers there. The day's aircraft losses were equal: German nine, British nine.

27 September

The final four days of September confirmed the growing superiority of Fighter Command. On 27 September came massive day thrusts on London and Bristol, challenging both 11 and 10 Groups. The fighters supposed to be shepherding the Ju 88s were just as savagely treated as the bombers themselves, with the eventual day's losses of German fifty-five, British twenty-eight.

Contributing to these figures were 12 Group.

The day marked the final large-scale Duxford Wing battle. They went up three times. At 9 am they did not meet the enemy. But at 11.42 am they were ordered off from Duxford to patrol the London area. On this sortie, the Wing comprised four squadrons: 242 and 310 of Hurricanes and 19 and 616 of Spitfires.

Bader heard over R/T:

'Bandits south-east of Estuary ...'

When he could not find them, the Duxford controller told him to return. Bader said:

'I'll just have one more swing round.'

Turning the Wing southwards and flying at 23,000 feet, he eventually sighted enemy aircraft apparently circling around the Dover/Canterbury/Dungeness triangle at 18,000–20,000 feet. They were Me 109s just milling about – a strange sight indeed. Visibility was good with a cloud layer higher at 25,000 feet. The sun lay behind the Wing, so Bader decided to dive into the attack. No formation or organised onslaught was either possible or desirable, so having manoeuvred himself into his up-sun position, he ordered the Wing to break up and attack as they liked. Bader chose a 109 which was passing underneath him. He turned behind and above the enemy, and got in a two-second strike with the instant result that the Messerschmitt dissolved into thick white smoke, turned over slowly, and took a vertical dive. Others of 242 confirmed this success.

A second 109 flew in front and below him, so Bader turned in behind. After a typical Bader burst, the 109 took evasive action by rolling on to its back and diving. Bader did the same but pulled out short and cut it off on the climb. The Hurricane had a long chase, finally getting in a long-distance squirt from 400 yards. A puff of white smoke slowed the 109 perceptibly. More bursts from the keen eye of Red 1. One missed completely but others hit. The last squirt produced black smoke from the port side of the fuselage: and Bader's Hurricane had its windscreen covered with oil from the 109. German oil. The enemy propeller stopped dead. The last seen of the 109 was as it glided down under control but with engine dead at a shallow angle into the Channel.

As Bader was on the edge of the coast and out of ammunition after all those squirts (his favourite word), he decided that discretion was required. He dived to ground level into the haze, went back to Gravesend and landed. This last combat finished somewhere off the coast between Dover and Ramsgate. Symbolic that Bader should be protecting his country actually over the white cliffs of Dover. Bader rearmed, refuelled, and had lunch with 66 Squadron.

But back in the air much was still happening or already had happened.

His Red 2 was P/O Stansfield, who chased an Me 109 across Dover and then lost sight of it. A Ju 88 crossed his sights so Red 2 fired from 200 yards. The enemy plodded on, smoking and turning now, flying parallel to the Kent coast eastwards. At about fifty feet from the bomber, Red 2 ran out of ammo. He did not see the Junkers crash, due to bad weather, but he felt convinced that it could not get home. Red 3 was Sergeant Lonsdale, who made no definite claims.

By Bader's standards, this was turning out to be rather an unpredictable patrol, although the results were coming in. This was because, in a complete 'shambles' with everyone manoeuvring in a confined air space and the enemy on the run, the chances of scoring were less than when a bomber group was being attacked further inland.

Flt Lt Ball got Bader's original 'Break up and attack' message along with the rest of them. He was Yellow 1. It was noon, roughly. Ball seemed to have chosen an experienced adversary, but eventually he got on the 109's tail and opened fire from 200 yards. But he had difficulty in closing due to their

On the way up – Spitfires of 19 Squadron.

relative speeds being virtually the same. He hit the cockpit of the 109. But Ball realised that he, too, had been hit – in the tank. He was in trouble. He tried to reach an aerodrome but the engine of his Hurricane started to catch fire. A few quick mental calculations and he knew he had to get down somehow – in seconds. He force-landed with the wheels still up in a field somewhere between Deal and Manston. In this case, a happy landing.

F/O Stan Turner was Blue Leader. Behind him at Blue 2 came P/O Bush. He found he was not in the right position to fire during that initial dive on the Me 109s. Climbing to gain precious height, he saw half a dozen of them about 3,000 feet above him. Not a nice sight. While Bush was still climbing to try for the rear one, their leader did a quick turn and dived on Bush.

The Hurricane pilot put his fighter into a spin and dived, only to find a 109 still after him. So he managed to conjure a quick turn and reverse their relative situations. He fired at the 109 and saw it plunge into the sea somewhere in the stretch between Dover and Gravesend. Blue 3 was P/O Hart. It was a rare occasion when one of Bader's best men did not happen to get near enough to connect with the enemy.

Green Section was the last one of 242 Squadron. P/O Tamblyn at Green 1 put his dogfight locale at 'Dover to mid-Channel'. As Tamblyn picked one, it throttled back and made for the sea. He found it hard to stay with the

Messerschmitt. The enemy evasive tactics consisted of skidding turns, porpoising, and violent climbing turns to 500 feet. The fight had descended all the way down from 12,000 feet to 100 feet! This called for some desperate precision flying. Tamblyn could see his shots hitting the 109 and eventually petrol or glycol was issuing out of the fighter. Tamblyn overshot on his last burst, so could not finally claim to have destroyed the enemy. He had forty rounds left in one gun but a stoppage prevented him firing them. Visibility was down to a mile or even less and so, reluctantly, he turned for home.

F/O M.G. Horner at Green 2 was missing …

P/O Latta at Green 3 was 21,000 feet up when he caught a 109 at 18,000 feet. As Latta got within range, however, the German levelled off and received a burst from astern. A direct hit on the petrol tank. The 109 crashed five to ten miles inland from Dover. That was the first of two 109s which Latta could claim on this sortie.

He spotted several making for the French coast in some disarray. Still having a height advantage, Latta was able to overtake one of them and close to fifty yards. Latta's aim appeared deadly, for once again the petrol tank sparked a general fire. The enemy maintained a fairly steep dive from 10,000 feet straight into the sea five miles or more off Dover. Although he did not know it then, Latta's Hurricane had sustained some damage both to its tail and one wing. Like Bader, he landed at Gravesend. The time: 1.15 pm.

Number 310 Squadron of Hurricanes destroyed one Me 109. So did 616 Squadron of Spitfires.

Number 19 Squadron had greater opportunities and took them. Flt Lt Lawson at Red 1 led an attack on a large group of 109s. He saw his tracer striking home on one of them. The enemy struggled to make headway for France but smoke started to be seen as it fell to an altitude of 3,000 feet. It dived into the sea about ten miles short of Cap Griz Nez. Lawson was close behind it all the way and only when he was satisfied it had crashed did he turn through 180 degrees and hurry for home.

Sergeant Blake at Red 2 also fired at a 109 as it turned across his bows. Eventually the machine hit the sea. Blake saw some other 109s speeding for home almost at sea level. He went on to attack one of these actually parallel to the surface of the sea. And in the confusion, the enemy pilot flew into it. Red 3 was P/O Bradil. He claimed damaging an Me 109 but not destroying it.

A pair of 109s were going for Yellow Section from above. Flt/Sgt Unwin at Yellow 1 gave one burst after burst. It writhed about trying to escape for ten minutes or more. At length, it stalled, seemed to hang in the air, and then spun into the sea. A worthy opponent.

At Yellow 2, Sergeant Jennings flew in fearlessly at the leader of a quintet of 109s. He hit one but could not follow it down further as he was set on by the other four Messerschmitts.

Sergeant Cox had a crash and was wounded. He was rushed to hospital.

Green 1 led an assault on eight 109s. Flt/Sgt Steere fired from 300 yards. Green 2, F/O Parrot, was about to follow Green 1 into the convergence on the same aircraft when it burst into flames, so perhaps Steere should have had credit for it. Green 2 got another 109 which went down, again near the golf course at Sandwich. Having lost the rest of his squadron, Parrot joined 616 Squadron for a head-on charge at other 109s. Green 3, Sergeant Plzak, fired at a 109 and followed it from 10,000 feet downwards. From Folkestone he saw it dive: the end of yet another 109.

Sqn Ldr Lane flew above the main formation and witnessed the small upper group of 109s preparing to attack. He went for two of them and pulled back his stick for a second go. His Spitfire failed to respond and he was unable to pull out of the dive until he came down as low as 3,000 feet. Then he did.

Green 4, P/O Burgoyne was missing ...

So counting the cost on both sides, the Duxford Wing claimed thirteen destroyed, five probables, three damaged. The Wing losses were five aircraft damaged or missing. The pilots lost or missing were three: Horner, Smith and Burgoyne. Luckily these losses were subsequently reduced. Duxford was delighted at the results but there was a sour postscript to these actions of 27 September. It was this.

They got a message from Air Vice-Marshal Park that they had been 'poaching' on 11 Group's preserves. Good for him, they thought – it was his way of congratulating them. But not long afterwards Bader discovered that this remark had been deadly serious and actually couched in the form of a complaint. Even so, Bader was prepared to make excuses for Park. But obviously the AVM still thought of it as a private war between Germany and 11 Group.

28 September
London and the Solent again. The figures for losses were 16-16, accounted for by an especially upsetting loss of Hurricanes and some pilots.

29 September
Now the scale was less intense and also the losses of German five, British five. The target turned out to be Liverpool, both by day and night. Fighters neutralized the daylight raid, and also minimized other lunges in East Anglia and south-east England. London was still taking it every single night.

30 September

Aerial signs were apparent in the Pas de Calais early on. About 8.30 am single decoy fighters came across the Channel and then recrossed it. At 9.30 am Ju 88s trundled over the customary crossing point of Dungeness-Dymchurch. Due to some mix-up with meeting their protective escorts, the Junkers found themselves on their own. A dozen-or-so squadrons from 11 Group were already en route to the 88s. Number 92 Squadron pounced on the bombers before enemy fighters arrived. This squadron was credited with nine of the twelve Ju 88s littered over the west Kent and east Sussex fields. The defenders accomplished their job of thwarting yet another attack on London, but 92 Squadron lost five Spitfires in the exchanges, and more pitifully, four of their pilots. A tragic day to die, so near the end of the daylight battle. But many more were to do so yet.

RAF Battle of Britain pilots, photographed with Air Chief Marshal Sir Hugh Dowding at the Ministry of Information, 14 September 1942. Left to right: Squadron Leader AC Bartley, D.F.C; Wing Commander D.F.B. Sheen, D.F.C; Wing Commander LR Gleed, D.S.O., D.F.C; Wing Commander Max Aitken, D.S.O., D.F.C; Wing Commander AG. Malan, D.S.O., D.F.C; Squadron Leader AC Deere, D.F.C, R.N.Z.A.F.; Air Chief Marshal Sir Hugh Dowding (in civilian clothes); Flight Officer E.C. Henderson, M.M., W.A.AF.; Flight Lieutenant RH. Hillary; Wing Commander J.A Kent, D.F.C, A.F.C, Wing Commander C.B.F. Kingcombe, D.F.C; Squadron Leader D.H. Watkins D.F.C; Warrant Officer R.H. Gretton, a sergeant-pilot in the Battle of Britain.

The rest of the large-scale action moved to 10 Group. Here, Heinkel IIIs went for Westlands factory at Yeovil, Somerset. Five squadrons from this Group positioned themselves between the Heinkels with escorting Me 110s and their destination. In another aerial prize fight with few rules, the RAF power prevailed. For the defending fighters it was a case of thinking while flying at 300 mph. The enemy were getting tired of this daily dose of having to endure the danger without apparent victory in view. Those not hit gave up their goal of Yeovil, settling instead for the Somerset and Dorset countryside. Suddenly their survival became a priority for them – instead of the Third Reich.

While all this was being slugged and slogged out, nineteen 110 fighter-bombers had peeled off to their plan, heading for a Bristol aircraft works. Again fighters stopped them, shooting down four of the force, including their leader. The losses in all for the day were German forty-eight, British twenty. The enemy decided that the price being paid was too high, particularly on 27 and 30 September. This marked the last of the mass daytime bomber raids on Britain. But there would be one more month before the final date drawing the line under the Battle of Britain. And eight months to the respite from night bombing – the Blitz. As if to stress this, on 30 September the night raids on London went on …

CHAPTER TWENTY

The Battle is Won

Even now the Battle of Britain was not over. Losses of aircraft for the month of October were German 318, British 144. An average per day of German ten, British 4–5. The main change of enemy plan was that they restricted raids by the principal quantities of their bombers to night-time. By day they relied on a combination of smaller Junkers 88 attacks, flying fast and often low, and an improved Me 109 capable of carrying one bomb. Virtually all the day raids this month featured one or other or both of these aircraft, often shielded by pure fighters flying still higher. The Me 110 fighter-bomber raids were mainly towards London. And by night the more massed raids went on – and on. The total sortie figures for enemy activity remained exhausting for the RAF to counter: up to 1,000 a day occasionally and about 150 bombers per night.

The feature that began to emerge from the first days of October was the difficulty defenders had in attaining some 30,000 feet altitude to get on equal terms with the opposition by day. That was an aspect of the fighter-bomber thrusts. Another move to be countered or conquered was dealing with the high-speed Junkers incursions. On 3 October, for instance, one bomber got through to the Hatfield factory of de Havillands, preparing the forthcoming Mosquito aircraft, and dropped just four bombs. These destroyed one of the key structures of the plan and caused major casualties. To try to combat the former raids by the 109 fighter-bombers, Park soon decided to return to putting up patrols in advance, so that some squadrons at least were ready at required altitudes. Losses for the first few days of the month read: 1 October German 6, British 4; 2 October, German 10, British 1; 3 October, German 9, British 1; 4 October, German 12, British 3.

On 5 October, Me 110s aimed for both West Malling and Detling, but after the attacks the fearsome Poles of 303 Squadron disposed of four or more of the 110s. Down westward, no interceptions impeded bombs falling on Southampton, while in vicious and violent exchanges over the idyllic

Swanage coastline, Hurricanes from 607 Squadron at Tangmere fought Me 109s. Losses were roughly equivalent on each side, though the difference being that the RAF men baling out or crash-landing all survived to fight again. The day's losses were German thirteen, British eight. The RAF made over one thousand sorties.

Next day, Biggin Hill, Northolt and Middle Wallop were all bombed from high-level, though on a restricted scale. Losses were German six, British one. On 7 October, Ju 88s with Me 109 watchdogs targeted Westlands at Yeovil, but their combined losses on this rather abortive attack were seven aircraft.

Spitfire on patrol over the coast.

On the same day, a Turner sky over the sea off Folkestone showed why the painter loved the light seen from this town. And on the famous Leas, looking out across the water, many of the population still living there saw Pilot Officer Kenneth Mackenzie, with all his ammo gone, pursue an Me 109 over the Channel and tilt it with one of his wings so that it crashed into the sea. Mackenzie steered his wrecked Hurricane to the shoreline, got out on the deserted beach, and when discovered on the Folkestone cliffs had lost some teeth and cut his lower lip. The day's losses: German twenty-one, British seventeen.

8 October: north-west bombing at Speke of Rootes' factory, with the day losses of German, 14 British 4. 9 October: RAF airfields hit in scattered forays, with losses of German 9, British 3. 10 October: German 4, British 4. 11 October: German 7, British 9. 12 October: Kenley and Biggin Hill raided yet again, with day losses of German 11, British 10. Piccadilly Circus was bombed, but the most significant event of the day went unknown to this country: that Hitler put off any possibility of invading until 1941 in the springtime.

But this did not mean any real respite for either side. On 13 October the losses in foggy autumn weather were German five, British two. Then on 14 October came two of the worst raids throughout the Battle of Britain – Coventry was bombed by night, including the strike at the symbolic cathedral, and London itself had to suffer its maximum raid to date. On the very next night, there rained down an even more drenching bomb-load from four hundred bombers over London. The loss in human terms was growing to massive proportions; and the material damage to railways and buildings in general was proportionate to the strength of the bomber force employed. Waterloo Station was one casualty. Aircraft losses: German 4, British O. 15 October: German 14, British 15. 16 October: German 13, British 1. 17 October: German 15, British 3.

During October 11 Group were of course still heavily engaged. And the Duxford Wing was ordered up about another dozen times. Yet the momentous days were already ending. Despite Bader's strong views on the subject of aerial warfare, even then he thought it only fair to remember that Dowding may have been considerably preoccupied in his daily contacts with the Air Staff, the War Cabinet, and indeed even the Prime Minister, Winston Churchill. Under such conditions of mental stress, it was reasonable and indeed excusable that he may have been unaware of the changing circumstances of the Battle of Britain. In this case, he failed in not appreciating the need for overall control from Fighter Command. He should have appointed a deputy, an Air Marshal, to coordinate and direct the battle.

What has been built into the Big Wing controversy stemmed from mutterings in the Mess by the pilots of the Duxford Wing against the

11 Group habit of calling them off the ground too late, so that they arrived in the battle area at a disadvantage. This was coupled with the fact that 11 Group headquarters used to complain when they were late – which was duly passed to them by 12 Group headquarters. The result was a vicious circle, with 11 Group saying that 12 Group took so long to get off the ground. Towards the latter part of the battle, matters did improve.

It should be remembered that the Duxford Wing went into action first as such on 7 September and that the big battles ceased after 21 September, so the period under discussion is only fourteen days. The difference of opinion had not been resolved by the end of the Battle of Britain. Park was opposed to the Big Wing ideas and to the general line adopted by Leigh-Mallory. Bader found that Leigh-Mallory had a quick, questing mind and a character of charm and understanding. He was tough, enthusiastic, and completely honest with his juniors. He cared about people. They mattered to him. Later Leigh-Mallory moved from Group Commander of 12 to 11 Group and subsequently Commander-in-Chief Fighter Command. Then as an Air Chief Marshal, he served as C-in-C Allied Air Forces Europe until he was killed with his wife in an air crash in 1944.

Bader found him an inspired leader. Leigh-Mallory's career after the Battle of Britain certainly confirmed that his ideas on fighter tactics were received with considerable sympathy and agreement by the Air Council. A famous meeting held on 17 October 1940 proved that the weight of opinion was with both Leigh-Mallory and Bader in the Air Council. Leigh-Mallory caused a minor stir by bringing Bader with him to such a high-level discussion in distinguished company. But the meeting vindicated them and their successful strategy of the Big Wing.

Although by this date, the Battle of Britain was assuredly won, neither the rest of the conflict nor the war in the air generally were over – and 12 Group suffered several tragic losses at this late phase of 1940. While Bader was in London on the very day of 17 October, Red Section of 242 Squadron got orders to orbit base at 8.40 am. And though instructions were given to pancake, these were cancelled and at 9.17 am Red Section received a vector. Flying at a height of about 7,000 feet, they saw a Dornier 17 cruising on a course some 3,000 feet below them. Visibility at 7,000 feet was good but at 3,000–4,000 feet there was 8/10th cloud. When first sighted the Dornier was making for a cloud.

They were thirty miles north-east of Yarmouth as Red 3, P/O Rogers, attacked from above and to starboard of Red 2. Red 3 got in a good burst. Then Red 2, P/O Brown, positioned himself dead astern of the enemy bomber and also got in a burst before experiencing fire from the enemy rear-gunner which connected with his throttle control. Red 2 was followed in line-astern by Red 1, P/O Campbell. Red 2 saw nothing further of Red 1 before breaking away. When he returned to attack, the enemy had vanished into the cloud and Red 2 made it back to base.

Red 3 followed the Dornier through a succession of clouds, catching occasional glimpses of all or part of it. But he failed to close in for a further effective burst and finally lost it altogether. When last seen by Red 3, the Dornier was still proceeding at a fairly slow speed on an easterly course in no apparent difficulties. Red 2 landed at 9.50 am. Red 3 landed at 10.20 am. Red 1 failed to land. P/O Campbell was posted as missing …

On the next day, 18 October, the Polish Squadron 302 suffered still more severely. Operating with 229 Squadron, they were told to scramble at 3 pm in poor weather and patrol Maidstone line at Angels One Five. Twelve fighters were airborne by 3.06 pm. They joined up with 229 Squadron over the base, 302 Squadron leading. After one or two varied manoeuvres and various vectors, Flt Lt Jathomson at Red 1 espied an enemy. He turned towards it and attacked three separate times. The first was from behind slightly above. The second and third followed vertically from above. During the first attack he met heavy enemy fire from machine guns, two of them in the rear-gunner's turret. The other two guns were located in 'blisters'. Many Hurricanes were also attacking enemy aircraft at the same time, so he broke off to avoid collision. His bandit scampered into clouds pursued by several Hurricanes. Red 2 attacked unsuccessfully. Red 3 was unable to fire at any enemy as he could not manoeuvre into a suitable position.

Yellow 1 was likewise unsuccessful. Yellow 2, Sergeant Nowakiewicz, closed on the enemy to a mere thirty yards. He broke away on a climbing turn after firing a burst. As he did so, he saw two men jump from the enemy aircraft and their parachutes open safely. The aeroplane dived rather gently towards earth. Yellow 3 could not place himself for an assault but confirmed the sight of the two parachutes.

No pilots in Blue or Green Sections who returned were able to attack. After the initial attack, the squadron reformed and Yellow 2 said that he was the last aircraft in the squadron. He counted ten others besides himself. The leader asked for his position and was told he was thirty miles from base at 4.26 pm.

The leader thinks he lost the last three sections when descending to Angels Five to investigate a bandit reported at that altitude at 4.30 pm. At 4.46 pm he asked for permission to land, as he had been up for one hour forty minutes. But he was told to orbit for two minutes as another bandit was nearby. Red Section eventually landed at Northolt at 5.08 pm.

The fate of the other sections was as follows:

Blue 1 landed at Cobham with one gallon of petrol left in his tank.

Blue 2, P/O Wapniarek, crashed at Cobham.

An eye-witness said he saw four aircraft flying overhead very low in and out of cloud. One of these detached itself and seemed to shut off its engine. A moment later it came out of the cloud and crashed, catching fire immediately.

Blue 3, P/O Zukowski, crashed and was killed near Detling.

Green 1, F/O Carter, and Green 2, F/O Borowski, both crashed at Kempton Park Race Course, within 200 yards of each other.

Green 2 and Yellow 3 both landed safely.

So four pilots were killed: Carter, Wapniarek, Borowski and Zukowski.

Equally tragic to Bader were the later losses of pilots from his original Canadian 242 Squadron. On 5 November, P/O N. Hart, to be followed by two others, P/O J.B. Latta and P/O Willie McKnight.

Opinion is still mixed over the question of the Big Wing tactics and it may be interesting to quote four Battle of Britain pilots on this question. Their comments are exclusive to the author:

Johnnie Johnson:

'Douglas was all for the Big Wings to counter the German formation. I think there was room for both tactics – the Big Wings and the small squadrons. The size of the fighting unit in 11 Group was conditioned by the time to intercept before the bombing. It might well have been fatal had Park always tried to get his squadrons into Balbos, for not only would they have taken longer to get to their height, but sixty or seventy packed climbing fighters could have been seen for miles and would have been sitting ducks for higher 109s. Also nothing would have pleased Göring more than for his 109s to pounce on large numbers of RAF fighters. Indeed Galland and Molders often complained about the elusiveness of Fighter Command and Park's brilliance was that by refusing to concentrate his force he preserved it throughout the Battle. This does not mean, as Bader pointed out at the time, that two or three Balbos from 10 and 12 Groups, gaining their height beyond the range of the 109s, would not have played a terrific part in the fighting. Park only had time to fight a defensive battle. The Balbos could have fought offensively. This was a matter for Fighter Command.'

Peter Townsend:

'Bader was a very great person, but of course he was involved in a highly controversial thing and in the judgment of many – and occasionally in my own judgment – he did infringe the rules. But I've let that be known in a very friendly way. He even visualized control of squadrons should have been handled from Fighter Command, even by Dowding himself. When I put this to Park, he said, "Well, I must say, that beats the band."

Sholto Douglas thought it ideal if Park's squadrons could attack the incoming bombers, with Leigh-Mallory's Wing harrying them as they retreated. Douglas Bader's idea was exactly the opposite: operating only from 12 Group or the flanks of 11 Group, Wings should take-off and gain height as the enemy was building up over France, and then advance in mass to attack them as they crossed the coast. Meanwhile, 11 Group squadrons climbing from forward airfields beneath the fray would tear into the retreating enemy. Bader never thought Wings could operate from 11 Group's forward airfields.'

Peter Brothers:

'There was a lot to be said for this Big Wing conception if they could be marshalled in time. But it obviously wouldn't work in 11 Group. But it could work in 12 Group. I flew in both Groups. Of course later on in the Battle, one was organized in Big Wings. You had that little bit more time to play. There was something to be said on each side. Park was quite right that it wouldn't work in 11 Group – they were too far forward. There was certainly a case when you were further back for a large formation.'

Alan Deere:

'I first met Douglas during Dunkirk operations, when I was operating at Hornchurch and he came down. When I first met him, I didn't know about his legs. I walked into the Mess. I can remember very distinctly. He was standing near the hatch where we got our drinks. He struck me at once in the way he attacked you, came at you. I met him and at that point I hadn't even heard of him before. He kept pumping me about tactics and shouting and all this sort of thing. Immediately he stood out as someone who was keen to get on with the job and wanted to find out all about it. That was in May 1940. I was shot down during those Dunkirk operations and don't recollect talking to him again at that time.

I heard about him during the Battle of Britain, because of these Wing tactics which are now so much in controversy. All I will say is that tactics will always remain a matter of opinion. But it is my opinion that the mass Wing formations of 12 Group could not have been successful in 11 Group. There just wasn't time to form up and get airborne. For example, when we were operating from Manston the most forward airfield in 11 Group – we actually had to fly inland to get our height before we could go back to meet the raids.'

But of course Bader never did advocate Big Wings from Kent or Surrey. But he did advocate an offensive attitude to the defence of Britain. No one can prove him finally right or wrong, but he had certainly scored substantial successes – for the minimum losses.

It was still 18 October. Losses on that day were German 15, British 4. Then 19 October: German 5, British 2. 20 October: German 14, British 4. 21 October: German 6, British 0. 22 October: German 11, British 5. 23 October: German 3, British 1. 24 October: German 8, British 4. 25 October: German 20, British 10. 26 October: German 10, British 4. During this spell, night raids visited Glasgow as well as London, and Montrose airfield also in Scotland.

In case anyone thought that the enemy air threat was ended, on 27 October the sheer statistics proved otherwise. The Luftwaffe pinpointed half-a-dozen or more RAF airfields and other targets in their running policy of hit-and-run raids plus the fast fighter-bomber bursts. This was a day when over 1,000 sorties were yet again needed by RAF fighters with the loss line: German 15, British 10. On 28 October it was German 11, British 2.

The last large-scale daylight attempts were on 29 October, with autumn already well advanced. A formation of thirty Me 109s flashed over the old fishing town of Deal; while a score of them took on Spitfires of 11 Group, two or three of the rest got through to London. From the original thirty 109s, the Spitfires shot five out of the mid-morning sky. The policy of Park to get the fighters up and patrolling as early as feasible paid off when the next 109s appeared. Five squadrons of Spitfires, aided and abetted by four of Hurricanes, caught the hundred-or-so fighter-bombers and escorts from above. In this well-prepared placing, the RAF took only six minutes to send eleven enemy plunging into the post-harvested fields. About half of these were confirmed as accredited to one squadron – 602. The rest of the enemy got rid of their remaining bombs anywhere and throttled south at speed.

Messerschmitt 109s and 110s, all with droppable armoury, made what was virtually the penultimate daylight outing – this time determined to reach North Weald. The purpose of these raids had become imprecise, even obscure, by now. But they forced a way through to catch 257 and 249 Squadrons of Hurricanes actually as they were being scrambled. The

Alan Deere being decorated by the King. He was the leading New Zealander in the Battle of Britain.

Irish ace Paddy Finucane in his shamrock-decorated fighter.

Another legend – Flying Officer 'Cobber' Kain.

Messerschmitts trapped a couple of Hurricanes amidst take-off and in the familiar fast, low-level appearance, inflicted damage on RAF North Weald itself.

The Germans lost aircraft. North Weald lost a score of ground staff. Portsmouth was another area of attention from the Luftwaffe. So 29 October ended with losses of German nine, British seven. Amid autumnal rain, a final and failed effort to reach London was made on 30 October, with losses totalling German eight, British five. October ended with a devastating total tally of civilian casualties from enemy air-raids. This read: over 13,000 killed and nearly 20,000 injured. And the last line of the battle was reached on 31 October. During that day, the respective aerial losses were: German 0, British 0. Officially this date marked the end of the Battle of Britain. The Royal Air Force had won. But the Blitz went on …

CHAPTER 21

The Blitz

B y mid-November 1940, when the Germans adopted a change of plans,
over 13,000 tons of high explosive and nearly 1,000,000 incendiaries had
fallen on London. Outside the capital there had been widespread
harassing activity by single aircraft, as well as fairly strong diversionary
attacks on Birmingham, Coventry and Liverpool, but no 'major raids'. The
London docks and railway communications – the enemy's favourite aiming
points – had taken a heavy pounding, and much damage had been done to the
railway system outside. In September there had been no fewer than 667 hits on
railways in Great Britain, and at one period between five and six thousand
wagons were standing idle from the effect of delayed-action bombs. The great
bulk of the traffic went on; and Londoners still got to work. For all the
destruction of life and property, London had adjusted itself to its new
existence with astonishing calm. Wardens, firemen, rescue and salvage teams,
repair gangs, bomb disposal squads, ambulance drivers, nurses – and plain
workers and housewives – all were cheating the Luftwaffe of its triumph.

More than 12,000 night sorties were flown by the Germans over Great
Britain during this phase of concentrated offensive against the capital. But in
the whole period from 7 September to 13 November the German night
casualty rate was less than one per cent of sorties. With a first-line strength of
1,400 long-range bombers, and some 300 emerging each month from the
factories, the enemy would have no difficulty in sustaining his attacks
indefinitely.

The forthcoming change in German objectives was sensed by our
Intelligence, and by 12 November we knew that three great attacks, called by
the Germans with unwonted humour 'Moonlight Sonata', 'Umbrella' and
'All One Price', were soon to be delivered against Coventry, Birmingham
and Wolverhampton.

Indeed, there was just time to plan a counter-operation – 'Cold Water' – by
which Bomber Command would simultaneously harass the enemy's

bomber airfields and retaliate against a selected German town. It is a striking illustration of the advantage then held by the Germans that though this information was in our hands, and though attacks against their airfields were duly carried out, Coventry and Birmingham were both heavily smitten within the next few nights. Wolverhampton, more fortunate, escaped. The sudden increase in its anti-aircraft defences was possibly observed by the enemy.

The new phase of the German offensive began on the night of 14/15 November, as the inhabitants of Coventry will long remember. The weather – full moon and good visibility – favoured the attack, and the German operation went more or less according to plan.

The first raiders crossed our coast at 6.17 pm when about a dozen enemy aircraft made landfall at Lyme Bay. They were He 111s of the unit which specialized in blind-bombing against precision targets. Their task was to find the target, shower it with incendiaries, and leave it well ablaze. The rest of the bomber force would follow up and bomb the fires.

The Heinkels arrived over Coventry at 8.15 pm. Meanwhile the main force was already approaching from a number of different directions. One stream led in across the Lincolnshire and Norfolk coasts: another between Selsey Bill and Portland: a third between Selsey Bill and Dungeness. All told, 437 enemy aircraft operated, keeping up the attack until shortly before 6 o'clock the following morning. Between them they dropped fifty-six tons of incendiaries, 394 tons of H.E. bombs and 127 parachute mines.

In view of our popular conception of this raid as a virtually indiscriminate assault on a city centre, it is not without interest to discover that many of the German aircraft were given specific targets: Standard Motor Company, Coventry Radiator and Press Company, Alvis aeroplane works, British Piston Ring Company, Daimler Works, and gas-holders in Hill Street. Most of these objectives were in fact fairly heavily hit.

Twelve important aircraft plants and nine other major industrial works suffered directly from the attack, but output was also affected by general damage to utilities. Only one power plant was actually hit, but many cables, pipes and lines were severed – there were nearly 200 fractures of gas mains – and the shortage of gas and water was felt for some time. Indeed several factories were compelled to suspend production solely for this reason. The disorganization of transport was another great handicap – all railway lines were blocked, and all road traffic except the most essential had to be diverted round the city – and the loss of some 500 retail shops greatly hampered the distribution of food.

Recovery from the general disorganization, however, was surprisingly quick. Help was rapidly forthcoming. All railway lines except one were

Coventry Cathedral in ruins after destruction in the air raid of 15 November.

reopened by 18 November. The large numbers of unexploded bombs were speedily dealt with, and within three or four days there was an excellent service of transport to take workers to the factories, evacuate the homeless, and disperse key tools from the damaged works. And despite the fact that 380 people had been killed and 800 seriously injured, morale remained unshaken. On the evening of 16 November arrangements were made to transport 10,000 people out of the centre of the city. Only 300 used them.

The results of the raid would, of course, have been much worse but for the fine work of the local civil defences and the voluntary helpers. The guns, too, had maintained a fierce barrage which kept the enemy high. Among the many who carried out their duties unflinchingly were the men of the Observer Corps, whose operations room was uncomfortably close to the blazing Cathedral. Mr Gilbert Dalton, a chief observer, has described how for twelve hours members of the Corps sat around the table and plotted the tracks of raiders:

'The building was frequently shaken by bombs; more than twenty detonated within a short distance – and surrounding buildings were on fire, but the work went on. Lights failed; candles were lit. Smoke drifted in through the ventilating system. Water from firemen's hoses swilled into the room. Telephones went dead; plots were still received and told to the RAF on the lines that remained. Men whose homes and families were in the city went on stolidly with their work; one member that night lost his house, his business and his car, but he reported for duty next day. A number of members got through as reliefs during the height of the blitz; one man took three hours to come two miles because of the fires and obstructions.'

The next two nights the enemy, anxious not to let the capital benefit unduly from his change of plan, reverted to attacks on London. On 17 November he struck at Southampton; then followed three nights of heavy raiding against Birmingham. In the last week of the month, Southampton, London, Liverpool, Bristol and Plymouth all received 'major raids'. Further ordeals followed in December, when Manchester and Sheffield were added to the list of stricken cities. The year went out with the City of London still smouldering from the fire-raising attack on 29 December. Who can ever forget that photographic imprint of the dome of St Paul's Cathedral engulfed by smoke, yet somehow surviving?

Symbolically standing out amid engulfing flames and smoke of the surrounding blazing buildings – the dome of St Paul's Cathedral during the great fire raid on London, 29 December.

The great fire raid on the City of London, 29 December.

Göring pursued the policy of ringing the changes between three main target groups until the latter part of February 1941. Of the thirty-one 'major raids' carried out between mid-November and that date, fourteen were on ports, nine on inland industrial towns, and eight on London. The enemy's effort was usually concentrated each night against a single centre; and he developed the unpleasant habit of bombing the same city twice or three times at brief intervals in the hope of impeding recovery. In January, though, three fresh centres Cardiff, Portsmouth and Avonmouth – had their first heavy night attack. But the German raids were much reduced by the weather. February saw a still further decline, with only 1,200 sorties as against over 6,000 in November and 4,000 in December. In the four months from the beginning of November to the end of February, the enemy put at least 12,000 sorties over this country, but the total number of aircraft claimed as destroyed by the defences was not more than seventy-five: two-thirds by guns, one-third by fighters.

The final phase of the Blitz began in late February 1941. When better weather again made intensive operations possible, the Luftwaffe turned in strength against the ports. Between 19 February and 12 May the enemy carried out sixty-one attacks involving more than fifty aircraft each. Seven of these – most of them very heavy – fell on London, five on Birmingham, two on Coventry, and one on Nottingham. The remaining forty-six were all directed against the ports. Portsmouth, Plymouth, Bristol and Avonmouth, Swansea, Merseyside, Belfast, Clydeside, were all heavily and repeatedly bombed. On the east coast, Hull became an increasingly favoured target, while Sunderland had one big raid and Newcastle two.

By March 1941, Fighter Command was changing night aircraft from Blenheims to Beaufighters. Hurricanes and Defiants allocated to night operations were gaining rapidly in skill and experience. During March, fighters claimed twenty-two of the night raiders to the guns seventeen. In April the figures were forty-eight to fighters, thirty-nine to guns. And in May a peak was reached with a claim of ninety-six to fighters and forty-two to all other means.

Squadron Leader John Cunningham and Sergeant C.F. Rawnsley soon began to achieve a reputation as the outstanding aircrew for night fighter operations – although of course there were many others.

John Cunningham commanded 604 Squadron. After the Battle of Britain, he turned to night flying, beginning his new career in the autumn of 1940. His first success had come on 19 November when he destroyed a Ju 88 over the East Midlands. By the beginning of 1941, the wintry weather, coupled with the better defences in anti-aircraft guns, barrage balloons and night-fighters, resulted in a change of enemy plans. Smaller groups of bombers were scheduled to reach their targets at successive periods to prolong the air-raid alarms. Barrage balloons and the guns kept the bombers high – and the night-fighters tackled them eagerly.

By Spring 1941, John Cunningham had become both busy and successful. One night he actually claimed three aircraft shot down. This was a different, alien world where impressions were muted. The cold clusters of stars and a milky moon were the only illumination from above. And below, the cities were blacked-out completely unless an occasional fire from enemy bombs broke the darkness.

Several miles up, Cunningham had to know exactly where he was all the time. A twenty-four-year-old pilot, he grew accustomed to the unlit universe. When an enemy raid was on, of course, there were also always the sudden stabs of searchlights ranging round for the bombers. And the curving tracer-sprays or shell-bursts far below. Or perhaps a pattern of coloured lights would mechanically dot the earth, denoting an airfield illuminated by ground lights to help one or more aeroplanes to land. Cunningham learned to absorb all these distant images instinctively and react to them rationally, rapidly.

He flew in a dim mixture of darkness and stellar sheen. He learned to recognize the ghostly glow of an aircraft bent on its bombing mission. His job was to keep it in range long enough for an attack: for an electrifying emission of fire through the icy night air. It hardly needs stressing how much more difficult was the art of night-fighting compared with daytime. But somehow Cunningham mastered all its hazards to become the greatest night-fighter ace of all. He represented all the night pilots who helped to foil the Blitz. Here are two typical sorties at the time.

Cunningham was airborne in a Bristol Beaufighter on the night of 11/12 April 1941. Base radio had just notified him of the approximate details of enemy bombers somewhere out there in the infinite night. He was within the network of the coastal ground control interception stations. Now he had to continue to be guided by base radio towards the enemy until the fighter's own radar-operator picked them up on the small screen. With him as usual on this flight was his faithful A.I. operator, Sergeant Rawnsley. This was what happened on the particular patrol, told in the tense, technical style of the report:

'Put on to north-bound raid 13,000 feet. Final vector 360 degrees and buster (full speed).

'Told to flash (to operate A.I.) but no contact received. G.CI. station then told me to alter course to 350 degrees and height 11,000 feet. While going from 13,000 to 11,000 feet a blip (flash of light in A.I. set) was picked up at max. range ahead. On operator's instructions I closed in and obtained a visual at 2,500 feet range (checked on A.I. set) and about 30 degrees up.

'Identified E/A as the He 111 which was flying just beneath cloud layer and occasionally going through wisps which allowed me to get within eighty yards of E/A and about twenty to thirty feet beneath before opening fire.

'Immediately there was a big white flash in the fuselage centre section and black pieces flew off the fuselage. E/A went into a vertical dive to the right, and about half a minute later the sky all around me was lit up by an enormous orange flash and glow. Bits of E/A were seen to be burning on the ground.

'I estimated my position to be about Shaftesbury but called Harlequin and asked for a fix so that my exact position could be checked.

'One He 111 destroyed. Rounds fired sixty-four.'

Cunningham made it all sound so easy. He found it fascinating to face the Nazis and the night. Flying by day in cloud was hard enough, doing this at night was immeasurably more so. As well as good eyesight, the pilot had to have other vital qualities for success or survival. The night-fighter pilots used to spend a short time before operations in dimly illuminated rooms, wearing dark glasses. But one of Cunningham's pet hates was to be referred to as 'Cat's Eyes' Cunningham.

As the Blitz went on and on, Cunningham and the other night-fighter pilots took off night after night. This was just one sortie, in his own words:

'Try to imagine the moonlit sky, with a white background of snow nearly six miles below. Somewhere near the centre of a toy town, a tiny

Firemen tackle the results of an incendiary raid on Great Yarmouth.

flare is burning. Several enemy bombers have come over, but only one fire has gained hold. After all the excitement of my combats, I can still see that amazing picture of London clearly in my mind.

'It was indeed the kind of night that we fly-by-nights pray for. I had been up about three-quarters of an hour before I found an enemy aircraft. I had searched all round the sky when I suddenly saw him ahead of me. I pulled the boost control to get the highest possible speed and catch him up. I felt my Hurricane vibrate all over as she responded and gave maximum power.

'I manoeuvred into position where I could see the enemy clearly with the least chance of his seeing me. As I caught him up I recognized him – a Dornier Flying Pencil. Before I spotted him I had been almost petrified with the cold. I was beginning to wonder if I should ever be able to feel my hands, feet or limbs again. But the excitement warmed me up.

'He was now nearly within range and was climbing to 30,000 feet. I knew the big moment had come. I daren't take my eyes off him, but just to make sure that everything was all right I took a frantic glance round the U office – that's what we call the cockpit and checked everything. Then I began to close in on the Dornier and found I was travelling much too fast. I throttled back and slowed up just in time. We are frighteningly close. Then I swung up, took aim, and fired my guns. Almost at once I saw little flashes of fire dancing along the fuselage and centre section. My bullets had found their mark.

The Battle by moonlight. Hurricane night fighter pilot about to take-off to intercept enemy raiders.

'I closed in again, when suddenly the bomber reared up in front of me. It was all I could do to avoid crashing into him. I heaved at the controls to prevent a collision, and in doing so I lost sight of him. I wondered if he was playing pussy and intending to jink away, come up on the other side, and take a crack at me, or whether he was hard hit. The next moment I saw him going down below me with a smoke trail pouring out.

'I felt a bit disappointed, because it looked as if my first shots had not been as effective as they appeared. Again I pulled the boost control and went down after him as fast as I knew how. I dived from 30,000 feet at such a speed that the bottom panel of the aircraft cracked, and as my ears were not used to such sudden changes of pressure I nearly lost the use of one of my drums. But there was no time to think of these things, I had to get that bomber. Then as I came nearer I saw he was on fire. Little flames were flicking around his fuselage and wings. Just as I closed in again, he jinked away in a steep climbing turn.

'I was going too fast again, so I pulled the stick back and went up after him in a screaming left-hand climbing turn. When he got to the top of his climb I was almost on him. I took sight very carefully and gave the button a quick squeeze. Once more I saw little dancing lights on his fuselage, but almost instantaneously they were swallowed in a burst of flames. I saw him twist gently earthwards and there was a spurt of fire as he touched the earth. He blew up and set a copse blazing.

'I circled down to see if any of the crew had got out, and then I suddenly remembered the London balloon barrage, so I climbed up and set course for home.

'I had time now to think about the action. My windscreen was covered with oil, which made flying uncomfortable, and I had a nasty feeling that I might have lost bits of my aircraft. I remembered seeing bits of Jerry flying past me. There were several good-sized holes in the fabric, which could have been caused only by hefty lumps of Dornier. Also the engine seemed to be running a bit roughly, but that turned out

West towers of St Paul's Cathedral seen through the arch of a bombed building.

to be my imagination. Anyway I soon landed, reported what had happened, had some refreshment, and then up in the air once more, southward ho! for London.

'Soon after, I was at 17,000 feet. It's a bit warmer there than 30,000. I slowed down and searched the sky. The next thing I knew a Heinkel was sitting right on my tail. I was certain he had seen me, and wondered how long he had been trailing me. I opened my throttle, got round on his tail and crept up. When I was about 400 yards away he opened fire - and missed. I checked my gadgets, then I closed up and snaked about so as to give him as difficult a target as possible. I got into a firing position, gave a quick burst of my guns and broke away.

'I came up again, and it looked as if my shots had had no effect. Before I could fire a second time, I saw his tracer bullets whizzing past me. I fired back and I knew at once that I had struck home. I saw a parachute open up on the port wing. One of the crew was baling out. He was quickly followed by another. The round white domes of the parachutes looked lovely in the moonlight.

'It was obvious now that the pilot would never get his aircraft home, and I, for my part, wanted this second machine to be a 'certainty' and not a 'probable'. So I gave another quick burst of my guns. Then to fool him I attacked from different angles. There was no doubt now that he was going down. White smoke was coming from one engine, but he was not yet on fire. I delivered seven more attacks, spending all my ammunition. Both his engines smoked as he got lower and lower. I followed him down a long way and as he flew over a dark patch of water I lost sight of him.

But I knew he had come down, and where he had come down - it was all confirmed later - and I returned to my base ready to tackle another one. But they told me all the Jerries had gone home. "Not all", I said, "two of them are here for keeps". So it went on.'

In the second half of April, London was twice raided with a greater weight of high explosive than ever before – 876 tons on the memorable Wednesday raid of 16 April and 1,010 tons on Saturday 19 April. On 17 April came the heavy raid on Portsmouth, when a diversionary tactic was employed by the defenders. An unpopulated part of nearby Hayling Island was purposely illuminated to deflect bombers from the main target.

Over on the Island, Major Jim Coates was commanding 219 Heavy Anti-Aircraft Battery. They occupied two sites on the island – at Sinah and North Hayling – each with four guns. The raid had started about 9 pm and the decoy fires were lit on the Hayling golf course as planned. The plan began to fulfil its purpose as the first of 170 bombs, thirty-two parachute mines, and some 5,000 incendiaries rained down on Hayling Island – attracted by the fires.

As the raid developed, one of the gun sites was fortunate in escaping serious damage. But not the HQ Sinah battery. Four 4.5-inch guns were ranged between Ferry Road and Sinah Lake, south of the golf course. When the raid was approaching its height at midnight, several landmines floated down towards them on the gun site. No one could get out of the way. Two or three of the mines dangled with their parachutes from trees, but one scored a direct hit on the gun battery and surrounding camp-site. Gun crew and other soldiers were all trapped in the blast of the one-ton mine, which flattened the entire headquarters. In its wake, it killed six men and wounded thirty-one. Although Jim Coates himself sustained minor injuries, he helped to organize the stream of ambulances – Service and Civilian – to take the wounded to various hospitals in the district. And still the raid went on ...

The damage done to Hayling and the casualties caused certainly saved worse suffering in densely-populated Portsmouth. But inevitably some damage to my beloved birthplace had been done by now. Commercial Road shops were flattened, including the Landport Drapery Bazaar. King's Road, Southsea, was no more – no more Dyer's department store. Portsmouth Hippodrome stood as a shell. The Guildhall had been hit. Then followed four grim nights for the port of Plymouth. The next month of May was ushered in by a sustained assault on Merseyside and by savage raids against Clydeside and Belfast. Diversionary measures deflected the enemy bombers from their next targets of Derby and Nottingham on the night of 8 May. Then in a final fling on 10 May London was treated to another 700 tons.

But by then German attention was veering eastward towards the imminent invasion of Russia. In the next two months, only four attacks of over a hundred tons were delivered against Britain. By the end of June, two-thirds of the Luftwaffe strength had been withdrawn east to Russia and south to the Mediterranean. Britain had time to count the cost in human suffering: 40,000 British civilians had been killed, 46,000 injured, and a million houses destroyed or damaged. Yet the Blitz was far from being a great strategic victory for the enemy, as they claimed.

The German night offensive of 1940–1941, like the daylight attacks in the Battle of Britain itself, suffered from confused direction. The enemy vacillated between attacks on our power installations; aircraft industry; and ports and dockyards – thus dissipating their overall effect. This could be compared to their fatal switch from attacking airfields to bombing London. Yet in the end nothing can ever detract from the immortal victory by the Royal Air Force in the Battle of Britain: one of the most crucial conflicts in the history of civilization.

Bibliography

The Royal Air Force 1939–1945 (HMSO)
The Battle of Britain (HMSO)
The Second World War Volume I by Winston Churchill
Royal Air Force 1939–45 Volume I by Denis Richards
Full Circle by Air Vice-Marshal J.E. Johnson
The Third Service by Air Chief Marshal Sir Philip Joubert de la Ferté
The Narrow Margin by Derek Wood and D. Dempster
Dowding and the Battle of Britain by Robert Wright
The Last Enemy by Richard Hillary
Nine Lives by Air Commodore Alan C. Deere
I had a row with a German by Group Captain T.P. Gleave
Duel of Eagles by Group Captain Peter Townsend
The Battle of Britain: The Jubilee History by Richard Hough and Denis Richards
The Battle of Britain 1940 by J.M. Spaight
So Few by David Masters
The Air Defence of Great Britain, Vol II: The Battle of Britain
Fight for the Sky by Douglas Bader (with John Frayn Turner)
Douglas Bader by John Frayn Turner
The Bader Wing by John Frayn Turner
VCs of the Air by John Frayn Turner
Famous Air Battles by John Frayn Turner
British Aircraft of World War 2 by John Frayn Turner
Eagle Day by Richard Collier
Heroic Flights by John Frayn Turner

Index